Praetorians, Profiteers or Professionals?

The **ISEAS – Yusof Ishak Institute** (formerly Institute of Southeast Asian Studies) is an autonomous organization established in 1968. It is a regional centre dedicated to the study of socio-political, security, and economic trends and developments in Southeast Asia and its wider geostrategic and economic environment. The Institute's research programmes are grouped under Regional Economic Studies (RES), Regional Strategic and Political Studies (RSPS), and Regional Social and Cultural Studies (RSCS). The Institute is also home to the ASEAN Studies Centre (ASC), the Singapore APEC Study Centre, and the Temasek History Research Centre (THRC).

ISEAS Publishing, an established academic press, has issued more than 2,000 books and journals. It is the largest scholarly publisher of research about Southeast Asia from within the region. ISEAS Publishing works with many other academic and trade publishers and distributors to disseminate important research and analyses from and about Southeast Asia to the rest of the world.

Praetorians, Profiteers or Professionals?

Studies on the Militaries of Myanmar and Thailand

EDITED BY
MICHAEL J. MONTESANO
TERENCE CHONG
PRAJAK KONGKIRATI

WITH AN EPILOGUE BY
ROBERT H. TAYLOR

First published in Singapore in 2020 by
ISEAS Publishing
30 Heng Mui Keng Terrace
Singapore 119614

E-mail: publish@iseas.edu.sg
Website: <http://bookshop.iseas.edu.sg>

All rights reserved. No part of this publication may be reproduced, stored in a retrieval system, or transmitted in any form or by any means, electronic, mechanical, photocopying, recording or otherwise, without the prior permission of the ISEAS – Yusof Ishak Institute.

© 2020 ISEAS – Yusof Ishak Institute, Singapore

The responsibility for facts and opinions in this publication rests exclusively with the authors and their interpretations do not necessarily reflect the views or the policy of the publisher or its supporters.

ISEAS Library Cataloguing-in-Publication Data

Name(s): Montesano, Michael J., editor. | Chong, Terence, editor. | Prajak Kongkirati, editor.
Title: Praetorians, profiteers or professionals? Studies on the militaries of Myanmar and Thailand / edited by Michael J. Montesano, Terence Chong and Prajak Kongkirati.
Description: Singapore : ISEAS – Yusof Ishak Institute, 2020. | Includes bibliographical references.
Identifiers: ISBN 978-981-4881-75-3 (soft cover) | 978-981-4881-76-0 (PDF)
Subjects: LCSH: Myanmar—Armed Forces. | Thailand—Armed Forces.
Classification: LCC UA853 B9P88

Typeset by International Typesetters Pte Ltd
Printed in Singapore by Markono Print Media Pte Ltd

CONTENTS

Acknowledgements		vi
About the Contributors		vii
1.	Introduction: Two Mainland Southeast Asian Militaries in Comparative Perspective Michael J. Montesano, Terence Chong and Prajak Kongkirati	1
2.	A New Tatmadaw with Old Characteristics Nay Yan Oo	30
3.	Thailand's Military: Ideology and Sense of Mission Paul Chambers	70
4.	The Defence Expenditures and Commercial Interests of the Tatmadaw Maung Aung Myoe	97
5.	The Economic Role of the Thai Military: A Commercial Logic to Coups? Kanda Naknoi	132
6.	Epilogue: Controlling or Playing Politics? Robert H. Taylor	150
Index		168

ACKNOWLEDGEMENTS

We thank Professor Suchit Bunbongkarn, a long-time friend of ISEAS and supporter of its work, for first proposing preparation of a comparative volume on the militaries of Myanmar and Thailand and former ISEAS Director Tan Chin Tiong for encouraging us to take this idea up. Without the trade-mark commitment, understanding, and professionalism of Ng Kok Kiong, Sheryl Sin Bing Peng and their colleagues at ISEAS Publishing, this book would have been impossible. Aung Aung Hlaing offered guidance on the transliteration of Myanmar-language terms, and Nursyazwani Jamaludin took charge of submitting the manuscript to ISEAS Publishing.

In addition to kindly contributing an epilogue, Professor Robert H. Taylor has been a mentor and guide to us in our work on the book. In the course of that work, both he and his fellow contributors have exemplified collegiality, scholarly dedication, and above all extreme patience. To collaborate with each of them has been a privilege for which we are grateful.

Michael J. Montesano
Terence Chong
Prajak Kongkirati

Tokyo, Singapore and Bangkok
March 2020

ABOUT THE CONTRIBUTORS

Maung Aung Myoe is Dean and Professor of International Relations, International University of Japan, Minami Uonuma, Niigata, Japan; email: maungmyoe@gmail.com.

Paul Chambers serves as Lecturer and Special Assistant on International Affairs, Center of ASEAN Community Studies, Faculty of Social Sciences, Naresuan University, Phitsanulok, Thailand; email: pwchambers@gmail.com.

Terence Chong is Deputy Director of the ISEAS – Yusof Ishak Institute, Singapore, and Head of ISEAS's Temasek History Research Centre; email: Terence_Chong@iseas.edu.sg.

Kanda Naknoi is Associate Professor in the Department of Economics, University of Connecticut, Storrs, Connecticut, USA; email: kanda.naknoi@uconn.edu.

Michael J. Montesano is Coordinator of the Thailand and Myanmar Studies Programmes, ISEAS – Yusof Ishak Institute, Singapore; email: Michael_Montesano@iseas.edu.sg.

Nay Yan Oo, formerly a resident fellow at Pacific Forum in Honolulu, Hawaii, is political analyst in Yangon; email: nayyanoo.mm@gmail.com.

Prajak Kongkirati is Director of the Direk Jayanama Research Center and Deputy Dean for Research and Academic Service, Faculty of Political Science, Thammasat University, Bangkok, Thailand; email: prajakk@yahoo.com.

Robert H. Taylor has served numerous terms as Visiting Senior Fellow at the ISEAS – Yusof Ishak Institute, Singapore. He is the author of *The State in Myanmar* (2009) and *General Ne Win: A Political Biography* (2015); email: dr.tinhla@googlemail.com.

1

INTRODUCTION: TWO MAINLAND SOUTHEAST ASIAN MILITARIES IN COMPARATIVE PERSPECTIVE

Michael J. Montesano, Terence Chong and Prajak Kongkirati

In 1959, Aguedo F. Agbayani of Pangasinan introduced to the Philippine Congress a bill "designed to prevent the growth of the power and influence of the military in this country, in order to spare our country from the tragic experiences of our Asian neighbors, recently in Burma and Thailand, where military dictatorship has marred their beautiful history" (Republic of the Philippines, House Bill 2220 [1959], quoted in Berlin 2008, p. 97).

Congressman Agbayani evidently had the keen sense of connections between the Philippines and the rest of Asia not uncommon among his countrymen in the post-war period. His reference to Burma, today's Myanmar, concerned the military's non-violent assumption of power in the country in October of the preceding year and to Chief of the General Staff Ne Win's consequent service as premier at the head of a "caretaker government" (Nakanishi 2013, pp. 84–88). In Thailand, Field

Marshal Sarit Thanarat had staged *coups d'état* in September 1957 and again in October 1958 (Thak 2007, pp. 78–80). Of course, Agbayani could not know that, following elections in early 1960, Ne Win would return power to a civilian government in Rangoon, only to mount a coup of his own in March 1962 and thus to initiate long-term military control of Burma, or that military rule in Bangkok was destined to last another fourteen years, until October 1973. These developments and their legacies account for the publication of the present volume, treating the same two states whose examples troubled Aguedo Agbayani sixty years ago.

The late Donald Berlin called attention to the congressman's 1959 bill in his landmark study of civil-military relations in the Philippines during the decades preceding President Ferdinand E. Marcos's declaration of martial law in September 1972 (Berlin 2008).[1] It was the contention of that study that—contrary to received wisdom, despite the absence of direct military control of the government in Manila, but very much as in other Southeast Asian states and societies—"military influence in Philippine state and society historically ha[d] been substantial" (Berlin 2008, p. 140). At the same time, the specific forms of that influence during the 1946–72 period proved varied. They depended on the circumstances and nature of successive administrations, and the backgrounds and networks of the presidents who led them.

While Berlin explicitly argued for continuities in the political influence of the Armed Forces of the Philippines, continuities that students of Myanmar and Thailand would find familiar, his equally strong emphasis on variation in the patterns of that influence also merits attention. Ukrist Pathmanand and Michael Connors suggest a way to think systematically about such variation (Ukrist and Connors 2019).[2] Seeking to understand the political role of the Thai military between 1992 and 2014, they ground their approach in Samuel P. Huntington's observation, "Military explanations do not explain military interventions" (Huntington 1968, p. 194). Rather, one must understand praetorianism in the context of societies marked by the politicization of a range of social forces, and not just of their militaries (Huntington 1968, p. 195). Huntington wrote with reference to "underdeveloped societies" that were "out-of-joint" (Huntington 1968, p. 194). Ukrist and Connors opt for less judgemental terminology. They propose the idea of the "ambivalent state", marked by unresolved competition among "actors who may seek in the long run to fully direct state apparatuses and to transform the state in accord with their respective ideological orientations and the interests of the broadly defined social bases that they serve" (Ukrist and Connors 2019, pp. 7–8).

Ukrist and Connors view the competing actors in this scenario as would-be "regime framers" (Ukrist and Connors 2019, pp. 7–8). The ongoing competition among them, not least insofar as they include militaries, constitutes the ambivalence of states to which this analysis might apply—in Berlin's account, the Philippines between 1946 and the last of Colonel Gregorio "Gringo" Honasan's and the Reform the Armed Forces Movement's coup attempts in 1990; in Ukrist's and Connors's analysis, Thailand between "Black May" of 1992 and the National Council for Peace and Order (NCPO) *putsch* of the same month twenty-two years later; and Myanmar in the wake of the Tatmadaw's post-2008 or post-2010–11 initiation of *abertura*.

The contending actors—would-be regime framers—in an ambivalent state seek "to advance their differential hegemonic projects and to bring to the state a coherent dominating line" (Ukrist and Connors 2019, p. 8). Some of those actors will advance their projects from positions that Ukrist and Connors label "partial regimes"—marked by "partial control over ... apparatuses of the state" (Ukrist and Connors 2019, p. 8).[3] To be sure, that control may also extend beyond state apparatuses. It may reach into domains like business, finance, the media, education, associational life, culture and society. Each of these domains figures in the contention to replace ambivalence with hegemony. In the context of an ambivalent state, both the measure of control of official apparatuses and the stake in some of these domains enjoyed by a contending actor like the military constitutes that actor's occupation of a partial regime.[4]

The four studies in the present volume address the ideological, organizational, and economic dimensions of the partial regimes that the militaries of Myanmar and Thailand have occupied. While their focus is above all on the most recent decades, the reality that ambivalence has marked the Thai state, where its armed forces are concerned, for at least nine decades means that the studies on Thailand take a somewhat more historical approach than do those on Myanmar.

The conception of this volume dates from a time just a few years ago when observers, above all in Thailand, often remarked with gallows humour that civil-military relations in Thailand and Myanmar seemed to be going in opposite, and ostensibly unfamiliar, directions. Many Thais had long viewed their neighbours to the west as the victims of isolation and poverty rooted in persistent military dictatorship. Now, however, Thais witnessed, and even partook of, the optimism engendered by the changes in Myanmar embodied by the national elections of November 2010, the accession to power in Naypyidaw of the apparently reformist government of President Thein Sein early the following year, the stunning re-entry into electoral politics of the National League for Democracy (NLD) under the leadership of the then still iconic Aung San Suu Kyi in by-elections held the year after that, and her party's landslide victory in elections held in November 2015. Thais recalled the now dashed hopes of the 1990s not only for political reform in their own far more prosperous country, but also for the relegation of its soldiers to life in the barracks. And they contrasted the optimism blanketing Myanmar with the Thai military's crude political manipulation in installing Abhisit Vejjajiva into the premiership in December 2008 (Stent 2012, p. 33), and above all with the coup mounted by General Prayut Chan-ocha and his confederates in May 2014 and the political repression that followed.[5]

Thai voters went to the polls in March 2019. But parliament's vote, after a delay of more than two months, to retain Prayut as prime minister has as of the time of writing convinced many in Thailand that their country effectively remains under military rule and may well do so for the foreseeable future. Events have thus done little to relieve the gloomy outlook for civil-military relations of several years ago. It is, in contrast, Myanmar that has betrayed the expectations of that earlier moment. In 2017, attacks spearheaded by its military precipitated the flight of some 700,000 Rohingya people from Myanmar's Rakhine State to neighbouring Bangladesh. These attacks left the Myanmar armed forces directly implicated in one of the gravest and saddest humanitarian crises of our times. To deepen international outrage, the country's authorities subsequently arrested, and its courts then convicted, two Myanmar journalists working for Reuters after their exposure of atrocities committed during the course of the security forces' operations in Rakhine State.[6] In the face of these assaults on helpless civilians and on committed reporters, the NLD government under Aung San Suu Kyi's leadership abandoned all semblance of commitment to principle; it failed to call out the country's military for its actions or to defend the Reuters journalists' effort to do their jobs. These developments and others like them have taken the shine off the Myanmar story.

That that story has proved less simple, happy and straightforward than the innocent readings of not long ago suggested only underlines the continued importance of efforts on the part of scholars to understand the Myanmar military, and above all the nature and dynamics of civil-military relations in post-2011 Myanmar. This imperative joins a parallel need to deepen the ongoing revival of a tradition of scholarship on the Thai military that the events of the past decade and a half have occasioned (Ukrist and Connors 2019, p. 6).[7] In responding in a modest way to each of these imperatives, the present volume also seeks to cultivate an at least tentative comparative perspective.

The Myanmar Tatmadaw: Transformation and Economic Interests

Burma's and, since 1989, Myanmar's armed forces, the Tatmadaw,[8] have stood at the centre of the country's affairs for fully six decades. General Ne Win's March 1962 coup led to the inauguration of a single-party socialist regime. In the event, Nakanishi Yoshihiro has argued persuasively, Ne Win's "revolution was a failure in terms of achieving socialism, but a success in creating an institutional basis for a robust military regime" (Nakanishi 2013, p. 25). The nominally ruling Burma Socialist Programme Party (BSPP) "could not grow out of its condition of being 'the tatmadaw's party'" (Nakanishi 2013, p. 278). The implication of Nakanishi's broad argument about Burma during the 1962–88 period is that its armed forces did not face competing actors or have to occupy only a partial regime.

Tensions resulting from the Ne Win/BSPP/Tatmadaw regime's removal from circulation of several denominations of bank notes in late 1987 led to student protests starting in March of 1988. After the effective failure of a brutal crackdown on mass protests in August of that year, the officers who had by that time risen to the top of the Tatmadaw abolished the socialist regime. They seized power in September. The State Law and Order Restoration Council (SLORC) junta, rechristened the State Peace and Development Council (SPDC) in 1997, imposed on the country direct military rule that would last for nearly a quarter-century, until 2011.

Following the junta's annulment of elections in 1990 in which the NLD scored a dramatic triumph, this period of military rule saw the Tatmadaw control Myanmar society through the use of force, draconian laws, and severe restrictions on civil liberties and freedom of expression. Scholars and other observers of the country came to view Myanmar politics as a prototype of long-lasting military authoritarianism, though the country's continued isolation perhaps led them to overlook what would prove the significant social and economic implications of the demise of the more than just officially socialist regime and the onset of naked military rule from the end of the 1980s.[9]

Since 2010–11, Myanmar has undergone a period of political liberalization under a Tatmadaw-designed constitution adopted in 2008. The period has seen general elections in 2010 and 2015 and a range of other political reforms. Nevertheless, in a context of transitional democracy, of continuing warfare among groups aiming to represent various ethnic nationalities, and of mounting Islamophobia among segments of the country's Buddhist majority, Myanmar's armed forces remain a powerful political force. They control a quarter of all seats in both houses of the national parliament,[10] thus retain veto power over constitutional amendments, and have the right to name the ministers of defence, home affairs, and border affairs. The persistence of institutionalized military influence and the Tatmadaw's expansive, if changing, role in Myanmar's politics, society, and economy point to its status during the past decade as the occupant of a rather well-defined partial regime. That persistence and that role are also the foci of the studies in this volume by Nay Yan Oo and Maung Aung Myoe.

Nay Yan Oo provides a comprehensive and effectively elaborated analysis of changes affecting the Tatmadaw since 2011. His study focuses on the Tatmadaw as a defence institution, rather than as a political or economic actor. It argues that, despite their progress toward becoming "a new Tatmadaw", Myanmar's armed forces have held fast to their old repressive traits. They have continued to suppress ethnic nationalities, to violate the human rights of civilians, and to enforce media censorship. Real transformation has not yet occurred.

Observing that three generations of officers have led Myanmar's defence institution since its creation during the Second World War, Nay Yan Oo considers the character of the country's armed forces as that character developed after the 1962 coup. Under General Ne

Win, a member of the first generation of those officers, Tatmadaw leaders perceived themselves as both the defenders of the nation and the administrators of the country. The suspicion toward non-Bamar ethnic groups and foreign powers fundamental to the mentality of all generations of Myanmar military leaders was already significant. Indeed, the recent experience of facing Western sanctions has joined historical experience in leaving subsequent generations of Tatmadaw officers paranoid about the influence of external powers in their country's domestic affairs. To understand the Tatmadaw's role in Myanmar, according to Nay Yan Oo's analysis, one needs to understand the three "National Causes" introduced by the second-generation officers of the SLORC/SPDC and still upheld by the armed forces. These causes are "non-disintegration of the Union, non-disintegration of national solidarity, and perpetuation of the Union's sovereignty". Both internal and external threats to these National Causes ensure a strong response on the part of the armed forces.

Nay Yan Oo explains that Senior General Min Aung Hlaing and the rest of the current, third-generation leadership of the Tatmadaw seek to transform it into a "Standard Army" through a tripartite focus on modernizing the armed forces, building the capacity of military personnel, and pursuing active military diplomacy. This leadership has thus recommitted the institution to defence functions rather than governance. At the same time, and crucially, the Standard Army now envisioned by the Tatmadaw's leadership is not the same as the professional militaries of democratic states, which accept civilian supremacy and are scrupulous in staying out of politics. Even though the "new" Tatmadaw assigns priority to its roles in national security and in the military domain and no longer involves itself in the day-to-day affairs of the government, Nay Yan Oo reports, its leaders continue to believe that they have a significant role to play in the newly-developed democracy to which Myanmar's reform process has given rise. Indeed, the 2008 constitution, drafted under the SPDC junta, mandated the armed forces to build a "discipline-flourishing democracy" in the country.

Nay Yan Oo's study takes a positive view of recent developments concerning the Myanmar armed forces *as armed forces*. Despite mounting Western criticism of the Tatmadaw over the appalling situation in Rakhine State and persistent violations of human rights more generally, he believes that the military has no intention to annul Myanmar's democratic reforms of the past decade. How to square the failure of its current leadership to appreciate the gravity of its conduct in Rakhine State in 2017, and indeed long before that, with its vision of a Standard Army remains an open question; one is justified in fearing that that leadership sees no contradiction between that conduct and that vision. But Nay Yan Oo contends that the evolving Tatmadaw can, not least with the affirmation of the West, have a place in the country's progress toward a successful democratic order. Only time will tell whether the new characteristics of a "strong, capable and modern patriotic" Tatmadaw are compatible with such an order.

Like Nay Yan Oo's study, Maung Aung Myoe's contribution to this volume—the second on the Tatmadaw here—is exceptionally well informed. And, while Aung Myoe joins Nay Yan Oo in closely scrutinizing Myanmar's recent history of arms procurement, he turns that scrutiny to a different purpose. It serves in his study as one foundation of a broad investigation into the economic and financial resources enjoyed, and even generated, by the Tatmadaw. Aung Myoe thus has two foci. His study addresses not only the budgetary allocations to and the defence expenditures of Myanmar's armed forces but also their commercial interests. Drawing extensively on both official sources and data available through other channels, and compiling this range of data in a thoughtful and systematic way, the study's author provides a clear picture of the Tatmadaw's economic means and its business interests.

Aung Myoe points out that the Myanmar armed forces rely on two main sources of financial support—allocations from the government budget and revenue from commercial activity. Since the country's independence in 1948, its defence expenditures have varied with the political climate and with military policy. Burma's defence budget was high during the first decade after independence, as the country found itself in a state of civil war and embarked upon the expansion of military units. Later, defence spending as a share of GDP would hover around 4.0 per cent in 1980–81, 3.0 per cent in 1987–88, 3.5 per cent in the early 1990s and 2.0 per cent in the late 2000s.

Aung Myoe notes that, for most of the past decade, defence spending has been about 14 per cent of Union Government Expenditure. Officially, the Tatmadaw requested a 2017–18 defence budget of 2,905.195 billion kyat, intended to further its leadership's project to build the capable, strong and modern Standard Army discussed in Nay Yan Oo's study. Nevertheless, Aung Myoe believes that there is reason to doubt that this figure reflects reality, as Myanmar's armed forces have since the early 1990s been on a spending spree for military hardware and facilities. Aung Myoe's study describes this spree in invaluable, eye-opening detail.

Besides the annual state budget, the heavy involvement of the Tatmadaw in business activities, dating in the first instance to the early 1950s, also makes a vital contribution to the resources available to it. In practical terms, revenue from business operations helps compensate for the Myanmar armed forces' budgetary constraints. Ideologically, too, the Tatmadaw views its economic activities as contributions to nation-building and economic development.

In independent Burma, military involvement in business began with the provision of consumer goods to members of the armed forces, before expanding to include activities ranging from banking, manufacturing, shipping and trading to publishing, retail business and others. By the late 1950s, the business enterprises of the military had, taken together, become the largest commercial undertaking in the country.

Circumstances changed significantly during the 1962–88 period, when the military had to refrain from commercial activities and support the country's socialist economic programme. But the Myanmar military revived its involvement in business activities after 1988. The Tatmadaw penetrated deeply into the economy and monopolized several business sectors through two military-owned firms—Union of Myanmar Economic Holdings Ltd. (UMEHL) and the Myanmar Economic Corporation (MEC). These firms enjoyed state protection and, until 2016, tax exemption. The two military conglomerates have also become vehicles for patronage.

To the degree that UMEHL and the MEC appear to exemplify the Tatmadaw's lack of accountability, it is easy to associate them with that institution's half-century-long domination of Myanmar politics. That they are in fact creatures of the post-1988 era underlines the need to appreciate the dynamic relationship among military, polity, society and economy in the country. Likewise, attention to the military conglomerates—actors in the economic domain—allows for a sharper recognition of the Tatmadaw's institutional interests than does continued hand-wringing over its persistent political role.

Along with direct ownership of firms active in many sectors of the economy, the Tatmadaw engages in lucrative business deals with the "cronies" whose rise—like that of UMEHL and the MEC—was a defining phenomenon of the country's post-1990 political economy (Jones 2014, pp. 148 ff). As Aung Myoe's study details, the Tatmadaw was also a notorious land-grabber during the SLORC/SPDC era. It utilized confiscated lands both for military facilities and for income generation. While this issue has, in its undeniable complexity, been the subject of investigation, resolution is nowhere in sight. Tatmadaw land-grabbing remains a source of extreme bitterness among many segments of rural society in Myanmar.

Aung Myoe takes the view that the Tatmadaw's broad but unstated policy of aiming for self-sufficiency—as if in scripted pursuit of a secure partial regime—makes the expectation that it will withdraw from economic activities unrealistic. He observes, intriguingly, that such a withdrawal might come at the risk of pushing soldiers into criminal activities, as they sought to make up for lost income. Constructively, then, he calls for the cultivation of transparency and improved public relations on the part of the military conglomerates. This call signals both the clear-headedness of Aung Myoe's analysis and its alignment with a continuing determination to see Myanmar's ongoing transition succeed.

Taken together, Aung Myoe's study in this volume and that of Nay Yan Oo offer a sharply drawn picture of the recent development and the fundamental characteristics of Myanmar's armed forces. Political reform and democratic transition since 2010–11 have been the outcome of the military's changing political strategy. They have left the Tatmadaw, for the first time in decades, the occupier of a partial regime. They have had an impact on its operation as a defence institution and, most recently, even seen it give up oversight of the General Administration Department—"Myanmar's paramount government agency, acting as the backbone of public administration" (Arnold 2019).[11] The Myanmar armed forces' current leadership speaks publicly of its ambition to modernize and transform the institution.

In embracing the goal of becoming a "Standard Army", the Tatmadaw does not signal acceptance of the idea, common in Western liberal democracies, of a professional army that steers clear of politics and accepts the principle of civilian supremacy over the military, and for that matter over all state institutions. If then, Myanmar has in the past decade witnessed a transition from military dictatorship to ambivalent state, the military architects of that transition have, to a striking degree, ensured that its armed forces would occupy, with almost unquestioned security, a partial regime. The long record of deep Tatmadaw involvement in political and economic affairs certainly matters, particularly as it shapes Myanmar people's understanding of their society. At the same time, the two studies on that institution in this volume argue for a rigorous understanding of the contemporary relationship between Myanmar's military on the one hand and its polity and society on the other.

"The Royal Thai Army": Political Ideology and Economic Interests

Surachart Bamrungsuk—the most eminent active student of the Thai Army, its politics, and its political role[12]—observes that, "[s]ince its break with the palace in 1932 and through its extended record of political intervention in subsequent decades, the Thai officer corps has held an undisputed role as a leading political actor in the country" (Surachart 2019, p. 171). Today, he asserts, "the Thai military's support is a basic prerequisite for the emergence of democratic rule" (ibid.). While not using such terminology, Surachart's observations describe the influential, perhaps singularly influential, occupant of a partial regime in a chronically ambivalent state.

Those observations characterize a position markedly different from—and less dominant than—that enjoyed by the Tatmadaw in the five decades after 1962. Put simply, the state in Thailand has a longer record of uninterrupted ambivalence than does the state in Myanmar. It is in that context that one must understand Surachart's observations, as they testify to the prominence of the Thai armed forces as a political actor for a period of at least ninety years. They suggest that what Congressman Agbayani decried as a regrettable and recent turn of events in fact exemplified a reality that many in Thailand, and many observers of Thailand, have taken essentially for granted.

But such easy acceptance of the expansive role of the Thai Army merits interrogation. How, one must ask, did the military and its officers attain lasting prominence as political actors in Thailand?

A second question, the basic one with which Robert Taylor opens the epilogue to this volume, is also instructive. "To whom or what does an army ... owe its loyalty?" Taylor argues that the answer to this question varies. It depends on the roles—whether perceived or conceived by soldiers themselves, or assigned to the military institution as a component part of the political regime—that armed forces play on the national landscape.

Taylor's argument highlights the implications of the two studies on Thailand's military in this volume. Those studies suggest that the genius of the country's Army is that it owes its loyalty not to one specific institution, ideal, community, or political group, but rather to any one of these or to some combination of them—depending on circumstances and need. It may at any given moment purport to be loyal to the Thai monarchy, to the principle of democracy, to the cause of national economic development, to the Thai people, or to all of these at the same time. The long-term ambivalence of the Thai state, dating at least to 1932, has both demanded this versatility and given the advantage to actors capable of demonstrating it. More than any other actor or institution in the country, the Thai Army has met the consequent challenge and seized the resultant opportunity. Its place of lasting prominence in the country's politics has been due to its ability to navigate the shoals of time and ideology by successfully claiming always to have the nation's interests at heart. Even as the Army has suffered fractious internal politics, nakedly pursued its own economic interests, and repeatedly used violence against Thai citizens, both its ability effortlessly to slip the jersey of national interests over its shoulders and the public's acquiescence have defined its long-term political relevance. That relevance embodies, in turn, the Thai Army's occupation of a partial regime.

Paul Chambers provides an invaluable chronology of the changing relationship of the Thai armed forces with the country's perpetually ambivalent state. His consideration of that relationship begins even before the end of Siam's absolute monarchy. He frames this relationship with reference to military ideology.

Chambers's analysis begins with the establishment of standing land and naval forces in the reign of King Chulalongkorn (1868–1910). It notes the significance of what Walter Vella termed the "nationalistic militarism" promoted during the reign of King Vajiravudh (1910–25)

(Vella 1978, pp. 87 ff.). But the real turning point was 1932. A group of soldiers and civilian officials replaced absolute monarchy with a constitutional regime, and the military's putative *raison d'être* first shifted from protection of the monarchy to defence of the nation. It was perhaps from that moment on that the Thai armed forces' continuing occupation of a partial regime within the Bangkok polity became an unmistakable reality in the life of that polity.

As the substance of that occupation evolved, Chambers notes another significant change in the Thai Army's ideological orientation during the 1950s, when it encountered a new and apparently formidable opponent—communism. With this new enemy came a new ally, the Americans, and the Army absorbed doctrines, modes of education and training, and equipment from that ally. This same era saw national security become the central plank in the military's ideology. Initially, that emphasis further eclipsed monarchism among members of the Thai officer corps. Strong anti-communist fervour was useful for congealing the relationship between the armed forces, including the police, and their American patrons. Nevertheless, and without sacrificing that patronage, Field Marshal Sarit Thanarat's seizure of power in 1957 heralded the arrival of developmentalism and, even more so, of monarchism as core elements of Army ideology.[13] A direct line connects the 1957–63 Sarit era with the Army's continuing role as what Chambers terms "the junior elite partner of the monarchy". This status crystallized, at the latest, in the aftermath of royal intervention to help end violence on the streets of central Bangkok in October 1973. The staunch royalism of former Army commander-in-chief General Prem Tinsulanonda during his 1980–88 premiership and his service as member and then chairman of the Privy Council until his death in 2019 only reinforced the partnership.

In 1992, during a time of rapid economic growth and unprecedented prosperity in which the threat of communism was but the faintest memory to most members of Thai society, the Army's image suffered a major blow. The bloody and sinister "Black May" crackdown of that year came after weeks of demonstrations and strikes in Bangkok. The protests arose in opposition to the attempt, following elections, of an Army faction—centred on the fifth cohort of the Chulachomklao Royal Military Academy to follow the academy's American-style curriculum—to hold onto the power that it had seized in its coup of February 1991.

The failed crackdown marked a low point in the armed forces' recent history. It gave rise to a spirit of reformism that resulted in the 1997 constitution. This charter, Chambers argues, enshrined an unprecedented "civilian orientation towards the armed forces".

The 2001–6 period, between the dramatic rise of Thaksin Shinawatra to the Thai premiership—and to a position of apparent political mastery in the country—and his equally dramatic fall following an Army *coup d'état*, saw an attempt to bring the military under the control of the government. The case of Thaksin may exemplify more than any other Thai elections' habit of bringing to power politicians whose interests, visions and, notionally, probity do not match those of the military. This habit has meant that electoral outcomes and some of the alleged traits of Thailand's political class help account for the military's renewed emphasis on the importance of defending the monarchy. That emphasis depends on a view of that class that assumes its thoroughgoing corruption, selfishness and irresponsibility—characteristics that stand in putative contrast to those of the country's royal and military institutions. In consequence, Chambers asserts, grasping the factors that triggered the September 2006 coup against Thaksin requires an understanding of the armed forces' belief that "developmental militarism could trump the inefficiencies of democracy". That belief was equally relevant in 2014, when the military accused elected politicians of populism, corruption and immorality and thus deemed yet another coup and the establishment of the NCPO junta necessary.

Kanda Naknoi's study of material underpinnings of the military's outsize long-term role in Thai life—and of the partial regime that it has occupied—complements Chambers's attention to the ideological dimensions of that role. Chambers in fact notes in his study the origins during the 1938–44 premiership of Field Marshal Plaek Phibunsongkhram of the Army's direct participation in the Thai economy. And, like his study, Kanda's also underlines the importance as a factor in recent Thai history of the Army's continuing pursuit of its institutional or corporate interests. Her contribution to this volume also serves to make her influential writing on the economic roles of the Thai military more widely available in English.[14]

Kanda premises her engrossing analysis of the military's evolving interests in various economic sectors on the elegantly drawn observation that it is both a consumer and producer of goods and services. She points out that many of the goods and services in question have essentially no relation to national security. Working entirely from publicly available data, she examines military involvement in banking and asset management, in radio and television, in real estate, and in several other sectors. Whether through a presence on boards of directors, major ownership stakes, or both, the Thai Army has long been able to ensure that the activities undertaken and decisions taken by a number of major Thai business concerns have secured and advanced its economic interests. The financial stakes involved have, as Kanda makes clear, been enormous, and it is impossible to understand either the resources available to, or the status of, the country's armed forces without taking those stakes into account.

Kanda's examination of military involvement in radio and television is particularly eye-opening. During the era of the Cold War, the Thai armed forces used the radio channels that they controlled for purposes relating to national security. The 1990s brought change, as these channels began to feature more commercial programming—offered through concessions to private companies, especially those in the music industry. In the even more important realm of television, 1957 saw establishment of the Royal Thai Army Television Station. Kanda tracks the growth and diversification of the Army's television business, each stage of which saw it maintain an important position in a sector whose dynamism one hardly associates with state-owned concerns. Successive changes in the policy regime governing television in Thailand have, to be sure, benefitted that business.

Indeed, it is perhaps the most significant contention of Kanda's study that the Thai military—and above all the Army—has functioned in areas unrelated to security both as service provider and as policymaker simultaneously. While scholars have paid scant attention to these twin roles, their significance and their complementarity demand that one understand the partial regime occupied by Thailand's armed forces with an eye to political economy, and not just to politics as narrowly defined.

Kanda's scrutiny of the Thai Army's roles as service provider and policymaker leads her to conclude that rules introduced by the military governments that have taken power following coups have worked to the advantage of military concerns operating in various significant sectors, above all banking and broadcasting. One of the functions, and perhaps one of the purposes, of such rules or regulations has been the restriction of new concerns' entry into these sectors. Army-affiliated firms have thus been able to operate in less competitive business environments than would have been the case in the absence of those rules and regulations. Kanda's findings lead her to posit "the possibility of a commercial logic to coups in Thailand". Her study calls for explicit and systematic attention to the political economy of military intervention in Thai politics, and of the opportunities for policymaking to which that intervention may lead. One expects, too, that this call has relevance to political interventions on the part of the armed forces that fall short of *coups d'état*.

Paul Chambers's and Kanda Naknoi's studies work together to frame a robust understanding of the persistent influence of the Thai Army, and of its position as the occupier of a partial regime. Central to that understanding is an ability to adapt to successive administrations and changing political, economic and even technological currents, many of them washing over Thailand from far beyond its borders.

Comparative Perspectives

In expressing his concern that undue military influence on Philippine politics could prove "tragic", and noting that military intervention had tarnished the "beautiful histories" of Burma and Thailand, Congressman Aguedo Agbayani explicitly adopted a comparative perspective. Donald Berlin's study of the involvement of the Armed Forces of the Philippines in politics benefitted from greater hindsight than was possible when the congressman introduced his bill to check such involvement in 1959. Developments in Myanmar and Thailand in the decades after 1960 certainly informed the assertion in the concluding passage of Berlin's study that "military influence in Philippine state and society historically has been substantial and thus constitutes additional evidence of this nation's Southeast Asian character" (Berlin 2008, p. 140).

Berlin extended that assertion to call for the cultivation of a comparative perspective in scholarship on "civil-military developments" in Southeast Asia (Berlin 2008, p. 140). Cultivating that perspective ranks among the goals of the present volume. But, just as Berlin did in scrutinizing the Philippines alone, the volume seeks to move beyond both generalizations about the Southeast Asian region and the all too common stylized treatments of the political roles of the Tatmadaw and the Thai Army in which journalists and even political scientists—the vast majority illiterate in the Myanmar and Thai languages—have often engaged.

In the opening lines of his epilogue to this volume, Robert Taylor characterizes the military as a nation's "sole legitimate yielder of violence". This trait means that armed forces' political roles are ultimately functions of their ability to threaten or practise the use of force against domestic opponents or potential opponents with less ability, let alone willingness, to use force. This reality obtains both in states under military control, like Burma and then Myanmar in 1962–2011 or Thailand most recently in 2014–19, and in those marked by the ambivalence that has marked Myanmar since 2011 and Thailand for—as Taylor notes—most of its post-1932 history. Ideological posturing on the part of soldiers as defenders of the nation or of its most important institutions, or as members of an organization uniquely capable of fostering development or modernization, cannot obscure importance of violence and the potential to use force as the bases of military influence in a country's political, economic and social affairs.

A corollary of this reality is that that influence goes hand in hand with illiberal urges or environments. It is the enemy of the open society. Comparative insight suggested by the studies presented in this volume reflects the deeply rooted, necessary antagonism between military roles outside the narrow sphere of national defence on the one side and the possibility of robust and secure liberal political orders on the other.

One must then, for example, understand the assumption of significant economic roles on the part of the Tatmadaw and the Thai Army with reference to political context. Both the UMEHL and the MEC are creatures of the repressive SLORC/SPDC era in Myanmar. Thai military involvement in business dates to the Phibun era. Field Marshal Phin Chunhawan's role in building the commercial empire of the War Veterans Organization of the Ministry of Defense was closely linked to his leadership of the coup of November 1947 that restored post-war Army domination of the government in Bangkok (Suehiro 1989, p. 136). Similarly, the Thai Army's activities in the fields of banking and television broadcasting took off during the authoritarian rule of Field Marshal Sarit Thanarat and his successor Field Marshal Thanom Kittikhachon, the latter in power during 1963–73.

Taylor also affirms the importance of militaries' institutional interests. One learns from Kanda's and Aung Myoe's studies, and from the comparison of the Myanmar and Thai cases that they make possible, that the breadth of those interests depends not least on the political environments that militaries themselves shape.

Another valuable point of comparison between Myanmar's and Thailand's armed forces lies in the realm of historical legacies. What Nakanishi observes for Burma and then Myanmar and for outright military regimes more generally proves equally relevant to Thailand and to military occupants of merely partial regimes: durability must be the object of explanatory effort (Nakanishi 2013, pp. 3–4, 283 ff.). But the legacies that undergird the persistent roles of the Tatmadaw and of the Thai Army in areas beyond the realm of national defence present contrasts that belie what cultural similarity and geographical proximity might lead one to expect.

Among those contrasting legacies, origins are case in point. The Tatmadaw traces its origins to Burma's or Myanmar's "first national army", established in 1941; it "fought for the freedom of the nation" against foreign powers, first the British Empire and then Imperial Japan (Nakanishi 2013, pp. 285, 292). On the other hand, and as Benedict Anderson persuasively argued, Thailand's modern armed forces originated at a time in the late nineteenth century when the British and French Empires guaranteed Siam's external security (Anderson 1978, p. 202). The most important initial functions of those forces were "*internal* royalist consolidation" and service as "an emblem of modernity for the outside world" (Anderson 1978, pp. 203–4). Chambers's study in this volume notes the subsequent formative influence of what was at the very least a quasi-empire, that of the United States, on those armed forces.

American influence on the Thai military came during what Douglas Blaufarb labelled "the counterinsurgency era" (Blaufarb 1977). And, indeed, the role of counterinsurgency in shaping both the Tatmadaw and the Thai Army figures as a second crucial pair of legacies.

The former force has confronted rival militaries operating within Burmese and Myanmar national territory, not least what one today calls "ethnic armed groups", since the months directly following independence from Britain in 1948.[15] Nakanishi notes pointedly that three decades of counterinsurgent warfare had forged the generation of officers who took control of the state in 1988 (Nakanishi 2013, p. 281).[16] The emphasis here must be on warfare, rather than on political approaches. The Tatmadaw did not adopt strategies of counterinsurgency grounded in "civic action", organicist conceptions of state-society relations, or what Mary Callahan calls "institutional reforms allowing more inclusionary politics" (Callahan 2004, p. 5). Instead, the 1960s saw it introduce an approach centred on "four cuts", on denying insurgents access to sources of "food, funds, intelligence, recruits" (International Crisis Group 2016, p. 7). Both as practice and as doctrine, violence and coercion would remain the Tatmadaw's enduring and unleavened mode of counterinsurgency (International Crisis Group 2016, p. 7; Abrahamian 2017).

Awareness of the choices that the Tatmadaw made in its approach to counterinsurgent operations serves understanding of the tragic ordeal of Rakhine State in recent years.[17] It also, Thant Myint-U argues, informs understanding of Myanmar's difficulty in coping with the cataclysmic impact of Cyclone Nargis in May 2008. Despite being "by far the best-equipped institution in the country", he writes, the Tatmadaw "was essentially a counterinsurgency force, with no experience or training in disaster relief" (Thant Myint-U 2020, p. 88).

During the recent era of state ambivalence, many observers have contended that battles with ethnic armed groups provide the Tatmadaw with a justification for its claims on government resources, and for its continued political role. The years ahead will clarify the implications of Senior General Min Aung Hlaing's vision of a Standard Army for any adjustment to the deeply rooted counterinsurgency orientation of Myanmar's armed forces.

Callahan contends that Myanmar's history of "war-induced state-building has solidified ... the 'command relationship' between state and society" in that country (Callahan 2004, p. 221).[18] Both the counterinsurgency experience of the Thai Army and its impact have been somewhat different. The contrast is manifest in a variety of areas. For one, the armed forces of the Communist Party of Thailand (CPT) did not threaten Bangkok's control of expanses of the national territory to a degree that recalls the situation faced by the Tatmadaw across the past seven decades. Yet the Thai Army, and the Thai state more generally, took very seriously the threat to the integrity of that state posed by those forces. The military's experience of besting Communist insurgents, as it did by the early 1980s, became central to its self-image.¹⁹ This remains true even despite its failure to bring to an end the bloody insurgency that has scarred South Thailand's Patani region for the past decade and a half.

More important than the impact of counterinsurgent campaigns against the forces of the CPT on the Thai Army's self-image was its fundamental and formative impact on Army thinking, and on the Thai state's relationship with Thai citizens. In contrast to the situation in Myanmar, that is, the most noteworthy legacy of Thailand's experience of counterinsurgency has little to do with actual warfare, or even with national security as traditionally understood. Rather, the significance of that experience lies in the socio-political vision to which it gave rise, and in the strategies and tactics of civic action, inclusion and incorporation, co-optation and control, and depoliticization that that vision informs. Those strategies and tactics remain central to the Thai Army's project of what Connors and Ukrist term regime-framing; they represent a factor in its continuing ability to occupy a partial regime in Thailand's ambivalent state. Indeed, appreciation of the quasi-organicist grounding of those strategies and tactics is central to any understanding of the Thai state's ambivalence today.²⁰

Two further kinds of legacy merit mention in a comparative discussion of the Tatmadaw and the Thai armed forces. One concerns the relationship between military officers and civilian officials in the Burmese and then Myanmar state and in the Thai state. While an "imbalance" between soldiers and civilians certainly has marked both those states during most of the past six decades,²¹ that imbalance has proved far more severe in the case of Burma and then Myanmar than in that of Thailand. The latter state has simply never witnessed the extensive substitution of military officers for civilian officials that occurred across the bureaucracy of the latter (Nakanishi 2013, pp. 27 and 142 ff.).²²

Then there is the legacy of royalism. Military officers figured prominently among the members of the *Khana ratsadon*, or People's Party, whose seizure of state power in Bangkok on 24 June 1932 brought Siam's absolute monarchy to an end. Determined to "place the King under the law" (Ferrara 2015, p. 5), the group did not intend to bring institutional change alone. With its composition of well educated, commoner officials—both civilian and military—and its emphasis on constitutionalism, its target was not only royal absolutism as a system of government but also royalism as a socio-political principle. Nevertheless, as Chambers's study in this volume makes clear, it is impossible to understand the Thai Army's conception of its role, and indeed of its mission, without taking the continued existence and—in the post-1957 and above all post-1973 periods—the renewed institutional and ideological prominence of the Thai monarchy into account. That prominence, and the influence and resources of the palace, means that the monarchy has occupied a partial regime of its own in Thailand. In the present century, the "monarchization" of the Thai military has, Chambers observes, reached perhaps unprecedented levels. It has, in fact, become a factor in renewed Army factionalism—a curse apparently alien to the history of the Tatmadaw (Nakanishi 2013, p. 285).[23]

To be sure, parallels between the hyper-royalism of the Thai military and the Tatmadaw's stake in Bamar Buddhist ethnic chauvinism merit attention from scholars. But for present purposes emphasis must be on the absence of royalism from the Myanmar political and ideological landscapes. In highlighting the contrasting situations of Thailand and Myanmar in this respect, Taylor recalls in his epilogue a conversation with a Tatmadaw officer who expressed his gratitude to the country's former British colonizers for abolishing—in 1885, at the conclusion of the brief Third Anglo-Burmese War—its monarchy. Taylor notes, too, that the military of Imperial Germany abandoned the Kaiser at the end of the First World War; the birth of the Weimar Republic would soon follow. Taylor's discussion touches on more than just the question of formal political regime, however. It calls attention to the reality that, as in the Siam of 1932, the institutional interests of armed forces and of reigning monarchies do not always coincide. The need to confront the divergence of those interests is not a legacy of the Tatmadaw's history.

On one level, the contrasting legacies that shape the Myanmar Tatmadaw and the Thai Army appear to pose a fundamental challenge to Berlin's stress, in his study of the Armed Forces of the Philippines, on the importance of a Southeast Asian context for military influence on and involvement in politics. On another level, however, they impel one to look harder in the search for commonality, or at least for comparative perspective.

It is the search for comparative perspective on the Southeast Asian context that leads Robert Taylor to consider the case of interwar Germany in this volume's epilogue. Recourse to the case of the Weimar

Republic is apropos. Its history of social turmoil and ideological contention certainly matches Ukrist's and Connors's characterization of an ambivalent state. Turning to the work of John Wheeler-Bennett to trace the German military's relationship to the fraught and hectic politics of that star-crossed polity, Taylor centres his discussion on the distinction that that scholar drew between the years during which that military controlled politics and those during which it made the mistake of playing politics.

In the Southeast Asian context, and understood with reference to Ukrist's and Connors's ideas, this distinction is both relevant and revealing. Taylor argues that the armed forces of six of the ten states that comprise the region today have largely avoided both trying to control politics and actively playing politics. He lists Malaysia, Singapore, Brunei, Cambodia, Laos and Vietnam. Indonesia, the Philippines, Myanmar and Thailand present a different picture.[24]

Comparing Myanmar and Thailand in particular, Taylor observes, "It would appear, on balance, that the army of Thailand has been more willing to play politics and less able to control the outcome of politics than the army of Myanmar". Taylor's broad conclusions map neatly onto ideas about ambivalent states and the contests to frame regimes that characterize those states. Simply put, the Thai Army's willingness, or need, to play politics has been a function of the chronic ambivalence of the Thai state. In contrast, for half a century the Tatmadaw framed the regime that governed Burma and then Myanmar, suffering no competing actors. In state ambivalence, or the periodic lack thereof, may lie the crucial commonality between the militaries of these two Mainland Southeast Asian neighbours and the political roles of those militaries.

The control of politics that the Tatmadaw exerted during that half-century, from the early 1960s, has in the last decade given way to the necessity that Myanmar's soldiers play politics. In a situation of their own making, and even as they may have designed the country's 2008 constitution to ensure continued military hegemony, theirs is now an ambivalent state. In moving in 2019 to amend that constitution and thus to reduce the political role of the Tatmadaw,[25] the NLD government sought nothing less than to reframe the regime. Now in the position of rival aspiring regime framer, the military, with its allies, found itself forced to join the ensuing political contest.

An analogous situation of political contestation obtained in Thailand at the same time. Submitting to close scrutiny the post-2014 regime of General Prayut and the NCPO, Prajak Kongkirati and Veerayooth Kanchoochat have exposed its effort to secure lasting control of Thailand's politics (Prajak and Veerayooth 2018). The junta's chosen means included attempting to depoliticize society, enhancing and embedding military power, designing the 2017 constitution to ensure lasting military influence, and recalibrating the role of big business in the Thai polity. But, in finally calling the elections of 24 March 2019, the Prayut regime effectively traded political control for the need to play politics.[26] Thailand again became an ambivalent state, in which contending occupiers of partial regimes—including not just the Thai Army but also the increasingly active monarchy—sought to frame the hegemonic regime.

Nothing illustrated this abrupt change so clearly as the emergence of the Future Forward Party. Both during the campaign for the 2019 polls and after taking its seats in parliament, the new party succeeded in putting onto the political agenda existential questions about the Army's prominence in the country's affairs.[27] It did so with remarkable deftness and timing. And the ferocious legal and political backlash on the part of the military and its allies that the upstart party thus provoked only called attention to the ongoing competition to frame the regime. It was a case of the Thai military playing politics, and certainly not controlling politics.

Ironically, both the SPDC and the NCPO juntas effected on timetables of their own choosing the 2010–11 and March 2019 "transitions" in their respective countries. It was these transitions that left them compelled to play rather than able to control politics. In normative terms, of course, neither a military that controls politics nor one that plays politics is acceptable. Like Filipinos, Indonesians, and their other Southeast Asian neighbours, citizens of Myanmar and Thailand deserve regimes and economies free of military interference and even influence. As Sam Huntington argued fifty years ago, however, achieving that objective is not a military matter. Rather, it requires overcoming obstacles in the social and political and other realms. The need to overcome those obstacles presents the most noteworthy commonality between Myanmar and Thailand, as the four important studies in this volume make evident.

NOTES

1. This book is the published version of Berlin (1982).
2. Note that page numbers in citations to Ukrist and Connors (2019) refer to the advance publication version of the article at https://doi.org/10.1080/00472336.2019.1635632.
3. Ukrist and Connors borrow this analytical approach from Brown (2016) (Ukrist and Connors 2019, p. 21 n. 6).
4. This usage of "occupation" is also drawn from Ukrist and Connors (2019, p. 8).
5. See the various chapters in Montesano, Chong, and Heng (2019).
6. See Wa Lone et al. (2018) and Lasseter (2018).
7. As the design of the cover of the present volume suggests, its editors would place it in the lineage of two important earlier ISEAS publications on the Thai military, Chai-anan (1982) and Suchit (1987).
8. The term refers to the armed forces as a whole, including the Army, Navy, and Air Force, though it is difficult to argue that the first of those services has not been the dominant branch of the Tatmadaw. Nakashi notes, for example, that as of 2012 or 2013 the manpower level of the Army stood at 375,00, while those of the Navy and Air Force stood at 16,000 and 15,000, respectively (Nakanishi 2013, p. 291).
9. On the abrupt launch of a more liberal economic order from late 1988, see Nakanishi (2013, p. 294).
10. The same is true at the level of state and regional assemblies.
11. What remains the best study of the General Administration Department is Kyi Pyar Chit Saw and Arnold (2014).
12. Among Thailand's three service branches, the Air Force has as an institution never played a political role, and the political role of the Navy, insignificant for many decades now, never seriously rivalled that of the Army. The commanders-in-chief of that latter branch or *phubanchakan thahan bok*, rather than the Thai military's inter-service supreme commander or *phubanchakan thahan sungsut*, is, likewise, the most powerful officer in the armed forces. Studies of the influence on and involvement of the military in Thai politics like those in this volume must therefore focus on the Army. While in English that dominant service affects the name "Royal Thai Army", its actual Thai name, *kongthap bok*, simply means "ground forces". That name contains no element relating to royalism or the monarchy; see *Kongthap bok* (n.d.).
13. See Thak (2007 [1979]) for a classic and long influential interpretation of the Sarit era.
14. For earlier Thai-language publications, see for example Kanda (2012a, 2012b); also see Kanda (2020) for a recent, related, paper in English.

15. See Callahan (2004, pp. 114 ff.).
16. Also see Nakanishi (2013, pp. 289–90).
17. For elaboration of this same point, see International Crisis Group (2016) and Abrahamian (2017).
18. Callahan here borrows terminology from Young (1988, p. 51).
19. The best-known statement of this case is probably Saiyud (1986). Also see Marks (1994); Chai-anan, Kusuma and Suchit (1990); Moore (2010); and Bergin (2016). Murray (1984), which gestures at a more balanced understanding of the end of the insurgency of the Communist Party of Thailand, also merits attention. On a related point, Kanda's study in this volume notes the early counterinsurgent role of military radio channels in Thailand.
20. See Puangthong (2017) and Puangthong (2019), each of which draws on the author's forthcoming book, *Infiltrating Society: The Thai Military's Internal Security Affairs*. Also see Montesano (2015, 2019a, 2019b, 2019c).
21. The term comes from Nakanishi (2013, p. 288).
22. See Riggs (1966) on the functioning of Thailand's "bureaucratic polity" in its heyday.
23. On Thailand's "monarchized military" and Chambers's extended analysis of Thai royalism in relation to the armed forces in the most recent period, see Chambers and Napisa (2016).
24. Both the Republic of Vietnam and pre-1975 Cambodia fall outside of the set of cases that Taylor considers.
25. See San Yamin Aung (2019).
26. On the Thai elections of March 2019 and their outcomes, see Pitch (2019) and McCargo (2019).
27. See *Bangkok Post* (2019).

REFERENCES

Abrahamian, Andray. 2017. "The Tatmadaw Returns to the 'Four Cuts' Doctrine". *The Lowy Interpreter*, 4 September 2017. https://www.lowyinstitute.org/the-interpreter/tadmadaw-ominous-return-four-cuts-doctrine (accessed 7 February 2020).

Anderson, Benedict R.O'G. 1978. "Studies of Thai State: The State of Thai Studies". In *The Study of Thailand: Analyses of Knowledge, Approaches, and Prospects in Anthropology, Art History, Economics, History, and Political Science*, edited by Eliezer B. Ayal, pp. 193–234. Athens, Ohio: Ohio University Center for International Studies, Southeast Asia Program.

Arnold, Matthew. 2019. "Why GAD Reform Matters to Myanmar". *East Asia Forum*, 24 August 2019. https://www.eastasiaforum.org/2019/08/24/why-gad-reform-matters-to-myanmar/ (accessed 9 September 2019).

Bangkok Post. 2019. "Defending the Indefensible?" 4 December 2019. https://www.bangkokpost.com/opinion/opinion/1807929/defending-the-indefensible- (accessed 5 December 2019).

Bergin, Bob. 2016. "Defeating an Insurgency—The Thai Effort against the Communist Party of Thailand, 1965–ca. 1982". *Studies in Intelligence* 60, no. 2 (Extracts, June): 25–36. https://www.cia.gov/library/center-for-the-study-of-intelligence/csi-publications/csi-studies/studies/vol-60-no-2/pdfs/Bergin-Defeating-Insurgency.pdf (accessed 20 November 2019).

Berlin, Donald L. 1982. "Prelude to Martial Law: An Examination of Pre-1972 Philippine Civil-Military Relations". Doctoral dissertation, University of South Carolina, 1982.

———. 2008. *Before Gringo: History of the Philippine Military, 1830-1972*. Manila: Anvil.

Blaufarb, Douglas S. 1977. *The Counterinsurgency Era: U.S. Doctrine and Performance, 1950 to the Present*. New York: The Free Press.

Brown, Andrew. 2016. "Political Regimes and Employment Relations in Thailand". *Journal of Industrial Relations* 58, no. 2 (March): 199–214.

Callahan, Mary P. 2004. *Making Enemies: War and State Building in Burma*. Ithaca, New York: Cornell University Press.

Chai-anan Samudavanija. 1982. *The Thai Young Turks*. Singapore: Institute of Southeast Asian Studies.

Chai-anan Samudavanija, Kusuma Snitwongse, and Suchit Bunbongkarn. 1990. *From Armed Suppression to Political Offensive: Attitudinal Transformation of Thai Military Officers since 1976*. Bangkok: Institute of Security and International Studies, Faculty of Political Science, Chulalongkorn University.

Chambers, Paul, and Napisa Waitoolkiat. 2016. "The Resilience of Monarchised Military in Thailand". *Journal of Contemporary Asia* 46, no. 3: 425–44.

Ferrara, Federico. 2015. *The Political Development of Modern Thailand*. Cambridge: Cambridge University Press.

Huntington, Samuel P. 1968. *Political Order in Changing Societies*. New Haven: Yale University Press.

International Crisis Group. 2016. "Myanmar: A New Muslim Insurgency in Rakhine State". *Asia Report*, no. 283 (15 December 2016). https://d2071andvip0wj.cloudfront.net/283-myanmar-a-new-muslim-insurgency-in-rakhine-state.pdf (accessed 7 February 2020).

Jones, Lee. 2014. "The Political Economy of Myanmar's Transition". *Journal of Contemporary Asia* 44, no. 1: 144–70.

Kanda Naknoi. 2012a. "Setthasat saman samnuek 55 pi thun kongthap thai (ton thi 1)" [Common-sense economics: 55 years of Thai military capital (part 1)]. *Prachatai*, 23 March 2012a. https://prachatai.com/journal/2012/03/39802 (accessed 25 June 2012).

———. 2012b. "Setthasat saman samnuek 55 pi thun kongthap thai (ton thi 2)" [Common-sense economics: 55 years of Thai military capital (part 2)]. *Prachatai*, 25 April 2012b. https://prachatai.com/journal/2012/04/40226 (accessed 25 June 2019).

———. 2020. "The Thai Military as a Business Group, 1940-2016". CEI Working Paper Series, No. 2019-14. Institute of Economic Research, Hitotsubashi University, February 2020. http://hermes-ir.lib.hit-u.ac.jp/rs/handle/10086/31030 (accessed 28 March 2020).

Kongthap bok. N.d. "Kongthap bok phuea chat sat kasat lae prachachon" [The Army: For nation, religion, king and people]. https://www.rta.mi.th/rta_website/ (accessed 18 October 2019).

Kyi Pyar Chit Saw and Matthew Arnold. 2014. "Administering the State in Myanmar: An Overview of the General Administration Department". Yangon: MDRI and the Asia Foundation, Discussion Paper No. 6, October 2014. https://asiafoundation.org/wp-content/uploads/2014/10/Administering-the-State-in-Myanmar.pdf (accessed 9 September 2019).

Lasseter, Tom. 2018. "Dangerous News: How Two Young Reporters Shook Myanmar". A Reuters Special Report. Reuters, 8 August 2018. https://www.reuters.com/investigates/special-report/myanmar-reporters-democracy/ (accessed 5 September 2019).

Marks, Tom. 1994. *Making Revolution: The Insurgency of the Communist Party of Thailand in Structural Perspective*. Bangkok: White Lotus.

McCargo, Duncan J., ed. 2019. "Roundtable: Thailand's Amazing 24 March 2019 Elections". *Contemporary Southeast Asia* 41, no. 2 (August): 153–222.

Montesano, Michael J. 2015. "Praetorianism and 'the People' in Late-Bhumibol Thailand". *SEATIDE Online Papers*, no. 10. www.seatide.eu/?content=activitiesandresults&group=3 (accessed 23 August 2018).

———. 2019a. "As Thai Military Holds on to Power, a 1980 Order by Former PM Prem Looms Large". *TODAY*, 6 June 2019a. https://www.todayonline.com/commentary/thai-military-holds-power-1980-order-former-pm-prem-looms-large (accessed 10 July 2019).

———. 2019b. "The Place of the Provinces in Thailand's Twenty-Year National Strategy: Toward Community Democracy in a Commercial Nation?" *ISEAS Perspective*, no. 2019/60, 8 August 2019b. https://www.iseas.edu.sg/images/pdf/ISEAS_Perspective_2019_60.pdf (accessed 20 November 2019).

———. 2019c. "National Security and 'Immunising' Thais to Political Conflict". *New Mandala*, 4 December 2019c. https://www.newmandala.org/national-security-and-immunising-thais-to-political-conflict/ (accessed 10 December 2019).

Montesano, Michael J., Pavin Chachavalpongpun, and Aekapol Chongvilaivan, eds. 2012. *Bangkok, May 2010: Perspectives on a Divided Thailand*. Singapore: Institute of Southeast Asian Studies, 2012.

Montesano, Michael J., Terence Chong, and Mark Heng. 2019. *After the Coup: The National Council for Peace and Order Era and the Future of Thailand*. Singapore: ISEAS – Yusof Ishak Institute.

Moore, Jeff M. 2010. "The Thai Way of Counterinsurgency". PhD dissertation, University of Exeter, UK. https://ore.exeter.ac.uk/repository/bitstream/handle/10036/3142/MooreJ%20.pdf?sequence=2.

Murray, Charles. 1984. "Thailand: The Domino That Didn't Fall". *The Atlantic Monthly* (November): 34–48.

Nakanishi Yoshihiro. 2013. *Strong Soldiers, Failed Revolution: The State and Military in Burma, 1962-1988*. Singapore and Kyoto: NUS Press and Kyoto University Press.

Pitch Pongsawat. 2019. "Kansueksa khwamkhlueanwai thangkanmueang lae phruetikam kanlueaktang samachik sapha phuthaen ratsadon 24 minakhom 2462 phuenthi krungthep mahanakhon" [A Study of Political Activity and Electoral Behaviour in Bangkok during the 24 March 2019 Parliamentary Elections]. Research report submitted to King Prajadhipok's Institute. Bangkok, October 2019.

Prajak Kongkirati and Veerayooth Kanchoochat. 2018. "The Prayuth Regime: Embedded Military and Hierarchical Capitalism in Thailand". *TRaNS: Trans-Regional and -National Studies of Southeast Asia* 6, no. 2 (July): 279–305.

Puangthong Pawakapan. 2017. "The Central Role of Thailand's Internal Security Operations Command in the Post-Counterinsurgency Period". Trends in Southeast Asia, no. 17/2017. Singapore: ISEAS – Yusof Ishak Institute, p. 7. https://www.iseas.edu.sg/images/pdf/TRS17_17.pdf (accessed 11 July 2019).

———. 2019. "Moradok khong phon ek Prem: kankhayai muanchon chattang khong rat" [The Legacy of General Prem: the expansion of the state's organized masses]. *The 101 World*, 4 June 2019. https://www.the101.world/heritage-of-prem-tinsulanonda/ (accessed 12 July 2019).

Republic of the Philippines. House Bill 2220. 1959. Introduced by Congressman A.F. Agbayani, Philippine House of Representatives, Fourth Congress of the Republic of the Philippines, Second Session.

Riggs, Fred W. 1966. *Thailand: The Modernization of a Bureaucratic Polity*. Honolulu: East-West Center Press.

Saiyud Kerdphol. 1986. *The Struggle for Thailand: Counter-insurgency 1965-1985*. Bangkok: S. Research Center.

San Yamin Aung. 2019. "Myanmar Parliament Approves Constitutional Amendment Committee Report". *The Irrawaddy*, 9 August 2019. https://www.irrawaddy.com/news/burma/myanmar-parliament-approves-constitutional-amendment-committee-report.html (accessed 5 December 2019).

Stent, James. 2012. "Thoughts on Thailand's Turmoil, 11 June 2010". In *Bangkok, May 2010: Perspectives on a Divided Thailand*, edited by Michael J. Montesano,

Pavin Chachavalpongpun, and Aekapol Chongvilaivan, pp. 15–41. Singapore: Institute of Southeast Asian Studies.

Suchit Bunbongkarn. 1987. *The Military in Thai Politics, 1981-1986*. Singapore: Institute of Southeast Asian Studies.

Suehiro Akira. 1989. *Capital Accumulation in Thailand, 1855-1985*. Tokyo: Centre for East Asian Cultural Studies, Toyo Bunko.

Surachart Bamrungsuk. 2019. "Thailand's Zig-Zag Road to Democracy: Continuity and Change in Military Intervention". In *After the Coup: The National Council for Peace and Order Era and the Future of Thailand*, edited by Michael J. Montesano, Terence Chong, and Mark Heng, pp. 170–74. Singapore: ISEAS – Yusof Ishak Institute.

Thak Chaloemtiarana. 2007 [1979]. *Thailand: The Politics of Despotic Paternalism*. Ithaca, New York: Cornell Southeast Asia Program.

Thant Myint-U. 2020. *The Hidden History of Burma: Race, Capitalism, and the Crisis of Democracy in the 21st Century*. New York: W.W. Norton.

Ukrist Pathmanand and Michael K. Connors. 2019. "Thailand's Public Secret: Military Wealth and the State". *Journal of Contemporary Asia*. Advance publication. https://doi.org/10.1080/00472336.2019.1635632.

Vella, Walter. 1978. *Chaiyo: King Vajiravudh and the Development of Thai Nationalism*. Honolulu: University of Hawai'i Press.

Wa Lone, Kyaw Soe Oo, Simon Lewis, and Antoni Slodkowski. 2018. "Massacre in Myanmar: How Myanmar Forces Burned, Looted and Killed in a Remote Village". A Reuters Special Report. Reuters, 8 February 2018. https://www.reuters.com/investigates/special-report/myanmar-rakhine-events/ (accessed 5 September 2019).

Young, Crawfurd. 1988. "The African Colonial State and Its Political Legacy". In *The Precarious Balance: State and Society in Africa*, edited by Donald Rothchild and Naomi Chazan, pp. 25–66. Boulder, Colorado: Westview Press.

2

A NEW TATMADAW WITH OLD CHARACTERISTICS

Nay Yan Oo

"New" and "old" are appropriate words to capture the democratic transition in Myanmar.[1]

In the years after the British left Burma on 4 January 1948, the newly independent nation seemed to number among those with the greatest potential for rapid development. Parliamentary democracy was functioning, and the country's democratic institutions, while still young, were gradually growing stronger. But the period of stability did not last long. On 2 March 1962, the army staged a *coup d'état* on the pretext of saving the country from disintegration. Repressive rule replaced democracy, and, with first the "Burmese Way to Socialism" and then crony capitalism, the country became an economic backwater. Self-imposed isolation from the 1960s to the 1980s, coupled with international sanctions in subsequent decades, made matters worse. The once promising country lagged far behind many of its Asian neighbours. Today Myanmar is one of the least developed countries in the world.

It took almost half a century for Myanmar to explore democracy again and to rethink the governance structure that had left it impoverished. The military junta designed a new constitution, the third one since independence, which was approved in a nationwide referendum on 29 May 2008. A general election, albeit a rigged one, was held two years later, in November 2010; the military-backed Union Solidarity and Development Party (USDP) won. As a result, a quasi-civilian administration came to power in March 2011. A new political system with separation of powers among the executive branch, the legislature and the judiciary emerged. At last, Myanmar had become free of military dictatorship.

However, old institutions from Myanmar's troubled history were still present. The bureaucracy, run by civil servants of uncertain competence and with former military officers occupying many senior positions, was inefficient. The rule of law remained fragile, as political influence and money continued to influence court decisions. Corruption was rampant. Myanmar was trying to find a new future, but the shadow of the past lingered.

This "new-and-old" and "somewhere-in-between" situation also applies to the country's military. Like other institutions in Myanmar, the armed forces, known as the Tatmadaw, are going through a transformation. Direct military rule over the country has ended. Yet the Tatmadaw has not fully returned to the barracks. Nor does it intend to do so in the near future. Article 6(f) of the 2008 constitution permits the Tatmadaw a leadership role in national politics. With 25 per cent of parliamentary seats held by men in uniform, the military holds a veto over amendment of the constitution, which requires more than 75 per cent of the legislature's support. The Tatmadaw is also in charge of three security-related ministries: Defence, Home Affairs and Border Affairs. The president of Myanmar is not the commander-in-chief of its armed forces; she or he cannot give them orders. Articles 417 and 418 of the constitution—included in Chapter 11, "Provisions on States of Emergency"—even allow the Tatmadaw to stage a coup in a time of crisis (Ministry of Information 2008).

While acknowledging the Tatmadaw's enormous power in governance, this chapter steps away from a focus on the role of the military in Myanmar's politics. Its primary focus is, rather, on the Tatmadaw as a defence institution. Since the political reforms of 2011, the Tatmadaw has been undertaking several changes to reflect the country's new democratic system. New leadership has emerged, and this leadership is directing the military to refocus on its primary functions of defence. In addition, the new leadership is reforming the Tatmadaw into a "Standard Army". In essence, Myanmar's armed forces have, or at least will, become a new Tatmadaw. However, their old behaviour, such as violating human rights and limiting freedom of the press, persists. The present chapter asserts that Myanmar's post-2011 military is a new Tatmadaw with old characteristics.

Emerging New Leadership

Three generations of leaders have commanded the Tatmadaw since its inception during the Second World War (Tin Maung Maung Than 2010, p. 134). On 27 December 1941, a group of Burmese nationalists known as the Thirty Comrades established the Burma Independence Army in Bangkok with the help of Japan, whose military trained the group on Hainan Island. The Thirty Comrades were the first generation of Tatmadaw leaders, and, among them, General Ne Win was appointed as chief of staff of the Burma Army after independence. He overthrew a democratically elected government in the *coup d'état* of March 1962.

Members of the second generation of the Tatmadaw's leadership built their military careers during the era of Ne Win's Burmese Way to Socialism. Under what amounted to a military dictatorship,[2] the country was isolated from the rest of the world, and Ne Win's closed-door policies resulted in a long period of economic stagnation. Burma was in turmoil by the late 1980s. University students in Rangoon started a series of protests in 1988, and the pro-democracy movement quickly spread to other parts of the country. Student leaders called for a nationwide demonstration on 8 August 1988, which would be later known as the 8888 Uprising. Unable to handle the situation, Ne Win asked the military to assume direct control of the state from his government. The Tatmadaw staged a coup on 18 September and set up the State Law and Order Restoration Council (SLORC). Ne Win tried to pull strings from behind the scenes, but by the early 1990s it was clear that Ne Win's influence was ebbing and that the Tatmadaw was controlled by its second-generation leaders.

The military junta renamed the SLORC the State Peace and Development Council (SPDC) in 1997 (Maung Aung Myoe 2009, pp. 1–2). From 1992, the junta's chairman was Senior General Than Shwe, who also succeeded General Saw Maung as Tatmadaw commander-in-chief in that year, when the latter's health deteriorated. Like Ne Win, Than Shwe was a military dictator who used a variety of methods, including patronage and punishment, in dealing with his subordinates and consolidating his hold on power (Win Min 2008). Than Shwe was careful and strategic in managing his rivals. He took early action when he felt that his power might come under threat, as when he ordered the arrest of General Khin Nyunt on charges of corruption in October 2004. The latter officer was the face of the military junta at the time, serving as both prime minister and head of military intelligence. A well-liked person, he had built a good reputation in diplomatic circles and among the general public. Than Shwe was troubled by Khin Nyunt's popularity and the powerful spy network that he controlled. Than Shwe knew that he needed to push Khin Nyunt aside before it became too late. He therefore not only had Khin Nyunt arrested but also went so far as to close down the Directorate of Defence Services Intelligence.

As the paramount leader of Myanmar, Than Shwe served as the SLORC/SPDC chairman and as Tatmadaw commander-in-chief for almost twenty years. However, by the early 2000s, he had begun to look for a way to leave power. He launched a grand plan centred on the design of a new political system that would protect him and his family from legal jeopardy and allow them to preserve their wealth (Callahan 2012). Than Shwe dissolved the SPDC on 30 March 2011, and transferred power to a government under the leadership of the military-backed USDP. Many analysts predicted that Than Shwe would become president in the post-SPDC government. Others speculated that he would remain in power as Tatmadaw commander-in-chief while appointing a puppet president. However, the dictator made an unexpected move. He simply stepped down and left power. Not only did Than Shwe himself retire, but he also arranged the retirement of Vice Senior General Maung Aye, the vice commander-in-chief and Than Shwe's immediate subordinate. Further, he forced the top brass to quit the military and assigned them to civilian posts. Parliament elected Prime Minister General Thein Sein president. Joint Chief of Staff General Shwe Mann became speaker of the Pyithu Hluttaw, the lower house of parliament, and General Tin Aung Myint Oo, the quartermaster general, became first vice president.

These moves saw Than Shwe replace the entire Tatmadaw leadership with members of the third generation of Myanmar military leaders. He had earlier assigned three lieutenant generals to work under his direct supervision. Thura Myint Aung was a member of the eighteenth intake of the prestigious Defence Services Academy. Min Aung Hlaing and Ko Ko were a year junior to him at the academy. Out of these three officers, Than Shwe handpicked Min Aung Hlaing to succeed him as Tatmadaw commander-in-chief, although Min Aung Hlaing was not the most senior on the shortlist. Seniority is not the only basis for promotion in the Tatmadaw. Other factors—for instance, competence and loyalty to superiors—are as important as experience for those who would reach higher positions in the Burmese military.

The Tatmadaw was in the hands of a new generation when Myanmar kicked off its democratic transition in early 2011. Younger generals had replaced older ones. The new commander-in-chief, Min Aung Hlaing, would soon let another batch of generals retire to run in the country's 2015 elections. Joint Chief of Staff General Hla Htay Win, Navy chief Vice Admiral Thura Thet Swe and Defence Minister Lieutenant General Wai Lwin joined the USDP, which ran a total of fifty-nine military candidates on its ticket in that year (Ei Ei Toe Lwin 2015).

The rise of Min Aung Hlaing and a younger generation to the top of the armed forces was of great significance for Myanmar and its armed forces. The new leadership undertook institutional changes. The new top brass set a mandatory retirement age for all military personnel and imposed limits on time-in-rank for high-ranking officers, including the top brass itself. There had been no mandatory retirement age in the Tatmadaw before. Although the Civil Services Personnel Law of 2013 mandates that all government officials retire at the age of sixty, it does not apply to members of the defence services. Article 291 of the 2008 constitution states that the nature of the work undertaken by military personnel is different from that of civil servants; relevant military laws therefore apply to military personnel (Ministry of Information 2008).

The Defence Services Act of 1959 regulates military affairs, such as recruitment, service privileges and procedures for courts martial. The Defence Services Council, formerly known as the War Office

Council, can pass bylaws in the form of directives. The council had already passed two directives concerning retirement before 2011. The first directive, the Defence Services Council Order 18/1973 or DSCO 18/1973, released in 1973, authorized lifetime employment in military service. Under the directive, military personnel could stay in the armed forces as long as the Tatmadaw needed them. The second directive, DSCO 6/1990, passed in 1990, allowed military personnel to retire after serving twenty years in the armed services. Neither directive explicitly specified regulations on mandatory retirement. According to the two directives, military personnel could still be on active duty even after they had served for twenty years.

Current military leaders are in their fifties. In contrast, Ne Win and Than Shwe occupied the office of commander-in-chief into their late seventies. Before 2011, it was not unusual for military leaders to hold senior positions for long periods of time. For instance, Than Shwe served as commander-in-chief for nearly two decades, from April 1992 to March 2011. But staying in office and dying in office are now no longer an option for members of the armed forces. After taking over in 2011, Min Aung Hlaing and the new Tatmadaw leadership began to review existing military laws and regulations. The new Defence Services Council concluded that serving in the military with no age limits was at odds with democratic principles. Therefore, in 2014 the council issued a new directive, DSCO 4/2014, setting the age of mandatory retirement from the Tatmadaw at sixty, as for civil servants. An exception applies to the two most senior positions. The commander-in-chief and vice commander-in-chief can serve until they reach sixty-five years of age. After that, they must also retire from the military.

Along with a mandatory retirement age, the Defence Services Council also adopted limits on time-in-rank for high-ranking members of the armed forces in 2016. DSCO 1/2016 instructs that a general must retire after serving four years in rank, a lieutenant general after five years, a major general after six years and a brigadier general after seven years.

The new Tatmadaw leadership has taken bold actions to set mandatory retirement and term limits for military personnel. Perhaps these measures represent just a small step toward building a democratic army, but they will certainly reduce the odds of another military strongman like Ne Win or Than Shwe emerging in Myanmar.

Defending the Country

With new leadership in place, the Tatmadaw has refocused its attention on protecting the country from internal and external threats. After the 1962 coup, the armed forces took on a dual role in society. They would both defend the nation and, in effect, run the government. In addition to playing its traditional role as a defence institution, the military had stepped into politics and taken full control of governance.[3] Cabinets were full of generals, and military personnel occupied senior positions in the civil service. The well-functioning bureaucracy inherited from the British deteriorated into a corrupt, inefficient institution over fifty years because of military favouritism. Since the start of democratic reforms in March 2011, however, the Tatmadaw has retreated into the domains of national security and military matters. The defence services are no longer involved in the day-to-day business of state administration, which now falls under the civilian government's authority.

The 2008 constitution describes the Tatmadaw's roles and responsibilities in the new democratic system. It mandates three major functions for the military in building "discipline-flourishing democracy" in Myanmar.

(a) Defence of the Nation
(b) Defence of National Interests and the Three Main National Causes
(c) Defence of the Constitution

Article 339 of the constitution states that the Tatmadaw will play a leading role in guarding the nation against all internal and external threats. Arms and armed groups are plentiful in many parts of Myanmar, even though possession of automatic weapons, grenades and explosives is illegal. The Myanmar Police Force and the pro-government militia, the People's Militia Forces, are legally allowed to bear arms. Other militias acquire weapons from the black market. In addition, there are dozens of ethnic armed organizations in the border areas, fighting for greater autonomy and some sort of federalism. Some of these organizations have already signed ceasefire agreements with the government but have not completely disarmed. Others have been transformed into units of the Border Guard Forces while maintaining their arsenals.[4] In view of this complex situation and the widespread distribution of arms, Article 338 of the 2008 constitution explicitly demands that all "armed organizations" be under the command of the Tatmadaw. Similarly, Article 20(c) states that the commander-in-chief of the Tatmadaw is the supreme commander of all the armed forces (Ministry of Information 2008). In other words, the Myanmar Police Force, People's Militia Forces and Border Guard Forces may enjoy some autonomy in their day-to-day operations, but in the end they all answer to the commander-in-chief and must obey the Tatmadaw's commands at all times.

To turn to defending national interests and the "Three Main National Causes", Article 337 of the constitution states that the main "armed forces" responsible for defending the nation are the Tatmadaw. The military will put itself in the first line of defence against all enemies. It will defend national interests and safeguard the Three Main National Causes. What are these, exactly?

Article 20(e) specifies that the Tatmadaw will ensure non-disintegration of the Union, non-disintegration of national solidarity and perpetuation of the Union's sovereignty—which are collectively known as the Three Main National Causes (Ministry of Information 2008). The 2015 Defence White Paper also states that, in order to build "a peaceful, modern developed and well-disciplined democratic state", Myanmar needs to protect and realize national interest by safeguarding the Three Main National Causes (Maung Aung Myoe 2016).

The Tatmadaw is concerned with the possible collapse of the nation, the breakdown of ethnic harmony and attacks on Myanmar's sovereignty. This concern is rooted in the military's bitter experience since the early years of the country's independence. A full-scale civil war broke out just three months after 4 January 1948. The Communist Party of Burma (CPB), known as the "white flag" communists, went underground in March 1948. Two battalions of the Burma Army joined the CPB. The other, "red flag", faction of the Communist Party had already been in revolt for a few years by that time. The white band faction of the People's Volunteer Organization, a paramilitary force formed by demobilized Second World War veterans, later joined the rebellion. Furthermore, the Karen National Union took up arms in January 1949 and seized Insein Township on the outskirts of Rangoon. The military was losing to "multi-colored insurgents" in many parts of the country. The foreign press mockingly called Burmese authorities "the Rangoon government" because the government only retained authority over the capital city (Maung Aung Myoe 2009, p. 16).

In the mid-1950s, the Tatmadaw was able to regain control of many insurgent-occupied areas. However, it would soon find itself fighting again, this time against a foreign army. After their side lost the civil war to the Chinese Communist Party, elements of Chinese Nationalist (Kuomintang or KMT) forces entered Burma's Shan State. With weapons and funds provided by the United States Central Intelligence Agency (CIA), these KMT troops were determined to launch offensive attacks into China's Yunnan Province from Burmese territory. The Rangoon government objected to the KMT entrenching itself on that territory and violating the country's sovereignty. It demanded the immediate departure of the KMT from Burmese soil. It took its case to the United Nations in order to put international pressure on both the Republic of China on Taiwan and on the United States. In the 1960s, when it was apparent that diplomatic actions would not work, the Tatmadaw initiated military operations to drive KMT forces from Burma.

These two chapters in independent Burma's early history have left the Tatmadaw perennially suspicious of Myanmar's ethnic minority groups and of foreign powers. It will respond with strong actions to challenges to any of the Three Main National Causes—the nation, ethnic unity and national sovereignty. It perceives any person or entity that harms any or all of these causes as an enemy. Such enemies may include individuals—for example, politicians, protestors or journalists. They may also include organizations like political parties, civil society organizations, the media, insurgent forces or terrorist groups; neighbouring or distant countries; or international institutions operating at the regional or global level.

The third constitutional function of the Tatmadaw is to preserve, protect and defend the constitution. Article 20(f) of the 2008 charter states that the military is responsible for safeguarding it. When it comes to matters of foreign policy and national security, the Tatmadaw follows the letter of the constitution. Article 41 states that Myanmar "practices an independent, active and non-aligned foreign policy aimed at world peace and friendly relations with nations and upholds the principles of peaceful co-existence among nations" (Ministry of Information 2008). Article 42(a) states that Myanmar will not commence aggression against any nation, and Article 42(b) that the deployment of foreign troops onto Myanmar's territory will not be permitted. The 2015 Defence White Paper repeats these points in its section on national defence policy (Republic of the Union of Myanmar 2015). The Tatmadaw will therefore maintain a position of neutrality in international affairs. It will not participate in military alliances between Myanmar and other nations or allow foreign troops to be stationed in Myanmar.

Defence Strategy

Enemies of or threats to the military fall into two groups: domestic or internal and foreign or external. On the domestic front, ethnic armed organizations and Rohingya militants cause the Tatmadaw great trouble. Perceived external threats include neighbouring states and great powers. The Tatmadaw has developed strategies to deal with each group.

Internal Threats
Ethnic Armed Organizations

Dozens of ethnic groups are fighting for autonomy and for Myanmar's adoption of a federal system of some kind, in what is considered the longest running internal armed conflict in the world. Some of these groups came into existence only after 1989, when the military's biggest foe, the CPB, collapsed as a result of a mutiny that paved the way for the creation of new groups among people that had been under the CPB's control. Other ethnic armed groups, such as the Karen National Union and the Kachin Independence Organization, have been fighting since the late 1940s or the 1950s and 1960s.

The Tatmadaw holds that armed conflicts started by ethic armed organizations pose a threat to Myanmar's internal security. It has pursued several approaches to ending these conflicts. It launched massive counter-insurgency operations in the 1960s and 1970s. However, this strategy failed to bring peace and stability. The Tatmadaw changed its approach in the 1990s and offered ceasefire deals to ethnic armed organizations. Many of the latter, mostly new armed groups born out of the collapse of the CPB, embraced the Tatmadaw's offer. It engineered a "ceasefire capitalism" scheme, in which the military government gave lucrative business deals to ethnic armed organizations and, in return, those groups stopped fighting. The scheme delivered peace in the 1990s and early 2000s. It was just a means of temporarily silencing the guns, however, and it did little to resolve the fundamental issues that had led the ethnic armed organizations to take up arms. Those issues included equal political rights for minority peoples and the redistribution of power in the country. The term "federalism" remained a political taboo, and there was no room for political dialogue on any sort of federal arrangements between the ethnic armed organizations and the military.

The ceasefire agreements broke down before the 2010 elections, when the military demanded that ethnic armed organizations transform themselves into Border Guard Forces. Intense fighting has since resumed in northern and eastern parts of Myanmar. Realizing that neither military operations nor business incentives could end the country's armed conflicts, which have lasted for seven decades, the Tatmadaw has revisited its strategy in the new democratic era. It states in the 2015 Defence White Paper that it will "end the [internal] conflicts through peaceful means, aiming at national reconciliation" (Maung Aung Myoe 2016, p. 6). Finding political solutions rather than using military means has become the Tatmadaw's official position on the need to address ethnic conflicts in Myanmar, although some senior officers still think that ethnic armed groups should be wiped out completely.

The Tatmadaw is supportive of the peace process on which Myanmar's civilian government is working. Eight ethnic armed organizations signed the Nationwide Ceasefire Agreement with the USDP government on 15 October 2015. Two more organizations joined the agreement on 13 February 2018, under the watch of the National League for Democracy government. The agreement is a landmark peace pact among the government, the Tatmadaw and ethnic insurgent groups. It is different from the bilateral ceasefire deals that the military initiated in the 1990s. It guarantees inclusive political dialogue, including a Union Peace Conference, to discuss the adoption of federal arrangements in Myanmar. The bilateral ceasefire deals of the previous decades did not have these elements.

The military has accepted the terms of the Nationwide Ceasefire Agreement and invited non-signatory ethnic armed organizations to join the agreement. It is willing to hold peace talks with any ethnic armed group, with the exceptions of the Myanmar National Democratic Alliance Army, the Ta'ang National Liberation Army and the Arakan Army. These groups emerged only after the new political system was installed in 2011, in contrast to other ethnic armed groups, whose existence dates back decades. The Tatmadaw's agreeing to discuss a federal system with ethnic armed organizations marks a significant departure from SPDC-era defence policy, under which the concept of federalism was completely unacceptable to the military.

Rohingya Militant Groups

In addition to ethnic insurgencies in eastern and northern Myanmar, the other challenge to internal security that the Tatmadaw faces today is Rohingya militant movements in the western part of the country. Rohingyas are a Muslim minority in Rakhine State, many of whom are stateless, as Myanmar's government stripped them of their citizenship. Attacks staged by Rohingya militant groups are not new. Mujahideen separatist movements were active in the late 1940s and early 1950s, when they fought to annex northern Rakhine State, where Muslims were the majority, to East Pakistan—today's Bangladesh. The Tatmadaw suppressed this rebellion in successful military operations against the mujahideen. New Rohingya armed groups were established in subsequent decades, such as the Rohingya Patriotic Front and the Rohingya Solidarity Organization, but these groups did not pose serious security threats.

The situation changed after June 2012. A series of episodes of communal violence between ethnic Rakhine people and Rohingya residents of northern Rakhine State caused 88 deaths and displaced more than 140,000 people, most of whom were Rohingya. The world suddenly noticed that successive Myanmar governments had suppressed Rohingyas. The Rohingya issue has since become a central focus of international human rights groups' human rights campaigns. Western countries are exerting strong pressure on the Tatmadaw and on the Myanmar government to end military action and discrimination against the Rohingyas.

Meanwhile, a new Rohingya militant force was quietly born, unbeknownst to the international community. Raised in a middle-class Rohingya family that had immigrated to the Pakistani port city of Karachi and later to Saudi Arabia, Ata Ullah decided to fight for Rohingya freedom after learning about the 2012 Rakhine State conflict. With millions of dollars contributed by Rohingya sympathizers, Ullah returned to Pakistan to seek guns, fighters and training from jihadi groups tied to the Taliban and to Kashmiri separatist groups like Lashkar-e-Taiba. Soon, Ullah realized that jihadi groups would only pay his cause lip service and not offer any real support. He therefore moved to Bangladesh and established himself near the Myanmar border, where he recruited and trained Rohingya soldiers. Under Ullah's leadership, the Harakah al-Yaqin (Faith Movement) was founded in 2014. It was later renamed the Arakan Rohingya Salvation Army (ARSA) (International Crisis Group 2016; Lintner 2017).

Unlike previous Rohingya militant groups, the ARSA is systematic in its recruitment and training of fighters. It has an effective propaganda machine to spread its messages to its followers and sympathizers. The ARSA carried out its first attack on 9 October 2016. Hundreds of Rohingya combatants attacked three Burmese police posts along the Bangladesh border, leaving nine officers dead. Two days later, further ARSA attacks left four more Burmese soldiers dead. The group undertook a larger operation on 25 August 2017, targeting 30 police posts and one army battalion. During these attacks, the ARSA killed 12 Burmese security officers and 99 civilians; the latter were all Hindus. The Tatmadaw launched a furious counteroffensive campaign and thus triggered a grave humanitarian crisis. Nearly 700,000 Rohingyas left their homes in northern Rakhine State and fled to refugee camps in Bangladesh. Human rights organizations accused the Tatmadaw of burning villages, raping Rohingya women and killing civilians in its "clearance operation". The United Nations called the military's atrocities against the Rohingya population a "textbook example" of ethnic cleansing (*UN News* 2017).

The Tatmadaw does not recognize the ARSA as a legitimate force that represents the interests of the Rohingyas. Myanmar's government officially declared the ARSA a terrorist organization. The military has said that it will not compromise with terrorist groups. It seems that the ARSA wants to hold peace talks with government officials to discuss Rohingya rights, but the Tatmadaw will never accept ARSA demands. Unlike the ethnic armed organizations with which the Tatmadaw is willing to meet in the Union Peace Conference, the ARSA is not a group that the armed forces have ever invited to sign the Nationwide Ceasefire Agreement. The only option that the Tatmadaw is willing to give the ARSA is a military one—defeat.

The reality, however, is that the Tatmadaw is not fully prepared to handle non-traditional security challenges like terrorism. It may know how to combat insurgent groups. Its "Four Cuts" strategy of severing militias' access to food, funds, information and recruitment successfully crushed communist rebels in the 1970s, for example. But the way in which the ARSA operates is different from that of earlier ethnic insurgencies. Transnational terrorist networks such as Al-Qaeda show support for the ARSA and have already threatened to carry out attacks in Myanmar. Islamic terrorism is something that the Tatmadaw does not know and with which it does not have prior experience. The

Tatmadaw and the Myanmar Police Force need to develop a national strategy to set policies, build up capacity and seek international assistance to combat potential terrorist actions.

External Threats

Burma's military fought for the country's independence against Britain and Japan in the 1940s, battled the KMT's CIA-backed invasion of Shan State in the 1950s, and engaged in counter-insurgency operations against the Chinese Communist Party-supported Communist Party of Burma in the 1970s. Moreover, the Tatmadaw suffered harsh Western sanctions against Myanmar throughout the 1990s and early 2000s. This history has left it suspicious of foreign countries and paranoid about the influence of external powers on Myanmar's internal affairs.

The Tatmadaw divides external powers into two groups: traditional enemies with armed strength roughly equal to its own and enemies with greater strength (Maung Aung Myoe 2009, p. 21). Thailand and Bangladesh are likely to fall into the first category, although the Tatmadaw does not make this judgement explicit in any official document. Military-to-military relations with Thailand have significantly improved over the years, despite heightened tensions between the two countries in the 1990s. However, relations with Bangladesh have rapidly deteriorated since 2012 because of the Rohingya issue. Bangladesh has condemned the Tatmadaw for alleged atrocities against Rohingya. Dhaka is pressing Naypyitaw hard to organize the return of almost a million Rohingya refugees now in various camps in Bangladesh. Bangladesh has joined the effort of the Organization of Islamic Cooperation to mobilize international pressure on Myanmar.

From Myanmar's perspective, Bangladesh is not a reliable neighbour. Officials of the Naypyitaw government have pointed out that Bangladeshi authorities are not cooperative in advancing the Rohingya repatriation process. The Burmese public in general and military personnel in particular have strong negative perceptions of Bangladesh. The public regards the neighbouring country as an opportunist that is exploiting Myanmar's internal problems for its own advantage. Border tensions escalated when the Tatmadaw built up forces near the border areas (BBC News 2018). In 2018, more than 6,500 Rohingyas were staying on Myanmar's side of the international border, refusing either to move to Bangladesh or to enter Myanmar territory. Myanmar's government accused Bangladesh of helping these people build illegal shelters on the "zero line" (*Asian Correspondent* 2018).

The Tatmadaw's strategy for handling "historical enemies with roughly equal strength" is to conduct conventional warfare under a total-war approach, "without giving up an inch of its territory to the enemy" (Maung Aung Myoe 2009, p. 22). Although Myanmar does not have any intention to commence aggression against any nation, as stated in Article 42(a) of the 2008 constitution and again in the 2015 Defence White Paper, the Tatmadaw is determined to respond accordingly if attacked by a foreign country. The response will be conventional warfare if the perpetrator is an "historical enemy" or any state with equal or less military strength.

However, the Tatmadaw understands that its power is inferior to that of some enemies or potential enemies. In the case of conflict with such militaries, Myanmar's armed forces will use guerilla warfare to resist offensive attacks. Over the years, the Tatmadaw has developed a military doctrine, known as People's War or the People's Militia, to protect Myanmar from external threats. Borrowing from Mao Zedong's military-political strategy, the Tatmadaw will mobilize "men, material, and [the] morale of the entire people" to engage in a combination of mobile-conventional and guerrilla warfare to resist foreign invasions (Maung Aung Myoe 2009, p. 27). It will turn to conventional warfare only at the last stage. Article 340 of the constitution allows the military to mobilize the entire country for national defence to carry out People's War. Similarly, Article 386, in the charter's chapter on the "Fundamental Rights and Duties of Citizens", mentions that every citizen is responsible for undergoing military training and serving in the armed forces to defend the country (Ministry of Information 2008).

The Tatmadaw will undertake national defence following the People's War strategy during invasions by great powers. However, in peacetime the military attempts a balancing act.[5] Its leadership is paranoid about what it calls the "neocolonialism" of Western countries. The 2015 Defence White Paper asserts that "some powerful states are now interfering with the internal affairs of smaller nations by using democratization, human rights, and humanitarian grounds as pretexts to influence geo-strategically important regions" (Republic of the Union of Myanmar 2015). This passage clearly refers to Western countries, and in particular to the United States, with which the Tatmadaw has not been comfortable dealing since the time of the SLORC/SPDC junta. Military commanders have been irrationally nervous about a potential American invasion in recent decades. Economic sanctions and arms embargoes on the part of the West hit Myanmar hard in the 1990s and early 2000s. To counter Western threats, the Tatmadaw tried to build strong and friendly relations with China and Russia. Heavy Chinese investment in the country saved Myanmar's economy from collapse. Russia supplied arms to the Tatmadaw. Both countries protected the SPDC regime in the United Nations Security Council.

After more than twenty years on this path, however, the Tatmadaw's leadership felt suffocated by Chinese power. China held all the cards in the Sino-Myanmar relationship, and a Burmese general publicly admitted that the junta "was afraid of China" (Kyaw Phyo Tha 2012). China's growing influence was bad for the country, and so Myanmar's military sought a way to balance China against the West. When the opportunity to do so emerged during the democratic transition, the Tatmadaw grasped it firmly. After 2011, Myanmar's relations with Western countries improved significantly. To reward positive developments in Myanmar, the United States and the European Union (EU) lifted almost all sanctions and increased their development assistance. Meanwhile, Myanmar tried to distance itself from China.

However, Myanmar's delicate relations with the West would soon sour. The United States and the EU have railed against Myanmar for alleged military violence against Rohingyas in the aftermath of the ARSA attacks of August 2017. Washington and Ottawa imposed targeted sanctions on the Tatmadaw, including visa bans for senior officials, and the EU ended engagement with the armed forces. Renewed pressure from the West has driven Myanmar back into the arms of its old allies China and Russia. China is giving full diplomatic support to Myanmar over the Rohingya issue, and Russia also sides with the Tatmadaw.

In summary, threats to Myanmar's military can be classified into two different categories: internal and external. Ethnic armed organizations and Rohingya militant groups fall into the first category. The Tatmadaw has made it clear that it will negotiate with organizations of the former sort to seek political solutions to end civil conflict. However, the military will never compromise with Rohingya militant forces like the ARSA. It seeks, rather, to defeat them by means of military operations. We may likewise see two groups of external threats: those coming from countries with military strength comparable to Myanmar's and those coming from great powers. The Tatmadaw will use conventional warfare to face attacks from enemies that have equal or less strength. But, if great powers make offensive attacks on the country, Myanmar's military will use the strategy of People's War to resist. That is at least the theory. In practice, the Tatmadaw seeks to balance one great power against another. For example, when China appears to have too much influence over Myanmar, the Tatmadaw tries to balance Chinese encroachment by moving closer to the West. In the same way, when the United States and the EU exert pressure on Myanmar, Naypyitaw embraces Beijing and Moscow once again. Table 2.1 summarizes defence strategy that the armed forces of Myanmar use to address different threat types.

TABLE 2.1
The Defence Strategy of Myanmar's Military

	Threats	Defence Strategy
Internal Threats	Ethnic Armed Organizations	Political Solutions
	Rohingya Militant Groups, ARSA	Military Means
External Threats	Historical Enemies with Roughly Equal Strength, Non-Great Powers	Conventional Warfare
	Enemies with Greater Strength, Great Powers	People's War, Geo-Political Balancing

Building a Standard Army

New leaders have emerged in Myanmar's armed forces, and the military has refocused its attention to concentrate primarily on defence functions. Additionally, the Tatmadaw is transforming itself into a "Standard Army". A key player pushing this ambitious project forward is none other than Commander-in-Chief Senior General Min Aung Hlaing.

Although he has not yet fully articulated what a Standard Army looks like, it is clearly not the same as a professional military in democratic states, where the armed forces stay out of politics and accept civilian supremacy. The Tatmadaw has remained intent on playing an important role in politics even after handing power to the civilian government in March 2011, and it is unwilling to come under civilian control. People in military circles do not accept the term "professional military" as a characterization of or goal for the Tatmadaw, because "professional" means "mercenary" to them. Many officers see themselves as patriots who joined the Tatmadaw to sacrifice their personal lives to defend the country.

It is clear that Min Aung Hlaing wants to build a "world-class Tatmadaw". Reviewing his speeches and interviews permits the inference that there are three central elements to his Standard Army reforms.

(a) modernizing the armed forces
(b) building the capacity of military personnel
(c) pursuing active military diplomacy

Modernizing the Armed Forces

Min Aung Hlaing's vision for developing the Standard Army aims at transforming the Tatmadaw into "a strong, capable and modern patriotic" military (Lawi Weng 2018). It is no secret that Myanmar's military has, in comparison with other regional militaries, historically been relatively ill-equipped. The 2015 Defence White Paper mentions that one of the main military challenges to Myanmar is the "military buildup" in neighbouring countries (Republic of the Union of Myanmar 2015). The Tatmadaw's leaders have long desired to modernize the armed forces to deter external threats and control internal insurgencies.

During the era of military rule, the defence budget was unknown. The SPDC junta basically determined the level of resources that it wanted to use for the armed forces. However, since the 2011–12 fiscal year this has no longer been the case. Under the 2008 constitution, the Tatmadaw must submit its annual budget plan to the Union Parliament for approval. Yet a detailed breakdown of military spending—how much is used for salaries, for buying weapons and so on—is still unknown. According to Tatmadaw data, Myanmar's defence budget has increased every year. It was less than US$1 billion in fiscal year

2011–12, but it doubled to US$2.11 billion in just four years, for fiscal year 2014–15. These budgets might appear modest in comparison with those of other Southeast Asian countries. But, relative to the size of the Myanmar economy, the sums involve represent a huge amount, accounting for 13 to 14 per cent of the entire government budget or more than the combined expenses of the Ministry of Education and the Ministry of Health and Sports.

TABLE 2.2
Myanmar's Defence Budget, 2011–18
(with currency conversions at a rate of 1 USD=1,300 MMK)

Fiscal Year	Myanmar Kyat	US Dollars	Percentage of Total Government Expenditure
2011–12	1.27 trillion	0.98 billion	14.73
2012–13	2.10 trillion	1.61 billion	14.57
2013–14	2.29 trillion	1.76 billion	13.81
2014–15	2.61 trillion	2.01 billion	13.44
2015–16	2.75 trillion	2.11 billion	13.34
2016–17	2.09 trillion	n.a	13.95
2017–18	n.a.	n.a.	13.95

Source: Myanmar Armed Forces data.

Replacing old defence equipment with new hardware and acquiring new weapons are major parts of the Standard Army reforms. At nearly US$700 million, arms imports to Myanmar hit an all-time high in 2011, the first year of Min Aung Hlaing's tenure as commander-in-chief. The value of arms imports was "more than double the highest annual figure since 1989" (Selth 2016, p. 7). From 2011 to 2017, Myanmar reportedly spent US$2.09 billion for arms acquisitions. Figure 2.1 shows the country's total arms imports from 1988 to 2017.

The Tatmadaw has been under various forms of Western arms embargoes since the 1990s. Australia imposed an embargo in 1991, and American sanctions followed in 1993. The EU has had a ban on the sale or transfer of arms and military expertise to Myanmar since

FIGURE 2.1
Total Arms Imports of Myanmar in US dollars, 1988–2017

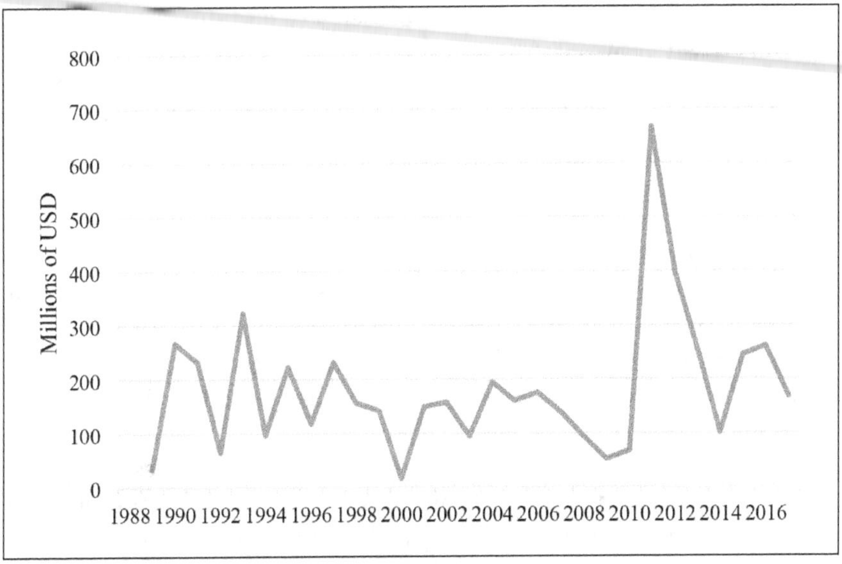

Source: Stockholm International Peace Research Institute (SIPRI), n.d.

October 1996. Additionally, Canada prohibited the export of arms and related material to Myanmar in 2007. Israel was long one of the few countries from which the Tatmadaw could seek arms. However, even Israel reportedly suspended weapons sales to Myanmar in late 2017, in the midst of the Rohingya crisis, as it wanted to appease the United States (Gross and TOI Staff 2017).

Because Western countries' arms embargoes have remained in effect even in the post-SPDC era, Myanmar has had to rely mainly on China and Russia as sources of weapons in recent years, although India, Ukraine and Belarus have also been sources of defence equipment. China is a major supplier to the Tatmadaw, providing armoured fighting vehicles, ships, aircraft, missiles, radar systems and rocket launchers. Although grateful to Beijing for its willingness to sell arms, Burmese generals are not happy with China's assistance to ethnic armed groups in northeast Myanmar. In addition, the quality of Chinese military products has been a matter of great concern. In recent years, aircraft bought from China were involved in several fatal accidents in Myanmar. A Chinese-made Shaanxi Y8-200F four-engine turboprop plane went missing over the Andaman Sea in July 2017 while carrying dozens of soldiers and members of their families. All 106 passengers and 14 crew members on board died in what was one of the worst aviation accidents in Myanmar history. The plane had been purchased from China just over a year earlier, in March 2016. Another Chinese-manufactured aircraft went down in April 2018. The pilot flying that F-7 fighter jet was killed in the crash.

Because of these issues, the Tatmadaw has sought alternative sources of arms. Russia is a natural fit for this goal, and Myanmar has bought military aircraft and missiles from that country in recent years. Additionally, it has purchased turbofan engines from Ukraine and Russian-made missiles from Belarus. India has also supplied air search radar, anti-submarine sonar and advanced lightweight torpedoes to Myanmar.

Traditionally, the Myanmar Army is the largest and best-equipped branch of the armed forces. Major steps toward Army modernization are taking place as renewed fighting with ethnic armed organizations in the country's Northeast has intensified in recent years. China delivered 50 main battle tanks (Type-90-2M/MBT-2000) and 76 infantry fighting vehicles (WZ-551/Type-92) to Myanmar in 2012–13. The Army also bought 10 new ZFB-05 armoured personnel carriers from China and 10 used M-3 VTT APCs from an unknown supplier, which is likely to have been Israel. Moreover, it acquired 20 self-propelled multiple rocket launchers (Type-81 122mm) and 100 armoured fire-support vehicles (WMA-301 Assaulters) from China. The Army now has a range of surface-to-air missiles that includes the second-hand Belarusian Kvadrat-M and the Chinese KS-1A missiles, as well as the Russian S-125 Pechora-2M and Igla-1/SA-16 portable surface-to-air missiles. Tata Motors, India's biggest automaker, has publicly stated that it is interested in supplying military vehicles to Myanmar. It has signed an agreement with a state-owned enterprise under the Ministry of Industry to build a factory for making heavy trucks in Myanmar.

In addition to acquiring arms from foreign sources, the Tatmadaw manufactures a wide range of defence products locally. Indigenous shipbuilding is a major component of the Myanmar Navy's modernization programme. The Navy is expanding its fleet to go beyond littoral environments, as it seeks to move "from brown water",

TABLE 2.3
Transfers of Major Weapons to Myanmar: Deals with Deliveries or Orders made during 2011–17

Supplier/ recipient (R)	Number ordered	Weapon designation	Weapon description	Year of order	Year of delivery	Number delivered	Comments
Belarus							
R: Myanmar	(100)	3M9/SA-6	SAM	(2014)	2015–2016	(100)	Second-hand (but modernized before delivery); for Kvadrat-M SAM systems; supplier uncertain
	(2)	Kvadrat-M	SAM system	2014	2016	(2)	Second-hand Kvadrat SAM system rebuilt to Kvadrat-M
China							
R: Myanmar	(1)	Aung Zeya	Frigate	2006	2011	1	
	(20)	C-802/CSS-N-8	Anti-ship missile	(2009)	2013–2014	(20)	For FAC-491 FAC
	(50)	K-8 Karakorum-8	Trainer/combat aircraft	2009	2011–2016	(24)	60 or 72 in number; assembled in Myanmar.
	(2)	NG-18 30mm	Naval gun	(2009)	2013–2014	(2)	For 2 FAC-491 FAC produced in Myanmar.
	(2)	Type-348	Sea search radar	(2009)	2013–2014	(2)	For 2 FAC-491 FAC produced in Myanmar.
	(50)	Type-90-2M/MBT-2000	Tank	2009	2012–2013	(50)	

TABLE 2.3 (continued)

Supplier/ recipient (R)	Number ordered	Weapon designation	Weapon description	Year of order	Year of delivery	Number delivered	Comments
	8	NG-18 30mm	Naval gun	(2010)	2014–2015	8	For 2 Kyan Sittha frigates produced in Myanmar; designation and supplier uncertain (perhaps AK-630 from Russia or other supplier).
	2	Type-347G	Fire control radar	(2010)	2014–2015	2	For 2 Kyan Sittha frigates produced in Myanmar; for use with 76mm gun.
	(2)	Type-360 Seagull	Air search radar	(2010)	2014–2015	2	Type-364 Seagull-C version; for 2 Kyan Sittha frigates produced in Myanmar.
	(20)	Type-81 122mm	Self-propelled MRL	(2010)	2012	(20)	
	(100)	WMA-301 Assaulter	AFSV	(2010)	2012–2015	(100)	
	(10)	ZFB-05	APC	(2010)	2011	(10)	
	(30)	C-802/CSS-N-8	Anti-ship missile	(2011)	2012	(30)	For Type-053 (Jianghu-2) frigates.
	(10)	C-802/CSS-N-8	Anti-ship missile	(2011)	2016	(10)	For Tabinshwehti corvette produced in Myanmar.

A New Tatmadaw with Old Characteristics

TABLE 2.3 (continued)

Supplier/ recipient (R)	Number ordered	Weapon designation	Weapon description	Year of order	Year of delivery	Number delivered	Comments
	(25)	HY-2/SY-1A/ CSS-N-2	Anti-ship missile	(2011)	2012	(25)	Probably second-hand; for Type-053 (Jianghu-2) frigates.
	(2)	NG-18 30mm	Naval gun	(2011)	2016	2	For 1 Tabinshwehti corvette produced in Myanmar; supplier possibly China.
	2	Type-53/Jianghu-1	Frigate	2011	2012	2	Second-hand; Type-053H1 (Jianghu-2) version.
	(76)	WZ-551/Type-92	IFV	(2011)	2012–2013	(76)	
	(12)	CH-3	UAV/UCAV	(2013)	2014–2015	(12)	
	(4)	KS-1A	SAM system	(2013)	2015–2016	(4)	
	(200)	KS-1A	SAM	(2013)	2015–2016	(200)	
	(16)	JF-17 Thunder/ FC-1	FGA aircraft	(2015)	2017	(4)	Possibly from Pakistani production line.
	2	Y-8	Transport aircraft	2015	2016	2	Y-8F-200W version.
France							
R: Myanmar	8	16PA4	Diesel engine	(2010)	2014–2015	8	For 2 Kyan Sittha frigates produced in Myanmar; probably from Chinese production line.

TABLE 2.3 (continued)

Supplier/ recipient (R)	Number ordered	Weapon designation	Weapon description	Year of order	Year of delivery	Number delivered	Comments
Germany (FRG)							
R: Myanmar	20	G-120TP	Trainer aircraft	(2014)	2015-2016	20	
India							
R: Myanmar	1	LW-04	Air search radar	(2006)	2013	1	For 1 Aung Zeya frigate from China.
	(1)	LW-04	Air search radar	(2011)	2016	1	RAWL-02 version; for Tabinshweti corvette produced in Myanmar.
	3	HMS-X	ASW sonar	2013	2015	(3)	For 1 Aung Zeya frigate from China and 2 Kyan Sittha frigates produced in Myanmar.
	3	LW-04	Air search radar	2013	2015-2016	3	RAWL-02 Mk-2 version; for 2 Kyan Sittha frigates and 1 Tabinshwehti corvette produced in Myanmar.
		Shyena	ASW torpedo	2017			US$38 m deal.
Israel							
R: Myanmar	1	Compact 76mm	Naval gun	(2006)	2011	1	Second-hand; for 1 Aung Zeya frigate from China; supplier uncertain (perhaps South Africa).
	6	Super Dvora	Patrol craft	(2015)	2017	(2)	Super Dvora Mk-3 version.

A New Tatmadaw with Old Characteristics 55

TABLE 2.3 (continued)

Supplier/ recipient (R)	Number ordered	Weapon designation	Weapon description	Year of order	Year of delivery	Number delivered	Comments
Netherlands							
R: Myanmar	2	Fokker-70	Transport aircraft	(2016)	2017	2	Second-hand; possibly for government VIP transport.
Russia							
R: Myanmar	(2000)	Igla-1/SA-16	Portable SAM	(2000)	2004–2014	(2000)	Including MADV AD systems produced in Myanmar.
	1	S-125 Pechora-2M	SAM system	(2008)	2012	(1)	Second-hand S-125 rebuilt to Pechora-M.
	(50)	V-601/SA-3B	SAM	(2008)	2012	(50)	Probably second-hand but modernized before delivery.
	(10)	Mi-24P/Mi-35P	Combat helicopter	2009	2010–2015	10	Probably second-hand but modernized before delivery; Mi-35P version.
	(14)	MiG-29	Fighter aircraft	2009	2011–2014	(14)	Part of US$570 m deal; including 4 MiG-29UB version.
	(6)	MiG-29S	FGA aircraft	2009	2011–2012	(6)	Part of US$570 m deal.
	12	Mi-2	Light helicopter	(2010)	2010–2011	(12)	Probably second-hand but modernized before delivery.
	(80)	R-27/AA-10	BVRAAM	(2010)	2011–2012	(80)	For MiG-29 combat aircraft.
	(150)	R-73/AA-11	SRAAM	(2010)	2011–2012	(150)	For MiG-29 combat aircraft.

TABLE 2.3 (continued)

Supplier/recipient (R)	Number ordered	Weapon designation	Weapon description	Year of order	Year of delivery	Number delivered	Comments
	(16)	RD-33	Turbofan	(2015)	2017	(4)	For 16 JF-17 combat aircraft from China.
	(12)	Yak-130	Trainer/combat ac	2015	2017	6	Delivery planned 2017–2018.
Ukraine							
R: Myanmar	(50)	AI-25	Turbofan	2009	2011–2016	(24)	For 50 K-8 trainer/combat aircraft from China; possibly WS-11 version from Chinese production line.
	(24)	AI-222	Turbofan	2015	2017	(12)	For Yak-130 trainer/combat aircraft from Russia.
Unknown supplier(s)							
R: Myanmar	(10)	M-3 VTT	APC	(2010)	2011	(10)	Second-hand but modernized before delivery; supplier probably Israel.

Note: The "Number delivered" and the "Year(s) of delivery" columns refer to all deliveries since the beginning of the contract. The "Comments" column includes publicly reported information on the value of deals. Information on the sources and methods used in the collection of the data, and explanations of the conventions, abbreviations and acronyms, can be found in the SIPRI Arms Transfers Database.

Source: Stockholm International Peace Research Institute (SIPRI), n.d.

or coastal areas, "to blue water", or oceans (Maung Aung Myoe 2009, p. 130). The Navy wants to build a blue-water maritime force capable of military operations across the deep waters of the Bay of Bengal and the Andaman Sea. Frigates are the most advanced warships in the Myanmar Navy, and all of its frigates, except the first, were commissioned in the post-SPDC era, on Min Aung Hlaing's watch. Out of Myanmar's five frigates, three were built in the Navy's own dockyard. The first locally built frigate is the Union of Myanmar Ship (UMS) *Aung Zeya* (F-11), which entered service in 2010. It was followed by the UMS *Kyan Sittha* (F-11) and the UMS *Sinbyushin* (F-14), which were launched in 2014 and 2015, respectively. China also delivered two second-hand Type 053H1 (Jianghu-II) frigates to Myanmar in 2012. They became the UMS *Mahar Bandoola* (F-21) and the UMS *Mahar Thiha Thura* (F-23).

TABLE 2.4
Frigates in the Myanmar Navy

No.	Name	Pennant	Class	Commissioned	Builder
1.	UMS *Aung Zeya*	F-11	Aung Zeya	2010	locally built
2.	UMS *Kyan Sittha*	F-12	Kyan Sittha	2014	locally built
3.	UMS *Sinbyushin*	F-14	Kyan Sittha	2015	locally built
4.	UMS *Mahar Bandoola*	F-21	Type 053H1 (Jianghu-II)	2012	China
5.	UMS *Mahar Thiha Thura*	F-23	Type 053H1 (Jianghu-II)	2012	China

Source: Myanmar Armed Forces data.

The Myanmar Navy launched a third locally built corvette, the UMS *Tabinshwehti* (773) in 2016. Fast attack craft, locally known as 5-series patrol boats, are being built in the Navy's dockyard, and 20 of them—christened UMS pennants 551 to 570—have already entered service. Moreover, seven new Myanmar-built vessels were commissioned in December 2017 to honour the seventieth anniversary of the Myanmar Navy. The Tatmadaw also ordered six Super Dvora Mark III-class patrol boats from Israel in 2015, and the first two were delivered in 2017.

In parallel to this naval buildup, the Myanmar Air Force regularly adds new aircraft to its complement of planes. It commissioned 51 airplanes and 10 helicopters between 2011 and 2016. An additional 10 airplanes—six Russian Yak-130 fighter jets, two Dutch Fokker-70 airliners and two French-Italian ATR 42-430 airliners—entered service in December 2017, on the seventieth anniversary of the Myanmar Air Force. The Tatmadaw made a US$570 million deal with Russia in 2009 to buy 20 MiG-29 fighter aircraft, which were delivered between 2011 and 2014. In January 2018, Myanmar ordered six Sukhoi Su-30 fighter aircraft from Russia, which will become the Air Force's most advanced fighter jets. In addition, China has sold Myanmar 16 fighter/ground attack aircraft (JF-17 Thunder/FC-1 type), which will be delivered in the years ahead.

Tatmadaw leaders had long wanted to upgrade the armed forces, but the modernization process began to speed up significantly from 2011 onward.

Building the Capacity of Military Personnel

Along with building up military hardware, developing the capacity of military personnel is another key aspect of the Standard Army reforms. Under the scheme of "from quantity to quality", the number of applicants accepted to officer-training schools—such as the Defence Services Academy, the Defence Services Medical Academy and the Defence Services Technological Academy—has been reduced. Starting in 1961, the military stopped recruiting women for non-medical services. However, in 2013, female officers were, for the first time in more than fifty years, welcomed into the Tatmadaw again. The first batch of female cadets graduated from the Army's Officer Training School in August 2014, and the Myanmar Air Force subsequently invited six of them to aviation training. The University Training Corps, closed in 1988, was reopened in the 2014–15 academic year. New uniforms were introduced in 2015 to increase the motivation of military personnel, and Commander-in-Chief Min Aung Hlaing has taken initiatives to provide a better welfare programme for military families (Selth 2016, p. 7).

The Tatmadaw is sending officers to foreign countries, above all Russia and China, for advanced degrees in science and engineering. The Russian Ministry of Education reports that 4,705 students from

Myanmar attended Russian universities between 1993 and 2013, and this number reached 6,000 in 2018. After those from Vietnam, students from Myanmar represent the second highest number from Southeast Asia pursuing degrees in Russia (Lutz Auras 2015; Aung Zaw 2018). Since 2015, Japan has invited two Tatmadaw officers each year to the National Defense Academy of Japan. The Nippon Foundation has also given ten scholarships to military officers from Myanmar to pursue a graduate degree in international relations at Japanese universities.

Further, the Tatmadaw is also conducting major exercises to strengthen its combat capabilities. Since 2014, the Navy has annually held a combined fleet exercise called "Sea Shield". More importantly, a major tri-service war exercise was conducted for the first time in more than twenty years in February 2018. The "Sinbyushin" drill was a combined exercise of the Army, the Navy and the Air Force aimed at improving the combat readiness of the armed forces for conventional warfare. Moreover, the Tatmadaw began taking part as an observer in the U.S.-led Cobra Gold, the largest Asia-Pacific military exercise, in 2013. It was, however, excluded from the drill in 2018 because of the Rohingya crisis.

Pursuing Active Military Diplomacy

In addition to military modernization and capacity-building projects, international engagement is one of the top priorities of Myanmar's military. The Tatmadaw has long wanted to have a better relationship with the West. Following democratic transition in 2011, the United States and the EU changed their policies toward the armed forces of Myanmar. Although arms embargoes were still in place, Western governments started engaging with the Tatmadaw, albeit slowly and cautiously.

American Secretary of State Hillary Clinton's 2011 trip to Myanmar included discussions on military cooperation between Myanmar and the United States. Officials from the Pentagon subsequently travelled to Myanmar for various meetings and trainings. The Myanmar-U.S. Human Rights Dialogue was held twice, in October 2012 and January 2014, and attended by representatives of the U.S. military and State Department. Lieutenant General Anthony Crutchfield, deputy commander of the U.S. Pacific Command, was one of the participants. He also delivered a speech at Myanmar's National Defence College in June 2014, becoming the first U.S. military officer to do so. The Defense POW/MIA Accounting Agency in Hawaii also resumed its operations in Kachin and Chin States of Myanmar. Moreover, the Daniel K. Inouye Asia-Pacific Center for Security Studies, a U.S. Department of Defense institution in Hawaii, has invited military officers and civilian officials from Myanmar for training since 2013. The U.S Navy expeditionary fast transport ship USS *Fall River* (T-EPF-4) made a goodwill visit to Yangon in March 2017—the first time that a U.S. Navy ship made an official port call to Myanmar since the era of the Second World War.

American lawmakers found other ways to formalize military-to-military engagement between the two countries. The National Defense Authorization Act for Fiscal Year 2015, sponsored by Senator Carl Levin and Representative Howard P. "Buck" McKeon, included a section that authorized the U.S. Department of Defense to provide training on human rights, the rule of law and civilian control of the military to Burmese officers; to deliver courses or workshops on the reform of defence institutions; and to assist with English language training and humanitarian or disaster relief (United States House of Representatives 2014, p. 128).

Like the United States, the EU was keen to engage with the Tatmadaw. The chairman of the EU Military Committee paid a visit to Naypyitaw in June 2016, and he invited the commander-in-chief of the Tatmadaw to make a reciprocal visit. This was a significant development because the EU has maintained a visa ban on Myanmar's military. But Senior General Min Aung Hlaing became the first Burmese military chief to visit Europe in decades. He addressed the EU Military Committee in Brussels in November 2016. Min Aung Hlaing was again invited to Europe a few months later, in April 2017, at the request of General Volker Wieker, chief of staff of the German armed forces. Accompanied by Joint Chief of Staff General Mya Tun Oo, Min Aung Hlaing also made a stop-over in Austria, where he received a guard-of-honour welcome and also toured Diamond Aircraft Industry. In Berlin, he spoke with German military leaders about combatting terrorism.

From 2012 to 2017, the Tatmadaw was able to build good relationships with the West. However, this thaw did not last very long. Western countries have more recently taken actions against Myanmar's military for its alleged atrocities in Rakhine State. The United Kingdom sent five Burmese military officers who were in England for training home in September 2017. The EU reviewed defence cooperation with the Myanmar Army and was poised to consider additional measures, if the situation in Rakhine State did not improve. It also suspended invitations to senior officers of the Myanmar Armed Forces. On 29 April 2019, the EU officially announced that it would extend its arms embargo on Myanmar (Parameswaran 2019).

Like the EU, the United States ended travel waivers for current and former senior leaders from Myanmar's military and rescinded invitations for senior Burmese security forces personnel to attend U.S.-sponsored events. No officers involved in military operations in northern Rakhine State will receive invitations to or be able to participate in any American assistance programmes. Moreover, in December 2017, using the Global Magnitsky Human Rights Accountability Act, the U.S. government sanctioned Major General Maung Maung Soe, who was the head of the Western Command of the Myanmar Army during clearance operations targeting the ARSA militant group.

American lawmakers have been furious about alleged human rights abuses on the part of the Tatmadaw in Rakhine State. The late Senator John McCain, a long-time supporter of Aung San Suu Kyi, expressed disappointment with her failure to condemn Myanmar's military for its actions there. He asked the U.S. Congress to remove the language related to expanding military-to-military cooperation between the United States and Myanmar from the National Defense Authorization Act for fiscal year 2018. He also sponsored the bipartisan S.2060 Burma Human Rights and Freedom Act of 2018 in the Senate. A companion bill, the H.R.5819 Burma Act of 2018, was introduced in the House of Representatives (*Mizzima* 2018).

Like the United States, Canada imposed targeted sanctions against Major General Maung Maung Soe under the February 2018 Justice for Victims of Corrupt Foreign Officials Act.

Although its military engagement with Western countries has—at least for now—come to an end, the Tatmadaw's ties with the militaries of regional powers have grown stronger over the years. President Xi Jinping invited Burmese Commander-in-Chief Min Aung Hlaing to China in November 2017, in the midst of the Rohingya crisis. China has sided with Myanmar over that crisis and the underlying issues. The two leaders had met in October 2013, but relations between the Tatmadaw and the People's Liberation Army (PLA) were tense for a time in 2015. Fighting between Burmese forces and those of the Myanmar National Democratic Alliance Army, a Chinese Kokang ethnic armed group, spilled over into Yunnan Province in that year, and the boom from a Myanmar fighter jet accidentally killed five Chinese and injured eight people. The PLA responded with an air-to-ground live-fire drill near the Myanmar border, sending the message that it would not tolerate such accidents in the future. The tension deescalated quickly, thanks to diplomatic efforts on both sides.

China is Myanmar's biggest arms supplier. According to Burmese sources, Beijing has also provided financial assistance to the country's intelligence agencies, such as the Office of Military Security Affairs and the Special Branch of the Myanmar Police Force. In addition, China held its first-ever naval exercise with Myanmar in May 2017. PLA Navy ships made a four-day port visit to Yangon, and a one-day joint naval exercise was conducted in the Gulf of Martaban. The frigate UMS *Aung Zeya* and the corvette UMS *Anawrahta* joined Chinese guided-missile destroyer *Changchun* (Hull 150), the guided-missile frigate *Jingzhou* (Hull 532) and the comprehensive supply ship *Chaohu* (Hull 890) for exercises including fleet communications, search and rescue operations, and formation manoeuvres. China is presenting itself as a reliable partner—unlike Western governments—to Myanmar and its military, because it has huge business interests in the country. Beijing has repeatedly called for closer cooperation between the two countries' armed forces and offered to provide training and technical exchanges to promote peace and stability along the China-Myanmar border.

Like China, India has sought to build strong ties with the Tatmadaw, partly because it wants to balance Chinese influence in the region and partly because it also has its own interests in Myanmar. Commander-in-Chief Min Aung Hlaing visited India in July 2015 and again two years later, in July 2017. On both trips, he met not only with Indian military leaders but also with Prime Minister Narendra Modi. India backs Myanmar's government on the Rohingya issue. It has sold radar systems and naval weapons to the Tatmadaw, and it is seeking to strengthen defence cooperation in the maritime sphere. The India-Myanmar Coordinated Patrol (IMCOR) exercise has been held annually since 2013, and a document on standard operating procedures for IMCOR was signed by the Indian Navy and the Myanmar Navy at the end of the fourth IMCOR, in 2016. Myanmar is only the third country with which India has signed a formal agreement for coordinated maritime patrols (Press Trust of India 2018).

Myanmar is also a regular participant in the biennial "Milan" naval exercise hosted by the Indian Navy. Moreover, the two countries' armies held the India-Myanmar Bilateral Military Exercise 2017 (IMBAX-2017) over six days in November of that year. This was the first military drill for United Nations peacekeeping operations between India and Myanmar. The first bilateral naval exercise, the India-Myanmar Naval Exercise 2018 (IMNEX-18), took place over nine days from late March to early April 2018. The frigate UMS *King Sin Phyu Shin* and the offshore patrol vessel UMS *Inlay* participated in exercises involving fleet manoeuvres, firing and coordinated anti-submarine drills.

Like Beijing and New Delhi, Moscow supports Naypyitaw on the Rohingya issue. Russia is the second largest arms supplier to the Tatmadaw after China, selling mostly the military aircraft that have become the primary fighter jets of the Myanmar Air Force. Moreover, Russia has trained thousands of Burmese officers in military technology, advanced engineering and nuclear science. A recent documentary, produced by a Russian Ministry of Defence television network with the Tatmadaw's cooperation, revealed that many Burmese military personnel spoke fluent Russian (*Mizzima* 2016). In June 2016, the defence ministries of Russia and Myanmar signed an agreement on cooperation in naval affairs, hydrography, topography, military medicine, military education and other promising fields (*Mizzima* 2016). A high-level delegation from Myanmar, headed by Major General Khin Aung Myint, chief of the Myanmar Air Force, toured the Kazan Helicopters facility of the Russian Helicopters Holding Company in July 2016.

A year later, in June 2017, Commander-in-Chief Min Aung Hlaing made an official visit to Moscow at the invitation of General Sergei K. Shoigu, the minister of defence of the Russian Federation. During the trip, Min Aung Hlaing discussed the promotion of bilateral military cooperation. The Russian defence minister made a reciprocal visit to Myanmar in January 2018, and his discussions there covered sending Tatmadaw military officers for military medical training in Russia, providing more scholarship opportunities to military officers from Myanmar to study at Russian universities and inviting high-ranking officials for state visits. Port visits on the part of naval vessels are an important part of Russia-Myanmar military relations, and the Russian destroyer *Admiral Panteleyev* and the tanker *Boris Butoma* visited the

Thilawa port near Yangon in December 2017. Moscow has also invited warships from the Myanmar Navy to make port visits to Russia. In addition, a Myanmar delegation participated in the Moscow Conference on International Security 2018 and in several events of the 2018 International Army Games.

In addition to strong military ties with China, India and Russia, the Tatmadaw also maintains an active role in Southeast Asian regional military affairs. Senior officials from the Myanmar Armed Forces regularly attend the Association of Southeast Asian Nations Defense Ministers' Meeting, which is the highest consultative and cooperative mechanism concerning defence in the region. The most remarkable outcome of this participation is that Myanmar has developed a strong and stable friendship with its historic rival Thailand.

Three factors may have contributed to strengthening this bond. First, the tradition of their armies' involvement in politics brought the two countries closer. Myanmar was under military rule for fifty years, and the most recent in a long line of military dictatorships held power in Thailand during 2014–19. Both the Tatmadaw and the Thai Army believe that they should not only act for national defence but should also be prepared to assume political authority in times of crisis. Those times include moments of massive political instability. Second, people-to-people relations between Myanmar and Thailand have become stronger because of low-cost airlines and agreements on visa-free travel. Bangkok is a weekend shopping destination for people from Myanmar, and Thai people make pilgrimages to various pagodas in Myanmar. Third, the "brothers-in-arms" bond between the two countries' military elites have played a central role in resetting relations between these historic adversaries. Soon after Min Aung Hlaing assumed leadership of the Tatmadaw, he built relations of lasting comradeship with Thai military leaders. Min Aung Hlaing met General Thanasak Patimaprakon, then the supreme commander of the Thai armed forces, in 2012, and they apparently became close. General Thanasak later introduced Min Aung Hlaing to other important figures in the Thai military. These included the late General Prem Tinsulanonda—a former Thai Army chief and former prime minister who subsequently served for two decades as the chairman of Thailand's Privy Council. It was reported that General Prem even adopted Min Aung Hlaing as his son (*The Irrawaddy* 2014). Because he did not have children of his own, General Prem, who had known Min Aung Hlaing's late father, happily accepted a request from the Burmese military chief to form this symbolic relationship. Min Aung Hlaing goes to Thailand several times a year to see Thai military commanders. Reciprocally, Thai generals make frequent visits to Myanmar for meetings. To honour Min Aung Hlaing's tireless efforts to build closer ties between the two militaries, Thailand awarded the Tatmadaw commander-in-chief a royal decoration in February 2018. Min Aung Hlaing became the first commander-in-chief of a foreign military to receive the Knight Grand Cross (First Class) of the Most Exalted Order of the White Elephant (Myanmar News Agency 2018a, 2018b).

Conclusion

Since Myanmar's democratic transition began in 2011, the country's armed forces have undertaken significant reforms. A new leadership is driving the Tatmadaw back into the defence sphere. Standard Army reform, comprised of three elements—military modernization, capacity building and active military-to-military engagement—is progressing well. One may argue that the Tatmadaw has become a new army because of the positive changes that it has carried out in recent years. However, the military still has old characteristics. The Tatmadaw is accused of having committed atrocities against the Rohingya population of Rakhine State. Also, in the northern and eastern parts of Myanmar, the military has reportedly committed human rights violations against civilians during its fight with ethnic armed forces. Back in the cities, the Tatmadaw has invoked the infamous Article 66D of the Telecommunications Act to sue dozens of journalists who wrote critical pieces about it. One of the worst cases was that of two Reuters journalists, Wa Lone and Kyaw Soe Oo, who were arrested in an alleged trap set by the Myanmar Police Force. The two journalists were covering the September 2017 Inn Din massacre, the extrajudicial killing of ten unarmed Rohingya people committed by Burmese soldiers. Wa Lone and Kyaw Soe Oo were charged under the colonial-era Official Secrets Act. The Tatmadaw used the case to send the message that it would not tolerate any behaviour that could harm the military's reputation or threaten the Three Main National Causes.

Notwithstanding its track record of human rights abuses, the leadership of the Tatmadaw is well aware that Myanmar is moving toward a democratic system. The armed forces have the capability to delay this process. Fortunately, military leaders do not have the will to nullify the democratic reforms of the past decade or to reverse their course. Building a modern military that has dignity, honour, and respect is more important to those leaders. Because the Tatmadaw wants to project a positive image to the rest of the world, appreciation and encouragement from the international community, especially the West, would deepen the Burmese military's commitment to supporting political transition. Diplomacy and engagement—not punishment and sanctions—would better help Myanmar establish a well-functioning democratic system.

NOTES

1. The State Law and Order Restoration Council junta changed the country's name in English from Burma to Myanmar in 1989. The word "Burma" is here used with reference to the period before 1989, and "Myanmar" with reference to the period after 1989. The word "Burmese", however, is used as an adjective in discussion of both periods.
2. See Nakanishi (2013), esp. Chapters 5 and 7.
3. See Nakanishi (2013).
4. Border Guard Forces are armed units that the Tatmadaw created in 2009 and 2010 from militia groups and ethnic armed organizations that had reached ceasefire agreements with the State Peace and Development Council junta. They are integrated into the formal command structure of the Tatmadaw, from which these armed groups receive financial and material support.
5. In fact, balancing one great power against another, especially China and the United States, is also the Myanmar government's *de facto*, albeit unofficial, foreign policy.

REFERENCES

Asian Correspondent. 2018. "Burma tells Bangladesh to Stop Aid to Rohingya in Zero Line", 21 February 2018. https://asiancorrespondent.com/2018/02/burma-tells-bangladesh-stop-aid-rohingya-zero-line/ (accessed 12 January 2020).

Aung Zaw. 2018. "Myanmar Seeks Advanced Weapons From Russia, But China Remains the Key Player". *The Irrawaddy*, 25 January 2018. https://www.irrawaddy.com/opinion/commentary/myanmar-seeks-advanced-weapons-russia-china-remains-key-player.html (accessed 12 January 2020).

BBC News. 2018. "Rohingya Crisis: Military Build-up on Myanmar Border with Bangladesh", 1 March 2018. https://www.bbc.com/news/world-asia-43248015 (accessed 12 January 2020).

Callahan, Mary. 2012. "The Generals Loosen Their Grip". *Journal of Democracy* 23, no. 4: 120–31.

Ei Ei Toe Lwin. 2015. "Ex-Generals Enter USDP, Election Fold". *Myanmar Times*, 14 August 2015. https://www.mmtimes.com/national-news/16000-ex-generals-enter-usdp-election-fold.html (accessed 12 January 2020).

Gross, Judah Ari, and TOI Staff. 2017. "Israel Says It Stopped Selling Weapons to Myanmar Months Ago". *The Times of Israel*, 30 November 2017. https://www.timesofisrael.com/israel-says-it-stopped-selling-weapons-to-myanmar-months-ago/ (accessed 12 January 2020).

International Crisis Group. 2016. "Myanmar: A New Muslim Insurgency in Rakhine State". *Asia Report*, no. 283 (15 December 2016). https://d2071andvip0wj.cloudfront.net/283-myanmar-a-new-muslim-insurgency-in-rakhine-state.pdf (accessed 19 March 2020).

The Irrawaddy. 2014. "Former Thai Army Chief is 'Godfather' to Burma's Top General", 16 July 2014. https://www.irrawaddy.com/news/burma/former-thai-army-chief-godfather-burmas-top-general.html (accessed 12 January 2020).

Kyaw Phyo Tha. 2012. "Fear of China Keeps Copper Mine Open: Aung Min". *The Irrawaddy*, 26 November 2012. https://www.irrawaddy.com/news/burma/fear-of-china-keeps-copper-mine-open-aung-min.html (accessed 12 January 2020).

Lawi Weng. 2018. "On Armed Forces Day, One Holiday, Two Visions". *The Irrawaddy*, 28 March 2018. https://www.irrawaddy.com/news/burma/armed-forces-day-one-holiday-two-visions.html (accessed 12 January 2020).

Lintner, Bertil. 2017. "The Truth behind Myanmar's Rohingya Insurgency". *Asia Times*, 20 September 2017. https://asiatimes.com/2017/09/truth-behind-myanmars-rohingya-insurgency/ (accessed 19 March 2020).

Lutz-Auras, Ludminla. 2015. "Russia and Myanmar — Friends in Need?" *The Journal of Current Southeast Asia Affairs* 34, no. 2: 165–98.

Maung Aung Myoe. 2009. *Building the Tatmadaw: Myanmar Armed Forces Since 1948*. Singapore: Institute of Southeast Asian Studies.

———. 2016. "Myanmar Military's White Paper Highlights Growing Openness". *Nikkei Asian Review*, 28 March 2016. https://asia.nikkei.com/Politics/Maung-Aung-Myoe-Myanmar-military-s-white-paper-highlights-growing-openness (accessed 19 March 2020).

Ministry of Information, Myanmar. 2008. *Constitution of the Republic of the Union of Myanmar (2008)*. Naypyitaw: Ministry of Information. https://www.burmalibrary.org/docs5/Myanmar_Constitution-2008-en.pdf (accessed 19 March 2020).

Mizzima. 2016. "Russia-Myanmar Military Cooperation Deal Signed", 17 June 2016. http://www.mizzima.com/news-domestic/russia-myanmar-military-cooperation-deal-signed (accessed 12 January 2020).

———. 2018. "US Passes Burma Human Rights and Freedom Act", 9 February 2018. http://www.mizzima.com/news-domestic/us-passes-burma-human-rights-and-freedom-act (accessed 12 January 2020).

Myanmar News Agency. 2018a. "Senior General Min Aung Hlaing to accept Knight Grand Cross (First Class) of the Most Exalted Order of the White Elephant". *The Global New Light of Myanmar*, 16 February 2018a. https://www.globalnewlightofmyanmar.com/senior-general-min-aung-hlaing-accept-knight-grand-cross-first-class-exalted-order-white-elephant/ (accessed 5 February 2020).

———. 2018b. "Thai King Confers Knight Grand Cross Honour on Senior General Min Aung Hlaing". *The Global New Light of Myanmar*, 17 February 2018b. https://www.globalnewlightofmyanmar.com/thai-king-confers-knight-grand-cross-honour-senior-general-min-aung-hlaing/ (accessed 12 January 2020).

Nakanishi Yoshihiro. 2013. *Strong Soldiers, Failed Revolution: The State and Military in Burma, 1962-1988*. Singapore and Kyoto: NUS Press and Kyoto University Press.

Parameswaran, Prashanth. 2019. "What's in the EU Myanmar Arms Embargo Extension?" *The Diplomat*, 2 May 2019. https://thediplomat.com/2019/05/whats-in-the-eu-myanmar-arms-embargo-extension/ (accessed 12 January 2020).

Press Trust of India. 2018. "India, Myanmar to Hold Coordinated Patrol in Andaman Sea, Bay of Bengal". *The Economic Times*, 12 July 2018. https://economictimes.indiatimes.com/news/defence/india-myanmar-to-hold-coordinated-patrol-in-andaman-sea-bay-of-bengal/articleshow/51044876.cms (accessed 12 January 2020).

Republic of the Union of Myanmar. 2015. *The Republic of the Union of Myanmar Defense White Paper (2015)*. Naypyitaw.

Selth, Andrew. 2016. "'Strong, Fully Efficient and Modern': Myanmar's New Look Armed Forces". Griffith Asia Institute Regional Outlook Paper 49. https://www.griffith.edu.au/__data/assets/pdf_file/0017/118313/Regional-Outlook-Paper-49-Selth-web.pdf (accessed 17 March 2020).

Stockholm International Peace Research Institute (SIPRI). N.d. "SIPRI Arms Transfers Database". https://www.sipri.org/databases/armstransfers/sources-and-methods (accessed 12 January 2020).

Tin Maung Maung Than. 2010. "Tatmadaw and Myanmar's Security Challenges". In *Asia Pacific Countries' Security Outlook and Its Implications for the Defense Sector*, pp. 123–40. NIDS Joint Research Series No. 5. Tokyo: The National Institute for Defense Studies. http://www.nids.mod.go.jp/english/publication/joint_research/series5/pdf/5-9.pdf (accessed 19 March 2020).

UN News. 2017. "UN Human Rights Chief Points to 'Textbook Example of Ethnic Cleansing' in Myanmar", 11 September 2017. https://news.un.org/en/story/2017/09/564622-un-human-rights-chief-points-textbook-example-ethnic-cleansing-myanmar (accessed 12 January 2020).

United States House of Representatives. 2014. "H.R.3979 - The Carl Levin and Howard P. 'Buck' Mckeon National Defense Authorization Act for Fiscal Year 2015". Washington: United States House of Representatives.

Win Min. 2008. "Internal Dynamics of the Burmese Military: Before, During and After the 2007 Demonstrations". In *Dictatorship, Disorder and Decline in Myanmar*, edited by Monique Skidmore and Trevor Wilson, pp. 29–47. Canberra: The Australian National University Press.

3

THAILAND'S MILITARY: IDEOLOGY AND SENSE OF MISSION

Paul Chambers

Ideology and sense of mission are, as reflections of the military mindset, fundamental to the shaping of military organization and behaviour—as that behaviour is directed either to guarding existing power structures or to changing them. The military mindset is a crucial element in gauging armed forces' collective perception of their preferences and goals, especially vis-à-vis notions of democracy and civilian control. Military mindset informs and is informed by ideology, which itself then shapes the sense of mission.

This study examines Thailand's military through reference to its ideology, the historical context in which it has evolved, and its contemporary sense of mission. The study stresses the degree to which ideological legacies have shaped and socialized the Thai armed forces and thus informed officers' understandings of their duties and roles in national life. These legacies have also served to clarify to military officers and to Thais more generally the fact that the country's military has a unique and serious political vision. The study argues that Thai military ideology has over time been constructed to rationalize the legitimacy of interventionism to rescue, defend and develop the nation, though variations in dogma relating to the prevailing cultural hegemony at different times in Thai history have also influenced this mindset (Gramsci 1971, p. 526). With an eye to maintaining its control over Thailand's hegemonic bloc, the monarchy has succeeded in dominating the armed forces by manipulating the values, beliefs and perceptions of soldiers and officers so that a monarchized worldview has become the socially accepted military ideology.

Thai military ideology, especially since 1980, has been a function of two related but sometimes countervailing conceptualizations. First, the armed forces are a "monarchised military"[1] which acts as a guardian of and mechanism serving palace interests. Second, the military sees itself as the nationalistic arbitrator of Thai politics. It is in that role responsible for ousting or installing governments as it deems such intervention necessary to protect Thai national security and development, correlating with an identity centred on Buddhism, monarchy and "Thai-ness".

But how has Thai military ideology evolved across time and to what extent has it become more cohesive?[2] What have been the most important dimensions of Thai military ideology since 2014, when the armed forces seized state power in Bangkok? How have ideological legacies informed the understandings, among both military officers and Thais in general, of the duties and roles of the military? To what extent will a cohesive military ideology drive the armed forces into the future? This study addresses these questions. It first looks at the evolution of Thai military ideology from 1852 until the time of the May 2014 coup. Second, it sketches the broad contours of military ideology since that putsch. It then considers the question of how this ideology influences the behaviour of military officers. Finally, the study's conclusion addresses potential future trends in Thai military ideology.

Thai Military Ideology since 1852

Throughout history, ideology has been a chief unifier of the Thai military machine. Thai military ideology has evolved along with and adapted itself to changes in the political landscape, whether under civilian-led or military-led regimes. There have been ten major eras of ideology across Thai military history.

In the first era, the evolution of Thai military thought commenced in 1852 with the establishment under King Mongkut (r. 1851–68) of the Royal Siamese Armed Forces as a rudimentary standing military force. The reign of King Chulalongkorn (r. 1868–1910) saw the more permanent establishment of land and naval forces and their unification under a War Department (*krom kalahom*). It also brought the creation of a military cadet school and the introduction of a system of universal conscription, with training by European officers. From the beginning, these forces located their ideological legitimacy in service to king and Buddhism. Almost all senior officers were princes; the core regiment was a King's Guard (*kong thahan mahatlek raksa phra-ong*), established in 1870; and the centralized loyalty of military to sovereign was meant to consolidate the palace's direct control over outlying principalities. At the same time, beginning as least as early as the second decade of the nineteenth century, royal decrees had declared the military a mechanism for safeguarding Buddhism, and various Buddhist monks extolled the virtues of the armed forces to the people (Battye 1974, p. 10). By the end of Chulalongkorn's reign, military ideology had crystallized around the notion of devotion to "king, nation and religion (Buddhism)" (Murashima 1986, p. 27). Sense of mission functioned to safeguard monarchy from perceived threats, both domestic and foreign. In later years, as the Navy and then the Air Force were established, they in turn adopted the same sense of mission. Such a royalist agenda helped to unite the military, even as the standards and ethics taught at Siam's cadet school clearly proscribed military involvement in politics.

Under King Vajiravudh (r. 1910–25), military ideology and sense of mission reflected most of all the concept that Vella labels "nationalistic militarism" (Vella 1978, p. 87). But such militarism remained tightly incorporated under monarchized absolutism. This "royal-centric military ideology" was closely tied to the expansion of monarchical power. Thus, Vajiravudh sought to develop an *esprit de corps* in which patriotism and nationalism centred directly on the sovereign. To this end he created a hand-picked personal detachment, called the "Wild Tigers" (*suea pa*), apart from the regular armed forces. Nevertheless, some disenchanted military factions began to believe that the king was promoting an ideology of loyalty to himself and to his Wild Tigers at the expense of national development. Partly because of this, a coup attempt occurred in 1912 (Greene 1999, pp. 51–52). And for the next twenty years the palace, in attempting to dominate the armed forces, allowed only members of royalty to fill positions of command. It also tried, more than ever, to inculcate an ideology of complete devotion to the palace on the part of Siam's military. But, by the early 1930s, and in the context of economic depression, many young officers had begun to believe that they themselves could guide the kingdom's national development better than the palace.

Turning to the second period in the evolution of Thai military ideology, in 1932 a group of soldiers and civilian bureaucrats overthrew the absolute monarchy to become the country's new ruling elite. They placed Siam under an authoritarian constitution which offered limited elections. The result, until 1944, was dictatorship by elements of the military-controlled *Khana ratsadon* or People's Party—an experience that helped to perpetuate a mindset in which the military saw itself as autonomous from elected civilian administrations and entitled to interfere in civilian politics. The key ideological notion in this period was to protect and nurture the Thai "nation" rather than the monarch. The prime military objective therefore became the eradication of any forces that might oppose the state-defined concept of a Thai race, as legitimized by supporting fascist dogma and reinforced through the use of suppression. This sense of mission became paramount during the militarist administration of Prime Minister Field Marshal Plaek Phibunsongkhram (1938–44), a period during which the armed forces underwent various purges and were extensively re-organized. The restructuring involved the adoption of nationalistic catch-phrases which, though acknowledging monarchy, primarily emphasized Phibun's "Era of Nation-building", constitutionalism, and the notion of "Thai-ness" (Wright 1991, pp. 97–98). The military-dominated regime wrapped itself in irredentist chauvinism, stressed Thailand's "national humiliation" in the form of territories "lost" to imperial powers of the West, and practised a form of state capitalism (Murashima 1986, p. 70). The bureaucracy's commanding role in economic affairs was spearheaded by security officials, in what might be termed "developmental militarism"—a notion which presumed that only security officials had the expertise and wherewithal to guide both the economy and state formation.

For the first time, the Thai military adopted the ideology of a "dual function". Calling it *dwifungsi*, the Indonesian military would adopt a similar concept later, in 1958. Under *dwifungsi*, soldiers play a crucial role in the realms both of defence and security and of socio-political affairs (Callahan 1999, p. 6). As later happened in Indonesia, the ideology of the military under Phibun allowed the armed forces to enmesh themselves into virtually all domains of Thai life. Accordingly, while operating in accordance with this new ideology, the military become the most powerful actor in Thai political history.

The brief third period in the development of Thai military ideology started with the fall of Phibun from power in 1944 and the defeat of the Axis powers, with which Phibun had sided, in 1945. This 1944–47 interlude witnessed a short-lived democracy led by civilian elites—most prominent among them Pridi Banomyong—who had been leading figures in the Seri Thai insurgent resistance to the Phibun-led military regime during the Pacific War. The democracy over which they presided was born from the simultaneous weakness of monarchical and military elites at a time when elected civilian rule appeared to be increasingly influential, both inside and outside of Thailand. Under civilian direction, the armed forces were downsized. The post of supreme commander was abolished, the military budget was drastically cut, and an ideology supporting democracy, civilian control and Asian nationalism permeated politics and the military itself. Yet this state of affairs frustrated many soldiers, many of whom increasingly supported the overthrow of democracy. They did not have to wait long.

A fourth period began in 1947, when a military coup led by General Phin Choonhavan and supported by Phibun was carried out against the elected civilian government. This putsch resurrected the military elite and transformed Thai military ideology, which increasingly "involved the trilogy of Nation, Religion (Buddhism), and King [with] the army's 'clientele' ... being these three" and the actions of civilian politicians seen as threats to this clientele (Thak 2007, p. 37). During this era, which lasted until 1951, the military's ideological focus spotlighted anti-communism, developmental militarism, and, to a lesser extent, monarchization. All three concepts helped to rationalize the armed forces' commanding role in politics—as national guardian against foreign (communist) encroachment, as facilitator of development in peripheral areas of the country and as protector of monarchy. In the context of the Cold War, such a posture earned the military amicable relationships with both the United States and the palace. In fact, it was in 1949 that the Thai military adopted an organizational and educational format borrowed from the American "West Point" model. The curriculum of the United States Military Academy offers four years of undergraduate education and encourages cadet initiative, intense subordination to group, and a spirit of camaraderie. With Thai military strategists having copied the U.S. military doctrine of containing communism, Thai security officers began to receive training from American military instructors (Surachart 1999, pp. 99–100).

By 1951, the "old guard" of the 1930s-era military was chafing at the monarchy's growing assertiveness. As a result, a 1951 "Radio Coup", in which military leaders scrapped the 1949 constitution in favour of the much more anti-royalist 1932 constitution, instituted a fifth period in the history of Thai military ideology. The period saw a drastic weakening of monarchization in Thai military discourse. To maintain U.S. support, the regime—nominally led by Phibun once again—and the armed forces continued generally to stress an ideology of strong anti-communism. During this period, the police also played a growing role in Thailand's national security apparatus, in part as a reflection of factionalism in the Thai armed forces. The powerful roles of the military and police in Thai society were reflected in a continuing emphasis on developmental militarism.

The coup of September 1957 abruptly transformed Thai military ideology for a sixth time. This putsch, led by Army Commander General Sarit Thanarat, immediately resulted in Washington's transferring the emphasis in its support for the Thai armed forces away from the police and toward the Army (Surachart 1999, p. 100). In the fifteen years that followed, anti-communism and developmental militarism became even more entrenched in the military mindset. Most significantly, new strongman Sarit re-established monarchization as part of the national credo. His emphasis on safeguarding royalty and royalism contributed to the king's becoming—once again—central to the ideology uniting Thai soldiers, and in fact the Thai people. The renewed importance of kingship to the Thai state—as undergirded by a monarchized military—strengthened the institutions of the monarchy and armed forces as entrenched elites across the nation. Though monarchical power grew, the military remained dominant, using the king as a legitimizing bridge to the populace. Sarit became the arch-royalist *phokhun upatham* or paternalistic despot of Thailand (Thak 2007, p. 119).

Anti-communism also now became a Cold War conceptual tool that bonded together the interests of the military, the monarchy and the United States. The military depicted communism as an external threat, one that endangered both the Thai monarchy and Thai identity. Its sense of mission during the 1958–73 period of overt military dominance was enunciated in the 1960 Defense Act. Article 4 of the act defined the role and duty of the Thai armed forces as defending and maintaining the stability of the kingdom from external and internal threats (Chambers 2013. p. 82). Communism was one of the kingdom's principal, albeit indirect, external threats. The military would be specifically utilized to safeguard the monarchy, combat insurrection, develop the country, and protect national interests.

Communism had first emerged in Siam in the 1920s. When the Communist Party of Thailand commenced armed insurgency in 1965, the military initially relied upon repression as the central plank in its programme for achieving victory, as reflected in Plan 09/10 of 1967 for waging counterinsurgency operations in the Northern and Northeastern Thailand and in the Deep South. Plan 110/2012 of 1969 kept the focus on a military solution to the problem of insurgency, but it placed more emphasis on development projects (Moore 2010, pp. 87–88). Indeed, in an attempt to stamp out rural support for the Communist Party of Thailand, the armed forces set out to "develop" rural areas, initiating numerous projects with U.S. support. Fears of a "red" menace and a focus on counterinsurgency objectives helped to solidify the unity of the armed forces behind the ideology of anti-communism. This effect lasted for more than three decades, from Sarit's 1957 putsch until the end of the Cold War in 1991.

The fall of the military dictatorship of Sarit's successors in 1973 left military ideology fractured. During the seventh period in its history, Army Commander General Krit Sivara supported an ideology of democracy under monarchy, but other officers, such as General Chalard Hiransiri, gave higher priority to anti-communism, monarchization, and militarism. Krit had ordered an end to the Army's repression of demonstrators on the streets of Bangkok on 14 October 1973, declaring, "These young people ... they are our children."[3] In 1975, he would issue a directive, entitled "An Approach to Communist Terrorist Suppression in Mountainous Areas", whose gist was that a greater emphasis on political measures must replace the use of direct force against communist insurgents. Beginning with Krit, a segment of the officer corps began to ideologically support a move from "armed suppression to political offensive" (Surachart 1999, pp. 104, 109). Yet Krit's sudden death in 1976 brought increased instability and factionalism to the Army.

The October 1976 coup overthrew Thai democracy, but only exacerbated the fractured state of military ideology. Incessant factionalism enabled the monarch to elevate Thanin Kraivichien, an arch-royalist palace advisor, to the post of prime minister. But severe frictions between Thanin and senior brass led to three coup attempts, the last of which was successful. The October 1977 coup, however, was not endorsed by the palace (Handley 2006, p. 267); it thus contributed to continuing tensions between palace and military.

Nevertheless, anti-communism, developmental militarism and monarchization continued to unify the Thai military mindset, even in the context of a lack of cohesion on other issues. Senior officers who had been allied to the 1958–73 military regime backed a return to the *status quo ante*. But many officers disagreed. These men included younger officers who were members of one or the other of two ideological factions, the "Young Turks" and the "Democratic Soldiers". The study returns to these cliques below.

Unity only returned to military ideology with the palace-engineered ascension to the premiership of General Prem Tinsulanonda in 1980, which inaugurated the eighth period in the history of Thai military ideology. Prem was an arch-royalist general popular in military circles, respected for his counter-insurgency leadership against the communists, and highly trusted by King Bhumibol. Under Prem, monarchization became the most important part of military ideology at any time since 1932. And it is since 1980 that the military has acted continuously as the junior elite partner of monarchy. Indeed, the nexus between Bhumibol and Prem ensured that the 1977 coup was the final putsch to succeed without the king's tacit support. Prem and his deputy General Chavalit Yongchaiyudh also embraced Krit's earlier counter-insurgency proposals for prioritizing political measures rather than using simple military force against insurgents.[4] This change in tactics contributed to the demise of the Communist Party of Thailand in 1983. Prem's service as Army commander (1978–81), prime minister (1980–88), and privy councillor (1988–2019) also contributed to his military faction becoming dominant across the armed forces. Despite the end of the Cold War in 1991, Thailand's national security state continued to prevail. From 1980 until 1992, monarchization, developmental militarism, and anti-communism remained dominant planks of military ideology.

After 1992—with the advent of elected civilian government, communism no longer a threat, and the military's own image tainted by its massacre of civilian demonstrators on the streets of Bangkok in May of that year—military ideology entered a ninth era. During this period, monarchization, followed by security sector reform and support for democracy, became the central features of military ideology. Thai military units became increasingly involved in United Nations peacekeeping operations, such as the 1999–2000 mission with the International Force for East Timor (INTERFET).[5] As the drafters of the 1997 constitution had been chosen while an elected civilian government was in power, it can be argued that this charter established, for the first time in Thailand's history, a civilian orientation toward the armed forces. Previous constitutions had been created either by regimes under direct military control, as in 1959 for example, or by military-appointed but civilian-led regimes, as in 1991. Yet in no part of the charter did the drafters specifically discuss the mission of the armed forces. This omission perhaps reflected fear of upsetting military leaders. Only in Section 72 was it declared that "the State shall arrange for the maintenance of the armed forces" (Kingdom of Thailand 1997).

At this same time, military leaders increasingly sought to streamline the military and make it more accountable. From 1998 until 2001, Army Commander General Surayud Chulanont instituted a series of modifications to the military, including a reduction in the size of all Thai security services, greater transparency in now reduced military budgets, and prosecutions of alleged crime in the military (Chambers 2013, pp. 244–45).

In 2001, following his election to the premiership, Thaksin Shinawatra tried to transform the military into more of an instrument of prime ministerial control than had historically been the case. Though monarchization and an emphasis on democracy remained strong elements of the military mindset, senior officers such as Army commanders-in-chief Generals Somdhat Attanand and Chaisit Shinawatra—the latter a cousin of Thaksin—prioritized civilian control, though perhaps for material or family reasons. The result was that democracy became a more important part of Thai military ideology. However, in the aftermath of an insurgent attack in Thailand's Deep South on 4 January 2004, the October 2004 Army reshuffle ensured the ascendance of a group of senior officers who favoured a stronger role for the armed forces in national development. The officers were led by Army commander-in-chief General Prawit Wongsuwan (2004–5) and his successor General Sonthi Boonyaratglin (2005–7). Under Sonthi's leadership, and with support from Privy Council Chairman Prem Tinsulanonda, the Army ousted Thaksin from office on 19 September 2006. This event put paid to backing for civilian control in the military's ideology once and for all.[6] According to their television announcement on the day of the putsch, the coup-makers' rationale for their move against the Thaksin government was that the elected Thai Rak Thai-led government had practised corruption, caused political fragmentation in the country, and challenged the king's power. Claiming that all other attempts to resolve Thailand's crisis had failed, they announced that the military had no choice but to usurp power (CNS 2006).

Since 2006, a tenth and final period in the history of its ideology, focusing on monarchization and developmental militarism, has dominated the mindset of the Thai military. The leaders of the junta in power during 2006–8 oversaw the enactment in 2007 of a new constitution that diminished elected civilian control over the upper house of parliament or Senate while weakening the power of parties in the lower house. The charter provided for greater military influence in the Senate, which would include 74 appointed and 76 elected members (Kingdom of Thailand 2007). Following elections in early 2008, 15.3 per cent of its total membership was now composed of retired military officials. As for the lower house of the Thai parliament, the 2007 reforms strengthened party factions while decentralizing party finance. In addition, this constitution even further insulated the Thai military from civilian control. Its provisions notwithstanding, pro-Thaksin parties succeeded in continuously winning general elections—in 2007, 2011 and 2014. Democracy became an extremely worrisome concept for the military, since governance on the part of the winners of elections appeared inimical to military interests. This is why, in its search for an alternative credo to democracy, the armed forces increasingly prioritized defence of monarchy. They used this rationale to explain the need to oust pro-Thaksin governments. The military also began to take a leading role in charging people with the crime of *lèse majesté* through the use of Article 112 of the Thai Criminal Code. Through coups and indictments under Article 112, the military sought to legitimize its role as defender of monarchy and thus to enhance military clout across society. The armed forces also grew intent on demonstrating that developmental militarism could trump the inefficiencies of democracy. Examples of this determination included the military's shaping of political development through the 2006 coup, its role in cobbling together a coalition government in 2008, and the 2014 coup. The ability of the military to assist victims of massive flooding in Central Thailand in 2011 earned it accolades and popular support (*Terra Daily* 2011). With King Bhumibol increasingly aged, sick, and frail after this latest coup, military ideology was presented as a form of substitute unifying guide through the political and economic turbulence that the Thai kingdom faced.

Military Ideology in Post-2014 Thailand

On 22 May 2014, Army commander-in-chief General Prayut Chan-ocha overthrew Thailand's elected government in the thirteenth overt military putsch in the country since 1932. In explaining the motive for the coup, Prayut said on television that immoral and corrupt elected politicians had, through political parties, established a parliamentary dictatorship and were implementing disruptive populist schemes which led to the partisan undermining of the executive, legislative, and judicial branches of government. The resultant disunity and conflict disturbed the political order under the monarchy and necessitated the coup, arrests of opponents to the new junta, and the ascendancy of military courts over the country (Ministry of Foreign Affairs 2014). It had been essential for the military to intervene in order to stabilize Thailand and establish a democratic process under greater guidance from monarchy and military. Prayut's rationale was similar to the declared motives for the coups of 1947, 1957, 1981, and 2006.

The National Council for Peace and Order (NCPO), as the junta called itself, immediately began to mandate an ideology for soldiers and civilians alike. It also ordained a sense of military mission that explicitly emphasized monarchization and developmental militarism under a national security state. Though the armed forces were answerable to the palace, the junta now directly administered Thailand. It was in no hurry to return the country to even partial elected governance—at least not until some guaranteed control could be placed upon electoral outcomes.

In a reflection of ideological monarchization, the junta tried symbolically to link the military to King Naresuan the Great, who lived between 1555 and 1605 and is perhaps the country's foremost nationalistic icon. The Thai armed forces have always regarded 18 January, the date on which Naresuan purportedly defeated a Burmese crown prince in battle, as Thai Military Day.[7] In a series of recent movies about Naresuan, the king is played by cavalry officer Wanchana Sawatdee, while his brother is portrayed by the NCPO spokesperson.[8] In 2015, the junta built Ratchaphak Park on military land in Hua Hin, Prachuap Khirikhan Province, to honour great Thai kings of the past. During the same year the NCPO visibly endorsed then Crown Prince Vajiralongkorn's "Bike for Dad" and "Bike for Mom" events. In a televised address in the 11 July 2014 instalment of the programme "Returning Happiness to the People", General Prayut announced twelve "core values" to which Thai people must adhere, and which children in schools must recite daily. They included upholding "nation, religion, and monarchy". These values correspond well with the expressed roles of the armed forces: "to safeguard independence, sovereignty, internal order, as well as protect the nation, religion, monarch, and the interests of the nation" (Ministry of Defense 2008, p. 33). Throughout the tenure of the junta, Prayut continued delivering weekly television addresses, on Friday evenings. These addresses served to connect the junta leader directly to the people. Among discussion topics, Prayut preached about loyalty to the monarch, security for the kingdom, and reconciliation under monarchy (Chambers and Napisa 2016, p. 437).

In terms of developmental militarism, "Reform", "Reconciliation", "Attitude adjustment", "Marching Thailand forward", "Bringing happiness back to the People", and "Thailand 4.0" all became catch-phrases in a ubiquitous junta-led campaign to manage the political and economic re-stabilization of Thailand while either trying to win over public opinion or justifying the need to imprison regime opponents. The NCPO's developmental militarism had two dimensions. First, it embodied authoritarian neo-liberalism in the sense that the junta welcomed massive investments, including investments in megaprojects, by domestic and foreign concerns alike. It often waived the need for environmental impact assessments and tolerated the displacement of local communities. Second, as if attempting to compete with the popularity of Thaksin's earlier populist policies, the regime devised reforms under an initiative that it labelled *Pracharat*, or State Populism. *Pracharat* differed from Thaksinomics in that it envisioned the distribution of state resources for welfare programmes to needy communities through state technocrats rather than elected politicians. Such a strategy was meant to help improve the junta's popularity (Kornkritch 2017).

Meanwhile, Section 52 of Thailand's 2017 constitution can be interpreted to grant the armed forces the right to intervene in Thai politics as well as a central role in the country's development.

> The State shall protect and uphold the institution of kingship, independence, sovereignty, integrity of the territories and the areas over which Thailand has the sovereignty rights, honor and interest of the Nation, security of the State, and public order. For these purposes, the State shall provide efficient military, diplomatic, and intelligence services. Armed forces shall also be deployed for the purpose of developing the country. (Kingdom of Thailand 2017)[9]

The NCPO's ideology of virulent royalism, developmental militarism, and disdain for the "chaos" of democracy was little different from that espoused by every Thai Army commander-in-chief since 2004, when Prawit Wongsuwan assumed the post, or from those in office between 1978 and 1992. It is reflected in the mission statements of the Thai security services as well as in that of the Ministry of Defense. All have ranked the safeguarding of monarchy and King Bhumibol's "sufficiency economy" as their most important mission. Units in the security bureaucracy also devoted themselves to backing the NCPO. For example, in the defense minister's 2016 policy statement, "Immediate Guideline 3.8" declared,

> Support the maintaining of peace as set forth by NCPO guidelines. This is achieved through supporting social order and controlling illegal activities in conjunction with propagating social awareness, for example, to help defuse student violent behaviors and aggressive acts. (Ministry of Defense 2016, p. 15)

In addition, Section 8 of the Administration of the Ministry of Defense Act of 2008 tasked the ministry with the following missions.

> To safeguard independence and security of the Kingdom from internal and external threats, protect the country and people from rebellion and disorder, safeguard and protect the institution of Monarchy as well as to support the mission of the institution of Monarchy, protect and safeguard the national interests and the democratic system of government with the King as Head of State, develop the country for security, support missions of the State in national development…. (Ministry of Defense 2008)

As these mission statements suggest, post-2014 Thailand is a national security state in which the principal objective of the military is to protect monarchical primacy—and in which democracy is but an afterthought—and in which the secondary objective is to manage national development.

The largest of the country's security services, the Royal Thai Army, itself prioritizes four principal missions. In order of importance, these are protecting and extolling monarchy, external defence, internal security, and supporting national development (Royal Thai Army n.d.). These missions and their ranking hark back to Thailand's pre-1992 period of military domination. The Army has specifically engaged in national development by emphasizing the Royally Initiated Projects (ibid.). Since 1951, over 3,000 Royally Initiated Projects, involving nearly eight million workers, have been undertaken. The projects are designed to improve the lives of impoverished people, mostly in Thailand's countryside, through the initiation of community development projects. A related objective is to bolster national security by winning the hearts and minds of impoverished people, mostly in Thailand's rural areas, who are potentially vulnerable to the spread of communism and other subversive ideologies. In practice, the military has been the prime engine to carry out the Royally Initiated Projects' objectives. In 2017, the Army was directly responsible for operations in 112 Royally Initiated Projects (ibid.). In addition, the Royal Thai Armed Forces have developed their own plans that reflect the initiative of the Royal Projects, or cooperate closely with them. Army involvement in the Royal Projects is often managed by "development for security" committees, established in each Army region with funding both from the palace and from the Army's general budget. The commanders of the Army regions are the heads of each regional committee. The palace's reliance on military implementation of Royal Projects and the legitimacy that such reliance then bestows on the military only further entrench the symbiotic relationship between the Thai monarchy and the military. The Royally Initiated Projects have thus enabled the armed forces to ride on the coattails of the monarch to extend their own influence.

As noted, aside from military collaboration in implementing the Royally Initiated Projects, independent military development projects have tended to dovetail with those projects. This followed from King Bhumibol's pronouncement that "combat" and "development" must be achieved simultaneously. Examples of past military development projects include the Five Provinces Bordering Forest Preservation Foundation in Eastern Thailand, the Doi Tung Development Project in the far North, the Pak Phanang River Basin Development Project in the Upper South, and the New Hope Project in the Deep South (Napisa and Chambers 2013, p. 81).

Recent national development and civic action programmes undertaken by the Thai military include directing relief operations following national disasters, helping farmers harvest their crops, and seeking ways to stabilize the prices of agricultural products (Ministry of Defense 2008, p. 68). As part of their development work, soldiers have also been instructed to inculcate political ideology and military notions of democracy (ibid., p. 45).

Today, the ideology of Thailand's armed forces, broadly speaking that of a "monarchized military", is reflected not only in their enshrined responsibilities and in the education offered at service academies but also in military songs, chants of allegiance, unit narratives and related discourse, uniforms, emblems, and awards. Indeed, "protecting and upholding the monarchy" remains the principal task of Thailand's armed forces (Ministry of Defense 2018, p. 11). The task of guarding the palace legitimizes the military in its task of spearheading the construction of the Thai nation.

The Influence of Military Ideology on Military Officers

Military ideology has both divided and made more cohesive Thailand's officer corps. Notions of arch-royalism and developmentalist nationalism superficially drape the armed forces in an appearance of unity that in itself creates a common ethos among soldiers. Yet such outwardly apparent concord conceals fissures within. A variety of ideological factions have been present in the Thai military. Evidence of ideological fissures can be found in the record of military support for or against coups and coup attempts across Thai history. While corporate interest has certainly accounted for many of these attempts to grab power, some have had at least partial ideological roots, as Table 3.1 suggests.

TABLE 3.1
Thai Coups and Coup Attempts Tied to Ideology-linked Motives

Year	Date	Coup Event	Ideology-linked Motive
1912	January 13	91 soldiers unsuccessfully tried to assassinate King Vajiravudh though the putsch was discovered and foiled before it could be carried out. In part, the plotters opposed the king's establishment of his Wild Tiger Corps.	Some participants favoured a move toward constitutional monarchy, and some even favoured republicanism.
1932	June 24	General Phraya Phahonphonphayuhasena successfully ousted Thailand's absolute monarchy at the head of "the Promoters".	An anti-monarchist move toward "constitutionalism".
1933	June 20	General Phraya Phahon led a successful coup against appointed royalist Prime Minister Phraya Manopakorn Nititada.	An anti-monarchist move toward "constitutionalism".
1933	October 11	Lieutenant Colonel Luang Phibunsongkhram led forces in putting down the royalist rebellion of Prince Boworadet.	The counter-rebellion proclaimed itself anti-communist and sought to resurrect arch-royalism.
1947	November 8	The military successfully carried out a coup against Pridi-aligned Prime Minister Thawan Thamrongnawasawat.	Coup leaders claimed the need to protect monarchy and to combat communism.

TABLE 3.1 (*continued*)

Year	Date	Coup Event	Ideology-linked Motive
1949, 1951	February 26; June 29	Pridi Banomyong led two Navy-assisted coup attempts.	Pridi was supporting greater democracy in Thailand.
1957	September 16	Army Commander General Sarit Thanarat usurps power.	Sarit claimed a need to protect the monarchy and restore order to the kingdom.
1973	October 14	Amid student demonstrations, Army Commander General Krit Sivara refused to support the military regime.	Krit claimed a need to support democracy.
1976	October 6	Following a massacre of university students, Admiral Sangad Chaloryu led a coup.	The coup leaders claimed a need to protect monarchy and Thailand from communism. The Young Turks supported the coup, seeking a move toward an efficient military regime.
1977, 1981, 1985	March 26, April 1, September 9, respectively	Thailand's "Young Turks" military faction supported or attempted coups.	The Young Turks saw the regimes in power as corrupt and malfeasant.
1991	February 23	The military overthrew an elected civilian government.	Coup leaders claimed a need to clean up corruption and malfeasance and to restore order to the kingdom.
2006	September 19	Army Commander General Sonthi Boonyaratglin led the overthrow of the elected Thaksin government.	Coup leaders claimed a need to restore order, "protect" monarchy and "end" corruption.
2014	May 22	Army Commander General Prayut Chan-ocha overthrew the caretaker Phuea Thai Party government.	Coup leaders claimed a need to restore order, "protect" monarchy and "end" corruption.

At least three important ideological factions have been present in the Thai military in recent times. The first was a grouping of junior officers known as the Young Military Officers Group (*Khana thahan num*), sometimes referred to as the Young Turks (Girling 1981, pp. 228–30). The Young Turks were graduates of Chulachomklao Royal Military Academy Class 7, which completed its studies at the academy in 1955. The group, which contained close to ninety middle-level officers by the late 1970s, was extremely anti-communist. But its members also castigated the exploitative capitalism of corrupt businesspeople and politicians for destroying the nation and thus giving communism greater appeal to the Thai peasantry. They thus believed that only under military tutelage could social reforms to bring order and unity to the country be instituted. During the 1970s, when the Thai military was particularly fragmented, the Young Turks were one of the more cohesive of its cliques. Notable Young Turks included Chamlong Srimuang, Manoon Rupkachorn, Pallop Pinmanee, Pridi Ramasoot and Prajak Sawangjit. The death in 1976 of General Krit, no hero to the Young Turks, allowed them to grow in importance, especially as theirs was the most cohesive among the cliques of the day.[10] These mid-level officers supported the 1976 coup, both an attempted and a successful coup in 1977, and attempted coups in 1981 and 1985. Yet these later failures did much to destroy the group.

A second ideological faction, also born in the late 1970s, was called the Democratic Soldiers. Comprised mostly of officers working in counter-insurgency operations at the Internal Security Operations Command or ISOC, this group promoted a transition toward "democratization", which would help develop the country while winning the hearts and minds of Thai communists. In addition, it promoted a more political approach to combating insurgency, prioritizing the rooting out of social injustices that led to support for insurrection rather than simply using military force to combat insurrection. Like the Young Turks, the Democratic Soldiers group was founded by mid-ranking officers. Its original members included Generals Harn Leelanon, Ravi Wanpen and Chavalit Yongchaiyudh (Suchit 1987, pp. 14–15). The political thought of the Democratic Soldiers became enmeshed in Thai electoral politics with the launch in 1990 of Chavalit's New Aspiration Party and his election as prime minister in 1996.

Arguably, the emergence of a third ideological grouping within the Thai armed forces accompanied the premiership of Thaksin Shinawatra. From 2001 until 2004, and despite opposition from Prem, Thaksin succeeded in promoting his loyalists and even kin to senior military positions. But his "Thaksinomics" was also popular with intermediate-level officers and enlisted personnel. Thaksin's populist welfare programmes earned him broad support among these soldiers as well as the general populace. Such officers and soldiers were known as "Watermelons" because they were "Red Shirts" wearing green military uniforms. Some "Watermelons", such as Khattiya Sawasdipol or "Seh Daeng", became high-profile participants in Red Shirt demonstrations. It has been alleged that some of these "Watermelon soldiers", appearing as "Men in Black", staged a nocturnal attack against a Thai Army regiment during demonstrations in Bangkok in April 2010 (Human Rights Watch 2011).

Finally, it must be emphasized that ideology has factionalized the military because of monarchization itself. Though the military as a whole gains legitimacy as a cohesive guardian of the palace, individual units also gain such legitimacy through their particular roles in relation to the monarchy. The 1st Infantry Battalion, Regiment and Division of Thailand's First Army Region were the original units called the "King's Guard", though the designation has now spread to other units within every military service. "King's Guard" soldiers are specifically tasked with personally protecting the king. The moniker corresponds to the *Wongthewan* ("Divine Progeny") Army faction, representing the old elite of the military establishment. *Wongthewan* is also the faction within which Thailand's current sovereign rose in the Army.

The "Queen's Tiger Guard" is a factional name referring to the 21st Infantry Regiment in the 2nd Division of the First Army Region. This regiment was created in 1950. Queen Sirikit became its honorary commandant eight years later. The "Queen's Guard" has been tasked with personally protecting the queen, who was herself quite close to some of the unit's leading officers (Chambers and Napisa 2016, p. 433). Members of this faction commanded the Army from 2007 until 2016, and they dominated the NCPO junta.

Yet another unit is Royal Guard 904, the Royal Guards Security Command, which is today under the direct control of King Vajiralongkorn.

Royal Guard 904, which comprises six battalions, is specifically charged with coordinating command and control regulatory practices designed for the protection of the king, as well as protecting the royal family. Its members are supposed to be the most elite of soldiers (Wassana 2014).

The advantage of ideology as a uniting factor is that it stresses common purpose at a particular time and can bring soldiers together around a shared course of action—mounting a putsch, for example. However, it is also the weakest bond among soldiers, as ideology—except for the unifying ideology of kingship—is in general only minimally valued in the factional politics of the military establishment. Indeed, ideological factions in Thailand's military have tended to be very fleeting.

Conclusion: Ideological Changes Ahead for the Military?

This study has argued that Thai military ideology has historically tended to rationalize direct intervention in politics and other areas of Thai life to rescue, defend, and develop the nation. At the same time, however, variations in dogma have influenced that mindset. Such dogma is linked to cultural hegemony at different points in Thai history. Prior to 1932, the dogma identified the nation directly with the absolute monarchy. After 1932, military ideology saw the armed forces as the champion of "Thai-ness", understood with reference to constitutionalism, sovereignty and national identity. This changed again in 1944, when the new civilian leadership of the country attempted to instil in the military an ideology of protecting elected civilian control and democracy. But a 1947 coup ended this attempt to ideologically "civilianize" the military. By 1957, the three pre-eminent ideological priorities were anti-communism, developmental militarism, and monarchization. The 1973–76 democratic interlude was too brief to affect military ideology and sense of mission. The 1980 ascension to power of arch-royalist General Prem Tinsulanonda as prime minister permitted the monarchy to become the most powerful institution in national politics, once and for all placing a palace-centred hegemonic bloc at the centre of military ideology and sense of mission. The end of the Cold War in the early 1990s and the "Black May" incident of 1992, the latter of which tarnished the military's image, compelled the armed forces to modify their ideological priorities. As a result, after

1992 the armed forces took an ideational "back seat" to democracy, while also participating in more United Nations peace-keeping missions and regional cooperation. The 2006 and 2014 coups occurred in the context of a heightened sense of monarchization and developmental militarism, which were now the centrepieces of Thai military ideology. The armed forces saw themselves as the protector of monarchy-centric national security, as legitimized through the *lèse-majesté* law. Especially as democracy had since 2001 consistently brought Thaksin Shinawatra or his supporters to power, it seemed to the military and its civilian allies that the only method to keep Thaksin at bay was to prevent democracy. Since the May 2014 putsch, "democracy" has become a term of anathema within Thai military ideology. By 2018, more than perhaps at any time since 1988, Thailand's armed forces were a "monarchised military", acting as a guardian and tool of palace interests. At the same time, the military now sees itself as the nationalistic arbitrator of Thai politics, responsible for ousting or putting in place governments as it deems necessary to protect Thai national security and development—understood with reference to an identity which prioritizes Buddhism, monarchy, and "Thai-ness". Perhaps this second role is most clearly seen in military's counter-insurgency efforts in the Deep South, where it is trying at all costs to keep the region under Thai sovereignty.

At the beginning of this study, four questions were asked. How has Thai military ideology evolved across time, and to what extent has it become more of a force for cohesion? What have been the dimensions of Thai military ideology since 2014? How have ideological legacies informed military officers' understandings of the duties and roles of the military? To what extent will a cohesive military ideology drive the armed forces into the future? In answer to the first question, Thai military ideology has evolved from arch-monarchization under absolute monarchy, to nationalistic developmental militarism (1932–44), to anti-communist, arch-monarchist developmental militarism (1957–73, 1980–92), to a greater emphasis on protecting democracy under monarchy (1992–2006). During this period, military ideology has become more coherent through its adulation of monarchy.

In answer to the second question, since 2014, and actually since the 2006 coup, the most important dimensions of Thai military ideology have been a focus on arch-monarchization and developmental militarism. After the 2014 coup, the NCPO sought to focus more coherently on these two ideological themes in order to win support for itself within the armed forces as well as among the civilian populace. Regarding the third question, military ideology has influenced the behaviour of military officers, producing both unity and disunity. Unity exists in the form of loyalty to the king and a determination to preserve order under his control: the institution of monarchy is more powerful than the military. However, division has been evident in several coups in Thai history which have been at least partly rationalized on ideological grounds. Furthermore, there have been several notable Thai military factions based upon ideology.

To turn to the final question, it can be said that, since King Vajiralongkorn ascended the throne in 2016, Thai military ideology and sense of mission have remained coherent in their emphasis on upholding monarchy and guiding the nation's development. However, one subtle change is that, since the royal succession, the military has appeared to become more visibly subservient to the monarch. For example, following the 2014 coup, the junta seemed to be more proactive in making decisions for the Thai nation, almost appearing to act a step ahead of the palace and the aged Privy Council Chairman Prem. This owed to the worsening health of King Bhumibol.

The new sovereign has, however, demonstrated that he will not be a pliant king, even placing the Royal Guard Command under his direct administrative control in 2017 (Lefevre 2017). Also, beneath the broad ideological unity of kingship, unit ideological differences abound. For example, men like former NCPO junta chief and Prime Minister Prayut, along with leading officers such as Army assistant commander-in-chief General Kukiat Srinaka, continue to be men with roots in the "Queen's Tiger Guard", while the "King's Guard" or *Wongthewan* represents the leading factional competitor to that former group. Yet, under the current royal potentate, the *Wongthewan* faction has seen the number of senior Army positions occupied by its members rise. In October 2018, the leader of *Wongthewan*, General Apirat Kongsompong, was appointed as Army commander-in-chief. Apirat's ascendancy appeared to represent the rise of a new Army faction, one that was perhaps more ultra-monarchist than any previously. In early March 2019, Apirat held an unprecedented oath-swearing ceremony in which he vowed to only back a government sufficiently loyal to royal family (Teeranai 2019).

Meanwhile, differences in political ideology among military officers continue to surface. Indeed, there are ever-present rumours about silent, pro-Thaksin "Watermelons"—soldiers who continue quietly to support Thaksin or democratic change. A number of officers with such views were arrested after the 2014 coup for allegedly plotting to overthrow the junta. Their group was branded the "Khon Kaen Model" (Jitima 2014). In 2019 there continued to be indications that many officers in a new "Young Turks" faction (*Krungthep thurakit* 2014) composed of younger, intermediate-level soldiers were unhappy with the lack of political progress and the regime's tardiness in re-establishing democracy.

Perhaps what is most noteworthy about Thai military ideology and sense of mission today is that they have become thoroughly monarchized—co-opted under the hegemonic control of the monarch and monarchical ideology. No military coup has succeeded without palace endorsement since 1977. In March 2019, a general election finally transformed the regime administering Thailand from a military dictatorship to a pseudo-democracy, one still highly overshadowed by the military. Despite continuing military influence, the military's ideology of subservience to monarchy informed a mindset and sense of mission whereby soldiers must always defer to palace intentions and preferences. Such an ideology created an anomalous form of "monarchical" civilian control, distinguishing Thailand from other countries with powerful militaries—such as Myanmar.

Acknowledgements

An earlier version of this study was presented at the annual meeting of the Council on Thai Studies (COTS), Los Angeles, California, 10–11 November 2017.

NOTES

1. See Chambers and Napisa (2016).
2. In this study "cohesion" refers to the extent to which the military as an institution, an individual unit or a faction can "stick together". Ideology is taken as conducive to this cohesion.
3. Cited in Wright (1991, p. 209).

4. Prem's issuance of Prime Minister's Office Orders 66/2523, 5/2524, and 66/2525 in 1980, 1981, and 1982, respectively, enshrined the change in Thai military doctrine and political thought regarding counter-insurgency; see Surachart (1999, pp. 113–16).
5. See Boonsrang (2002).
6. On 14 July 2006, Prem publicly offered his metaphorical view of Thai civil-military relations. "In horseracing, horse owners hire jockeys to ride the horses. The jockeys do not own the horses. They just ride them. A government is like a jockey. It supervises soldiers but the real owners are the country and the King. The government supervises and employs us in compliance with the policy declared to parliament ... What I mean is that we are the country's soldiers. Governments come and go." (Sutichai 2006).
7. In 2017, the military accused the renowned royalist intellectual Sulak Sivaraksa of *lèse majesté* for publicly doubting the veracity of Naresuan's elephant-back duel with the Burmese prince (Pravit 2017).
8. Wanchana was also allegedly on the verge of portraying in film the late Colonel Romklao Tuwatham, a hero of the Army's leading Queen's Tiger Guard faction who fell during 2010 protests in Bangkok; that faction dominated the NCPO.
9. Section 52 of the 2017 constitution replicates sections of earlier constitutions: Section 77 of the 2007 constitution, Section 72 of the 1997 constitution, Sections 59–60 of the 1991 constitution, and others. See Kingdom of Thailand 1991, Kingdom of Thailand 1997, Kingdom of Thailand 2007, and Kingdom of Thailand 2017.
10. See Chai-anan (1982).

REFERENCES

Battye, Noel. 1974. "The Military, Government and Society in Siam, 1868-1910: Politics and Military Reform during the Reign of King Chulalongkorn". Doctoral dissertation, Cornell University.

Boonsrang Niumpradit. 2002. *410 Days in East Timor: A Peacekeeper's Diary*. Bangkok: Darnsutha Press.

Callahan, Mary P. 1999. "Civil-Military Relations in Indonesia: *Reformasi* and Beyond". Occasional Paper no. 4, Center for Civil-Military Relations, Naval Postgraduate School, Monterey, California, September 1999. http://www.ccmr.org/public/images/download/indonesia.pdf (accessed 2 February 2015).

Chai-anan Samudavanija. 1982. *The Thai Young Turks*. Singapore: Institute of Southeast Asian Studies.

Chambers, Paul. 2013. "A Short History of Military Influence in Thailand". In *Knights of the Realm: Thailand's Military and Police, Then and Now*, edited by Paul Chambers, pp. 109–446. Bangkok: White Lotus Press.

Chambers, Paul, and Napisa Waitoolkiat. 2016. "The Resilience of Monarchised Military in Thailand". *Journal of Contemporary Asia* 46, no. 3: 425–44.

CNS (Council for National Security). 2006. "Thai Coup: First Announcement of Reasons for Coup", 19 September 2006. https://www.youtube.com/watch?v=ZS-4WKiTnx8 (accessed 2 July 2017).

Girling, John L.S. 1981. *Thailand: Society and Politics*. Ithaca, New York: Cornell University Press.

Gramsci, Antonio. 1971. *Selections from The Prison Notebooks of Antonio Gramsci*, edited by Quentin Hoare and Geoffrey Nowell Smith. London: Lawrence and Wishart.

Greene, Stephen Lyon Wakeman. 1999. *Absolute Dreams: Thai Government under Rama VI, 1910-1925*. Bangkok: White Lotus.

Handley, Paul M. 2006. *The King Never Smiles: A Biography of Thailand's Bhumibol Adulyadej*. New Haven: Yale University Press.

Human Rights Watch. 2011. "Descent into Chaos: Thailand's 2010 Red Shirt Protests and the Government Crackdown", 3 May 2011. https://www.hrw.org/report/2011/05/03/descent-chaos/thailands-2010-red-shirt-protests-and-government-crackdown (accessed 22 November 2013).

Jitima Janphrom. 2014. "Khon Kaen Model Suspects Deny All Charges, Including Uprising Plot". *The Nation*, 22 October 2014. http://www.nationmultimedia.com/detail/national/30245999 (accessed 1 September 2015).

Kingdom of Thailand. 1991. "Constitution of the Kingdom of Thailand", 9 December 1991. http://www.thailaws.com/law/t_laws/claw0015.pdf (accessed 14 April 2015).

———. 1997. "Constitution of the Kingdom of Thailand", 11 October 1997. http://www.asianlii.org/th/legis/const/1997/1.html (accessed 2 January 2015).

———. 2007. "Constitution of the Kingdom of Thailand", 24 August 2007. http://www.asianlii.org/th/legis/const/2007/1.html (accessed 5 January 2015).

———. 2017. "Constitution of the Kingdom of Thailand", 6 April 2017. http://www. CONSTITUTION+OF+THE+KINGDOM+OF+THAILAND+(B.E.+2560+(2017))_3 (accessed 1 June 2017).

Kornkritch Somjittranukit. 2017. "What Has Ruling Junta Learnt from 'Wasted' Coup in 2006??" *Prachatai*, 21 September 2017. https://prachatai.com/english/node/7390 (accessed 4 October 2017).

Krungthep thurakit. 2014. "Samoraphum daeng thi aksa pharakit raek 'phukan Daeng'" [Red battlefield at the crossroads: the first mission of Commander "Red" (Apirat Kongsompong)], 5 April 2014. http://www.bangkokbiznews.com/news/detail/573539 (accessed 20 June 2019).

Lefevre, Amy Sawitta. 2017. "Thai Royal Agencies Brought under Control of New King". Reuters, 21 April 2017. https://www.reuters.com/article/us-thailand-king/thai-royal-agencies-brought-under-control-of-new-king-idUSKBN17N0O6 (accessed 5 July 2017).
Ministry of Defense, Thailand. Defense Ministry Administration Act (2008), Article 8, published by Thailand Lawyer Center. http://www.thailandlawyercenter.com/index.php?lay=show&ac=article&Id=538974219&Ntype=19 (accessed 5 May 2010).
———. 2008. *The Defense of Thailand* (White Paper). Bangkok: Ministry of Defense.
———. 2016. Minister of Defense Policy Statement. www.mod.go.th/ (accessed 5 May 2017).
———. 2018. "Immediate Policy of the Minister of Defense for Fiscal Year 2019 (1st October 2018 – 30th September 2019)". https://www.mod.go.th/Policy/Policy/policy-of-mod_58_en.aspx (accessed 10 March 2019).
Ministry of Foreign Affairs, Thailand. 2014. "National Broadcast by Gen. Prayuth Chan-ocha, Head of the National Council for Peace and Order", 6 June 2014. http://www.mfa.go.th/main/en/media-center/3756/46368-Unofficial-translation-National-Broadcast-by-Gener.html (accessed 7 July 2014).
Moore, Jeff M. 2010. "The Thai Way of Counterinsurgency". PhD dissertation, University of Exeter, UK. https://ore.exeter.ac.uk/repository/bitstream/handle/10036/3142/MooreJ%20.pdf?sequence=2.
Murashima Eiji. 1986. *Political Thoughts of the Thai Military in Historical Perspective*. Tokyo: Institute of Developing Economies.
Napisa Waitoolkiat and Paul Chambers. 2013. "Khaki Veto Power: The Organization of Thailand's Armed Forces". In *Knights of the Realm: Thailand's Military and Police, Then and Now*, edited by Paul Chambers, pp. 1–107. Bangkok: White Lotus Press.
Pravit Rojanaphruk. 2017. "112 Case Moves Forward Against Historian for Doubting 16th Century 'Elephant Duel'". *Khao sot*, 6 October 2017. http://www.khaosodenglish.com/news/international/2017/10/06/military-try-historian-doubting-16th-century-elephant-duel/ (accessed 7 October 2017).
Royal Thai Army. N.d. "Information". http://eng.rta.mi.th/information/ (accessed 8 October 2017).
Suchit Boonbongkarn. 1987. *The Military in Thai Politics, 1981-86*. Singapore: Institute of Southeast Asian Studies.
Surachart Bamrungsuk. 1999. "From Dominance to Power-Sharing: The Military and Politics in Thailand". Doctoral dissertation, Columbia University.
Sutichai Yoon. 2006. "Thai Talk: Old Soldiers Never Die, They Raise 'Career' Thoroughbreds". *The Nation*, 20 July 2006. http://www.nationmultimedia.com (accessed 8 November 2010).

Teeranai Charuvastra. 2019. "Army Chief Swears to Back Only Government Loyal to King". *Khao sot*, 7 March 2019. http://www.khaosodenglish.com/politics/2019/03/07/army-chief-swears-to-only-back-govt-loyal-to-king/ (accessed 20 June 2019).

Terra Daily. 2011. "Floods Help Thai Army Clean Up Reputation", 19 November 2011. http://www.terradaily.com/reports/Floods_help_Thai_army_clean_up_reputation_999.html (accessed 2 April 2012).

Thak Chaloemtiarana. 2007 [1979]. *Thailand: The Politics of Despotic Paternalism*. Ithaca, New York: Cornell Southeast Asia Program Publications.

Vella, Walter. 1978. *Chaiyo: King Vajiravudh and the Development of Thai Nationalism*. Honolulu: University of Hawai'i Press.

Wassana Nanuam. 2014. "Elite Royal Guards Go on Defence Ministry Payroll". *Bangkok Post*, 13 February 2014. http://www.bangkokpost.com/print/394760/ (accessed 20 February 2014).

Wright, Joseph J. 1991. *The Balancing Act: A History of Modern Thailand*. Oakland, California: Pacific Rim Press.

4

THE DEFENCE EXPENDITURES AND COMMERCIAL INTERESTS OF THE TATMADAW

Maung Aung Myoe

From a relatively small number of troops at the time of the country's independence in 1948, the Tatmadaw, or Myanmar Armed Forces, has grown into one of Southeast Asia's formidable militaries, even while details on the total number of troops and units are difficult to ascertain. Indeed, they remain a matter of secrecy. Undoubtedly, the Tatmadaw is today far better equipped than it was when it took over the state three decades ago, in September 1988, in the name of the State Law and Order Restoration Council (SLORC)—to become the State Peace and Development Council (SPDC) in 1997. The cash-strapped socialist regime of the Burma Socialist Programme Party (BSPP), which ran the country from 1974 to 1988, had, despite its best effort to look after the military, done little to modernize the Tatmadaw. The latter thus remained a poorly equipped force, relative to its peers in the region. It was essentially a counter-insurgency force with almost no capability to engage in conventional warfare.

Since the early 1990s, the Tatmadaw has pursued a force modernization programme, procured military hardware from various foreign sources, and expanded Myanmar's defence-industrial bases. In the last five years, Commander-in-Chief Senior General Min Aung Hlaing has repeatedly confirmed his commitment to build the Tatmadaw into a "Standard Army", although the concept has never been properly defined. In recent years, the Tatmadaw has received some of the advanced weapon systems, fighter aircraft and warships available on the international arms market. In addition, it has improved troops' combat gear and equipment. All of this has required an injection of large amount of money into defence spending.

Throughout 1990s and 2000s, the Tatmadaw leadership repeatedly reminded its commanders that the force had to be built by four means: administration, training, welfare, and morale. Troops' welfare is thus an essential part of building a "modern, strong and highly capable" Tatmadaw. In his address at the fifty-fourth Armed Forces Day Parade on 27 March 1999, Commander-in-Chief Senior General Than Shwe explained what he meant by building the Tatmadaw by means of welfare.

> Welfare is also an organizational activity. It supplements discipline. It also boosts morale. Therefore, welfare is essential in strengthening the Tatmadaw's capabilities. Welfare must be properly and correctly provided for Tatmadaw personnel who not only have to sacrifice life and limb but also have to live away from their families, going through much hardship, and also for their families in the units. (*Myanma Alin* 1999)

Welfare for troops, however, has not been part of the defence budget as reflected in the official documents. Rather, building the Tatmadaw through welfare has involved measures ranging from forming military-managed or military-backed companies at the ministry level to running small-scale businesses at the level of the individual unit.

In other words, the Tatmadaw relies on two sources of financial support: its budget and its business activities. This study therefore addresses the Tatmadaw's defence expenditure and its commercial interests.

The Defence Budget

To discuss the defence expenditure of any country is a challenge. In the case of Myanmar, especially during the SLORC/SPDC era, this challenge is particularly great. Publicly available figures, released by the Myanmar government, are questionable and largely fail to reflect reality. Moreover, in the period between 2000 and 2010, the Statistical Yearbook published annually by the Central Statistical Organization (CSO) omitted figures on the state's financial situation after 2000. Only in the 2010 edition of the yearbook did the government release figures on the state's finances.

In the first two years immediately after the country's independence in 1948, defence expenditure amounted to 40 per cent of the Union Government Expenditure. This high proportion of total expenditure was due mainly to the outbreak of civil war. Defence expenditure remained relatively high throughout the 1950s—about 32 per cent of the Union Government Expenditure on average—as the Tatmadaw needed to fund purchases of military hardware, the drastic expansion of military units, and military operations.[1] Between 1948 and 1961, the Myanmar government spent 4,067.7 million kyat (in current prices) or 880.0 million kyat (in 1960 constant prices) on defence (Maung Aung Myoe 2009, p. 164). According to the Stockholm International Peace Research Institute (SIPRI), Myanmar's military expenditure in the period between 1962 and 1975 amounted to about 7,055 million kyat (in current prices) or US$1,425.1 million (in 1970 constant prices). Defence expenditure as a percentage of GDP declined from an average of 6.5 per cent in early 1960s to an average of 5.5 per cent in the late 1960s and early 1970s. In the period between 1975 and 1980, while defence expenditure continued to grow in both current and constant price terms, its share of GDP declined and remained at an average of about 4.0 per cent.

Since the 1978–79 fiscal year, Myanmar government statistics have shown two measures of expenditure: Union Government Expenditure and State Administrative Organizations Expenditure. The latter did not cover expenditure on state-owned economic enterprises, such as factories under various ministries. It is therefore much smaller than Union

TABLE 4.1
Myanmar Defence Expenditure, 1962–80

Year	Current Price (Million Kyat)	1970 Constant Price (Million US$)	1980 Constant Price (Million US$)	Percentage of GDP
1962	432.0	89.5		6.3
1963	478.0	90.5		6.4
1964	455.0	97.7		6.5
1965	511.0	107.0		6.6
1966	502.0	105.2		5.7
1967	486.0	101.8		5.7
1968	498.0	104.3		5.3
1969	545.0	114.1		5.4
1970	582.0	121.9		5.7
1971	599.0	125.5		5.7
1972	581.0	121.7		5.3
1973	739.0	117.1		5.9
1974	647.0	128.8		4.3
1975	886.0		162.0	3.9
1976	1,041.0		156.0	3.9
1977	1,197.0		181.0	4.1
1978	1,320.0		213.0	4.2
1979	1,491.0		227.0	4.3
1980	1,622.0		246.0	4.3

Source: SIPRI Yearbook, various years.

Government Expenditure. Depending on the measure of expenditure used, either Union Government Expenditure or State Administrative Organizations Expenditure, the percentage of the budget devoted to defence varies significantly.[2]

TABLE 4.2
Defence Expenditure, in Union Government Expenditure (UGE) and State Administrative Organizations Expenditure (SAOE) and as Percentage of GDP, 1980–88
(Millions of Kyat, in current prices)

Year	UGE	Defence	%	GDP	%	SAOE	Defence	%
1980–81	27,632.6	1,538.1	5.6	38,609	3.98	5,499.0	1,341.2	24.4
1981–82	31,748.9	1,730.8	5.5	42,879	4.04	6,146.4	1,500.1	24.4
1982–83	34,544.6	1,773.2	5.1	46,811	3.79	6,961.0	1,498.7	21.5
1983–84	33,184.9	1,795.7	5.4	49,823	3.60	7,123.1	1,540.1	21.6
1984–85	34,671.5	1,826.3	5.3	53,597	3.41	7,463.8	1,576.0	21.1
1985–86	34,668.6	1,924.9	5.6	55,989	3.44	7,886.5	1,698.0	21.5
1986–87	33,194.3	1,868.2	5.6	59,025	3.17	8,691.7	1,699.8	19.6
1987–88	33,052.0	2,089.6	6.3	68,698	3.04	8,453.8	1,239.9	14.7

Source: Central Statistical Organization, Myanmar.

Until the collapse of the BSPP government, defence spending between 1980 and 1988 was roughly 5.5 per cent of the Union Government Expenditure or 21 per cent of the State Administrative Organizations Expenditure. Its share of the GDP declined steadily from around 4.0 per cent in 1980–81 to around 3.0 per cent in 1987–88.

TABLE 4.3
Defence Expenditure, in Union Government Expenditure (UGE) and State Administrative Organizations Expenditure (SAOE) and as Percentage of GDP, 1988–2011 (Millions of Kyat, in current prices)

Year	UGE	Defence	%	GDP	%	SAOE	Defence	%
1988–89	31,451.6	2,131.4	6.8	76,243	2.80	8,362.6	1,762.9	21.1
1989–90	45,656.1	4,614.8	10.1	124,666	3.70	16,959.5	4,330.8	25.5
1990–91	58,981.1	5,436.2	9.2	151,941	3.58	23,367.5	5,436.2	23.3
1991–92	66,379.2	6,086.2	9.2	186,802	3.26	26,978.0	6,086.2	22.6
1992–93	75,692.8	9,126.7	12.1	249,395	3.66	27,827.4	9,126.7	32.8
1993–94	95,811.2	13,884.1	14.5	360,321	3.85	35,594.6	13,884.1	39.0
1994–95	134,501.4	17,694.1	13.2	472,774	3.74	47,887.8	17,694.1	36.9
1995–96	165,558.1	23,812.8	14.4	604,729	3.94	64,723.9	23,812.8	36.8
1996–97	214,233.6	28,951.5	13.5	791,980	3.66	79,945.5	28,951.5	36.2
1997–98	330,894.3	30,135.0	9.1	1,119,509	2.69	98,232.0	30,135.0	30.7
1998–99	452,161.5	39,626.6	8.8	1,609,776	2.46	123,906.7	39,626.6	32.0
1999–2000	532,147.3	38,037.5	7.1	2,190,320	1.74	145,051.3	38,037.5	26.2
2000–1	632,940.6	63,453.0	10.0	2552732.5	2.49	221,014.8	63,453.0	28.7
2001–2	721,159.7	64,015.1	8.9	3548472.2	1.80	271,142.9	64,015.1	23.6
2002–3	911,835.9	74,426.5	8.2	5625254.7	1.32	353,351.1	76,080.8	21.5
2003–4	1,353,771.3	172,632.9	12.8	7716616.2	2.24	590,480.0	172,632.9	29.2
2004–5	1,692,403.8	173,558.3	10.3	9078928.5	1.91	766,434.2	173,558.3	22.6
2005–6	2,353,407.0	197,792.6	8.4	12286765.4	1.61	1,007,733.7	197,792.6	19.6
2006–7	3,692,854.4	317,844.2	8.6	16852757.8	1.89	1,684,630.3	317,844.2	18.9
2007–8	4,900,862.7	384,138.2	7.8	23336112.7	1.65	2,199,079.8	384,138.2	17.5
2008–9	7,458,811.0	465,147.3	6.2	29233288	1.59	2,326,318.1	465,147.3	20.0
2009–10	6,256,077.5	657,299.2	10.5	33905665.6	1.94	3,178,269.2	657,299.2	20.7
2010–11	7,505,719.6	1,297,050.9	17.3	39776764.9	3.26	7,506,500.7	1,297,050.9	17.3

Source: Central Statistical Organization, Myanmar.

TABLE 4.4
Defence Expenditure in Union Government Expenditure (UGE) and State Administrative Organizations Expenditure (SAOE) and as Percentage of GDP, 2011–18
(Millions of Kyat, in current prices)

Year	UGE	Defence	%	GDP	%	SAOE	Defence	%
2011–12	8,205,280.6	1,269,705.4	15.5	46,307,887.7	2.74	4,526,812.1	1,269,705.4	28.0
2012–13	11,665,668.2	1,887,415.4	16.2	51,259,260.0	3.68	6,927,727.2	1,887,415.4	27.2
2013–14	14,280,208.6	2,222,582.0	15.6	58,011,626.0	3.83	7,629,437.9	2,222,582.0	29.1
2014–15	21,291,551.3	2,471,340.9	11.6	65,261,890.2	3.79	9,702,833.6	2,471,340.9	25.5
2015–16	18,923,646.6	3,141,147.3	16.6	72,714,021.2	4.32	11,539,161.3	3,141,147.3	27.2
2016–17	21,105,589.6	3,000,664.8	14.2	79,720,897.9	3.76		3,000,664.8	
2017–18	20,594,164.8	2,915,427.4	14.1	90,319,432.7	3.23		2,915,427.4	

Source: Central Statistical Organization, Myanmar.

According to available data, defence expenditure in the period between 2000 and 2010 was about 10 per cent of Union Government Expenditure. However, some observers dispute these spending figures. The share of GDP indicated by the data—an average of 3.5 per cent in the early 1990s and 2.0 per cent in the late 1990s and the 2000s—was far below what some observers believe.

While current expenditure is generally slightly higher than capital expenditure, in some years the difference is huge. In the 2003–4 and 2010–11 fiscal years, capital expenditure was double current expenditure. In the 2010–11 fiscal year, defence spending accounted for 17.26 per cent of the Union Government Expenditure. The total amount was almost double the figure for the preceding fiscal year. One of the reasons for this sudden jump in spending was the new military pay scale introduced in April 2010. The introduction of this scale also triggered higher inflation for goods and services. The same was true for the 2006–7 fiscal year, as a new pay scale was also introduced in April 2006. Defence expenditure since the 2011–12 fiscal year has been around 15 per cent of the Union Government Expenditure. The Union Solidarity and Development Party (USDP) government, in office from April 2011 to March 2016, tried to be more transparent in budgetary matters. Its budgets were subject to approval by the Hluttaw, or parliament. The latter requested that ministers or deputy ministers from various ministries and committees, including the Ministry of Defence, explain planned spending.

In the budget bill submitted to the parliament in January 2017, the Tatmadaw requested a total of 2,905.195 billion kyat for fiscal year 2017–18. Deputy Defence Minister Rear Admiral Myint Nwe explained that current expenditure would be 1,654.33 billion kyat and capital expenditure would be 1,250.865 billion kyat. He further explained that the estimated capital expenditure for 2017–18 would be 86.533 billion kyat less than the previous year (*Kyemon* 2017a, p. 5). In fact, he proudly claimed that the proposed defence budget for the year was less than those for the two previous fiscal years (Min Min 2017).[3] In his presentation, Myint Nwe reported that the current account spending was for salaries and allowances, military equipment, logistics, engineering work, factories and workshops, and military operations. A figure of 4.203 billion kyat was earmarked for military operations in the proposed budget. The capital expenditure was, the deputy minister explained, for construction work and military hardware.

TABLE 4.5
Current and Capital Expenditure in Defence Spending, 2000–18
(Billions of Kyat)

Year	Current Expenditure	Capital Expenditure	Total Expenditure
2000–1	35	28	63
2001–2	38	26	64
2002–3	43	33	76
2003–4	58	115	173
2004–5	87	86	173
2005–6	93	105	198
2006–7	291	99	390
2007–8	249	135	384
2008–9	249	216	465
2009–10	300	357	657
2010–11	401	896	1,297
2011–12	413	856	1,269
2012–13	861	1,026	1,887
2013–14	993	1,229	2,222
2014–15	1,158	1,313	2,471
2015–16	1,552	1,590	3,141
2016–17*	1,664	1,337	3,001
2017–18*	1,664	1,251	2,915

Note: Asterisks indicate years for which figures show provisional data.
Source: Central Statistical Organization, Myanmar.

In order to justify the proposed budget, Myint Nwe told the Hluttaw that, in the process of building a "Standard Army, Navy and Air Force", the Tatmadaw needed to be strong, capable and modern armed forces, in order to be able to safeguard "our three main national causes" of non-disintegration of the Union, non-disintegration of national solidarity, and the perpetuation of sovereignty. It also needed to be able to perform nation-building and national defence based on the people's war strategy that rested on the participation of the entire people and centred on the Tatmadaw (*Kyemon* 2017a). Despite cuts of more than 300 billion kyat in the overall state budget, from 20,896 billion to 20,594 billion kyat, defence expenditure was to remain intact (Nyein Nyein 2017; Min Min 2017).

On 16 January 2018, when the government's decision to change the Myanmar fiscal year from April–March to October–September required submission of a six-month interim budget bill, Rear Admiral Myint Nwe again explained proposed defence expenditure. The proposed expenditure for the six-month period was 1,334.194 billion kyat: 723.107 billion for current expenditure and 611.087 billion for capital expenditure. The proposed current expenditure included 2.107 billion kyat for military operations (*Kyemon* 2018, p. 7).

TABLE 4.6
Proposed Military Expenditure, April–September 2018
(Millions of Kyat)

No.	Item	Current Expenditure	Capital Expenditure	Total Expenditure
1	Salaries and Allowances	372,238.593		
2	Equipment	171,173.819		
3	Transportation/Logistics	10,065.827		
4	Engineering work	28,034.990		
5	General	73,591.500		
6	Military Operations	2,106.786		
7	Industry/Workshops	63,083.929		
8	Interest on Loans	2,811.328		
9	Construction Work		105,538.566	
10	Military Hardware		505,148.800	
11	Others		400.000	
	TOTAL	723,106.772	611,087.366	13,314,194.138

Source: Myanmar Ministry of Defence data.

An interesting point in the data presented in Table 4.6 concerns the capital expenditure on military hardware. A total of 505,148 million kyat was at the current exchange rate around US$370 million. Since no details are available, one could wonder what this spending was for.

In a discussion of defence spending, several factors need to be considered. First, figures could be under-stated, especially those for the SLORC/SPDC period. Second, dubious foreign exchange rates could be applied. For instance, in the market the exchange rate for one US dollar was about 1,200 kyat in that same period. However, available data may reflect calculations at the rate of six kyat to the dollar, 200 times lower than the market rate. Third, defence spending could come under different ministries. Fourth, there could be off-budget measures, possibly financed through military-owned and military-backed companies. Fifth, it is also possible that some spending could be covered by crony business firms in exchange for business opportunities, such as land development, monopolies in the import and export of certain products, and so on.

Considering the spending spree on military hardware and other facilities since the early 1990s, one could find it rather difficult to believe that the official figures reflect the reality. Within the last ten years, for instance, the Tatmadaw has procured considerable military hardware. In 2009 and 2010, the Myanmar Air Force (MAF) bought 50 K-8 trainer aircraft from China to be assembled in Myanmar, possibly to replace its ageing PT-6 planes. At about the same time, the MAF also signed a contract to acquire 20 MiG-29 multirole fighters with a total price tag of US$570 million (*The Irrawaddy* 2010). The year 2015 was a watershed year for the MAF as it decided to make major purchases of aircraft. In June 2015, the MAF reportedly bought 12 Yakovlev Yak-130 combat training aircraft from Russia, with a price tag of US$15 million per unit, to be delivered within the next three years (Russian Aviation 2016, 2017a, 2017b).[4] At about the same time, the Tatmadaw also signed a contract to buy 16 JF-17 fighter aircraft from Pakistan with a price tag of US$16 million each (*Mizzima* 2017).[5] In the same year, it was reported that German aircraft manufacturer GROB had delivered half of the 20 new G120TP turboprop trainers ordered by the Myanmar Air Force (*Flight Global* 2015). It appeared that all 20 of these aircraft had already been commissioned. Moreover, in the same year the MAF also bought 10 MiL Mi-24P/35P planes from Russia (Fuller 2017; Grevatt 2017). In January 2018, during the visit of its defence minister to Myanmar, Russia agreed to supply six Su-30 fighter jets in a deal worth at least US$204 million (about 274.7 trillion kyat) (*Frontier Myanmar* 2018). In addition, the list of aircraft commissioned in this decade includes four ATR42/72 transport aircraft, six Y-8/12 transport aircraft, seven Beech 1900D light transport aircraft, three Bell-206 helicopters, two Fokker transport aircraft, and eight EUROCOPTER helicopters.

In the wake of Cyclone Nargis and a close encounter with Bangladeshi warships in the disputed Special Economic Zone in 2008, the Myanmar Navy also pursued an aggressive naval expansion programme. Within the last ten years, it has commissioned five frigates; one corvette, MNS *Tabinshwehti* – 773; one offshore patrol vessel, MNS *Innlay* – 54; ten 47m-missile and one 49m-missile fast attack craft; four landing craft tanks (56m); 16 landing craft mechanized (29m); and one torpedo boat (T201), among other vessels. Except for two frigates—the Jianghu-II class F-21 and F-23 from China—all of these vessels were locally built. The Myanmar Navy also ordered six Super Dvora Mk-III patrol boats from Israel in 2015 (*WeapoNews* 2017). Two were commissioned on 24 December 2016. The navy also procured a floating dry dock—FD-01 *Saya Shan*—for ship-building from China.

While most of the Myanmar Army's small arms and mortars are locally produced, it has imported air defence missile systems, heavy artillery, tanks, and armoured personnel carriers from China, Russia, South Korea, Brazil, and South Africa. While details on the quantity of this hardware remains unknown, one can generally estimate the number of pieces required to arm ten artillery divisions, ten armoured divisions, and six air defence divisions. Force modernization in recent years, under the banner of "Building a Standard Army", has thus led some observers to wonder whether the official defence budget is really big enough to cover the buying spree for military hardware.

The Tatmadaw's Commercial Activities

The origins of the Tatmadaw's commercial activities lie in both ideological conviction and practical purpose. Ideologically, these activities reflect its dual function—to play a role not only in defence against internal enemies but also in internal security and nation-building. As the Tatmadaw was an army fighting against a communist campaign of armed struggle, it was thought necessary for it to engage in development activities, nation-building, and state-building. In this sense, its participation in the national economy was in its view natural and legitimate. In practical terms, the financial incentive to transcend its budgetary constraints, to enhance the welfare and well-being of service personnel and their families, and to strengthen the corporate interests of the military as a viable and credible national institution were the primary rationales for undertaking commercial activity.

In the early 1950s, the Tatmadaw established the Defence Services Institute (DSI) to provide inexpensive consumer goods to the members of the armed forces. This line of business soon expanded to incorporate a wider range of economic activities. By the late 1950s, the DSI had probably become the largest commercial enterprise in Myanmar. Many military businesses were rather successful in those days, partly because of the DSI's status under the Special Company Act of 1950. The DSI ran banking, shipping, trading, manufacturing, publishing, and retail businesses, among others.[6] It used income generated from these commercial enterprises for the welfare and well-being of its service personnel and their families. Some of the businesses did not have purely commercial purposes. For instance, the DSI-owned Myawaddy Press published two monthly magazines, *Myawaddy* and *Ngwetaryi*. *Myawaddy* magazine in particular was an instrument of psychological warfare, used to voice the interests of the military. The Tatmadaw also published the *Guardian Newspaper* and *Guardian Magazine*, each of which reflected a pro-military view and enjoyed a substantial circulation, on a commercial basis.

In the early 1960s, while a few enterprises remained under the DSI, many were placed under the Tatmadaw's newly established Burma Economic Development Corporation (BEDC). The BEDC's operations were far more extensive than those of the DSI; it even maintained overseas branches. However, after the Tatmadaw staged a military *coup d'état* on 2 March 1962, in the name of the Revolutionary Council, and eventually introduced a state-owned socialist economic system under the Burmese Way to Socialism, these military enterprises were among the first to fall under the state's nationalization programme. After the nationalization of private and foreign banks and schools in early 1963, the Revolutionary Council decided to nationalize the businesses of the Tatmadaw. On 20 October 1963, the Revolutionary Council government nationalized all assets and firms owned by the DSI and the BEDC, forty-seven in total.

At the time of nationalization, there were five firms under the DSI: the Defence Services Institute Head Office, DSI No. 1 and General Provision Store and Canteen, Beatrice Food (Burma) Limited, Burma Orchids Limited, and Burma International Inspection Company Limited. Beatrice Food (Burma) Limited was known for its dairy products. Table 4.7 lists the forty-two firms under the BEDC that the Revolutionary Council nationalized.

TABLE 4.7
BEDC Firms Nationalized by the Revolutionary Council, 1963

BEDC Head Office	Burma Beverage Co.
Mandalay Brewery and Distillery	Burma Chemical Industries Ltd.
Burma Paints Ltd.	Burma Pharmaceutical Industries
Centrade Polyproducts Ltd.	Burma Canning Factory
Burma Shoes Ltd.	Garment Factory Ltd.
Lodge Plug (Burma) Ltd.	Mechanical and Electrical Ltd.
Multitex Co. Ltd.	Burma Farms Ltd.
Burma Fisheries Ltd.	Burma National Housing and Construction Co. Ltd.
Ava House (Bookstore)	Myawaddy Press
Burma Five Star Line Ltd.	Rangoon Agencies Ltd.
Diesel and General Services Ltd.	Burma Hotels Ltd.
Hotel International Ltd.	Tourist (Burma) Ltd.
Strand Hotel Ltd.	Ava Insurance Ltd.
People's Loan Co. Ltd.	Rangoon Drug House
Rowe & Company Ltd.	Burma Asiatic Co. Ltd.
Burma Teak and Plywood Trading Co. Ltd.	Continental Trading House
Burma Trading House Ltd.	Dalhousie Stores Ltd.
General Trading House Co. Ltd.	International Trading House Co. Ltd.
Motor House Co. Ltd.	S. Openheimer & Co. Ltd.
United Coal and Coke Suppliers and General Trading Co. Ltd.	BEDC Branch Office (Tokyo, Japan)
Economic Development Fisheries Ltd.	Burma Trade (London)

Source: San Nyein and Mya Han (1993), pp. 283–86.

The Tatmadaw-owned Ava Bank had been nationalized at an earlier date, and both the *Guardian Newspaper* and *Guardian Magazine* experienced the same fate in 1964. Following the loss of all these sources of off-budget financial support, the Tatmadaw's expenditure and welfare services were covered by the government; there is no evidence to suggest that it maintained independent sources of financial support. Moreover, the Tatmadaw also ended the policy of "Saving for the General Providence Fund", for the post-retirement financial support of its personnel.

During the period of Revolutionary Council rule (1962–74), General Ne Win and the rest of the Tatmadaw's leadership transformed it into the "Pyithu Tatmadaw", or People's Army. They made it a key institution in Myanmar's march toward the goal of socialism. When the Burmese Way to Socialism was officially announced on 30 April 1962, it was as a result of the endorsement of the annual Commanding Officer Conference. Again, when the BSPP was founded as an elite cadre (embryo) party in July 1962, all of its leading members were senior military officials. In fact, the BSPP was founded by the Tatmadaw. Through the BSPP's Tatmadaw Organizing Committee, the party recruited military officers into its ranks.

When the BSPP was transformed from an elite cadre party into a mass party in the early 1970s, it set up a Tatmadaw Party Committee to control the military, reflecting a pattern of civil-military relations in which the party governed the army. The general secretary of the BSPP was the chairman of the Tatmadaw Party Committee, and the joint general secretary of the BSPP and a member of the Central Executive Committee (CEC) of the BSPP were members; the chief-of-staff of the Defence Services was the secretary. Therefore, between 1974 and 1981, the BSPP's General Secretary U San Yu was the chairman of the Tatmadaw Party Committee, Joint General Secretary U Thaung Kyi and CEC member U Kyaw Soe were members, and Chief-of-Staff General Thura Tin Oo and then General Thura Kyaw Htin served as its secretary. Below this Tatmadaw Party Committee was the Tatmadaw Organizing Committee, chaired by the chief-of-staff and with the deputy chiefs-of-staff representing the three services as members and the military secretary as its secretary. Operating under this Tatmadaw Organizing Committee, party organizing committees were formed at various levels down to the battalion level and even in smaller units commanded by officers entrusted with command authorities. Unlike the situation in some communist countries, instead of party cadres serving as political commissars in military units, in socialist Burma unit commanders were concurrently made chairmen of the units' organizing committees (BSPP 1971).

Throughout the socialist era (1962–88), the Tatmadaw was required to refrain from engaging in substantial commercial activities; it had no commercial enterprises. Yet the Tatmadaw was involved in the production of basic commodities, mostly for the welfare of its members and their families, and essentially on an individual-unit basis, on a much smaller scale. Military units, such as battalions, for example, would grow rice and vegetables and raise poultry and fish and operate canteens, liquor houses, video houses, and cottage industries such as candle factories or cheroot factories, all funded by the Regimental Fund.

As the backbone of the BSPP, the vanguard of the socialist revolution in Myanmar, and the institution for building and protecting the socialist economic system, the Pyithu Tatmadaw needed to participate in socialist economic production. It was not to own any major means of production. Rather, its economic contribution was mainly in the form of the production of agricultural produce and livestock. For mostly symbolic reasons, in the 1980s the Tatmadaw was mobilized to participate in seasonal paddy production: *Mya Sein Yaung* operations at the start of growing season and *Shwe War Myay* operations at the start of the harvest.

The Tatmadaw's economic activities during the socialist era were confined to cottage industry and self-sufficiency in the context of the state ownership of the means of production. Only after the Tatmadaw's takeover of the state in September 1988 were the military's commercial interests revived on a large scale.

Since the 1990s, working primarily through two business entities, the Tatmadaw has penetrated deeply into the Myanmar economy and practically monopolized several lines of profitable business. These entities are the Union of Myanmar Economic Holdings Ltd. (UMEHL) and the Myanmar Economic Corporation (MEC). In some business areas, these two firms hold a near-monopoly. For instance, UMEHL's fully-owned Mandalay Brewery and joint venture Myanmar Brewery, which markets the famous MYANMAR BEER and other brands including the Japanese KIRIN beer, and MEC's Dagon Brewery together hold a total monopoly over local beer production. Likewise, UMEHL and MEC are engaged in the profitable insurance business. UMEHL's Aung Thit Sar Oo Insurance and MEC's Aung Myint Mo Min Insurance have enjoyed considerable earnings. As a recent article in the *International New York Times* commented,

> Two secretive conglomerates, the Union of Myanmar Economic Holdings Limited and Myanmar Economic Corporation, operate subsidiaries in jade mining, gem production, wood industries, energy and banking. Military personnel can invest in the two companies, giving them a stake in the success of Tatmadaw business operations. (Paddock 2018)

Union of Myanmar Economic Holdings Ltd. was the first business venture established by the Tatmadaw after its takeover of the state in 1988. Formed in 1990, under the 1950 Special Company Act, UMEHL is a military-managed business. As a special company, UMEHL until recently enjoyed the privilege of tax exemption for its fully owned firms and subsidiaries, though not for affiliated firms. One of its main objectives is to support regimental welfare organizations, in-service and retired military personnel, and veterans' organizations. The UMEHL's shares are non-redeemable, but they may be transferred to family members. To date, UMEHL has provided a 30 per cent dividend; the investment in shares is thus recouped within four years. When UMEHL was established, the Tatmadaw's leadership was taking serious interest in reinstating the policy of Saving for the General Providence Fund in the aftermath of the collapse of the socialist regime; thus welfare is the first priority. Besides, the stated objectives of UMEHL also include "to support the welfare of general public and to support national economic development" (UMEHL 2002, p. 1).

Between 1990 and 2007, UMEHL formed a total of 77 firms. These may be classified as fully owned firms, subsidiary firms, and affiliated firms. By 2007, the group only had a total of 51 firms: 35 fully owned enterprises, nine subsidiary firms, and seven affiliated firms. It had liquidated 26 firms. In 2017, according to some observers, UMEHL appeared to operate 38 fully owned firms, 10 subsidiary firms, and nine affiliated firms.

TABLE 4.8
Number of Firms under UMEHL, 1999–2017

Sr.	Type of Firm	1999–2000	2006–7	2016–17
1	Fully-Owned	15	35	38
2	Partnership (Subsidiary)	18	9	10
3	Partnership (Affiliation)	7	7	9
	TOTAL	40	51	57

Source: UMEHL General Annual Reports, various years.

Under the management of the Office of the Adjutant General, UMEHL is engaged in small and medium-sized commercial enterprises and industries.[7] Its commercial interests include gem production and marketing, garment factories, wood and wood-based industries, food and beverage and other trading, and supermarkets, banking, hotels and tourism, transportation and shipping, construction, real estate, the steel industry, cement production, automobiles, and so on.[8] Myawaddy Trading and Myawaddy Bank are perhaps its best known firms. Its Gandamar Wholesale centres in Yangon and Mandalay are popular among shoppers for their low prices. UMEHL also runs a dozen rice mills and engages in trading agricultural produce. Knowledgeable observers believe that UMEHL's two most profitable businesses are Myanmar Beer and Red Ruby and Premium Gold cigarettes.

At the same time, some of UMEHL's business activities—for instance, its copper mining projects at Letpadaung, Kyesindaung, and Sabaedaung—are controversial. Criticisms focus on the lack of environmental, social, and health impact assessments and, more importantly, on the inadequate compensation of local people for these impacts. Some observers believe that the Tatmadaw simply grabbed land in the project areas and entered into joint ventures with Chinese firms. It was reported that the Tatmadaw claimed about 6,000 acres of land in Kyesindaung-Sabaedaung and entered into a joint venture with Yang Tse Mining Ltd., a subsidiary of China's NORINCO, and that the proceeds of this production-sharing contract go only to the Tatmadaw and the Chinese firm, not to the Myanmar government (*Democratic Voice* of Burma 2015; Han Zar Myay Mon 2016). Likewise, in the case of the controversial Letpadaung copper mine project, it is alleged that the Tatmadaw seized 7,868 acres for the project, including 5,057 acres of cultivated land, with just token compensation, and that it did business with Wanbao Mining Ltd., another subsidiary of NORINCO (Ei Ei Toe Lwin 2013). After a 2013 investigation, an additional 3,166.154 million kyat in additional compensation was paid to 1,163 farmers for the area of 3,065.15 acres taken from them (*Kyemon* 2013a, p. 7).

As a special company formed under the 1950 Special Company Act, UMEHL enjoyed tax exemption for its fully owned and subsidiary firms until March 2016, when it was transformed into a public company. While its stated objective is to support regimental welfare organizations, in-service and retired military personnel, and veterans' organizations, UMEHL also serves as an instrument of political patronage. It enjoyed monopolies in a number of business sectors, such as the importation of cooking oil and of vehicles from overseas. In 2007, it had an allotted capital of 39 billion kyat. Ten years later, that figure had risen fourfold.

The Myanmar Economic Corporation is a second major military-managed economic organization. It engages in large-scale industries and projects. It enjoys the privilege of doing business in areas exclusively reserved for state enterprises. In March 1989, the SLORC government enacted SLORC Law No. 9/89, the State-Owned Economic Enterprise Law, which stated that the government had the sole right to carry out economic activities in twelve broad sectors through state-owned enterprises, and that it could form joint ventures with any other person or any other economic organization. This law was superseded on 4 March 1997 by SLORC Law No. 6/97, with a new clause stating the following:

> In order to contribute towards the development of the State economy, to mitigate the expenditure from State finances and in the interests of the welfare of State employees, the Government may, by notification, constitute any organization to enable economic enterprises to be carried out without subscribing from State finances but by causing investment [to] be made from the funds owned by the relevant employees' organization.

Several days later, the government issued SLORC Notification No. 4/97, forming the Myanmar Economic Corporation (MEC) under the Ministry of Defence, with the following stated purpose.

In order to contribute towards the development of the State economy, to decrease defence expenditure by fulfilling the needs of the Tatmadaw, to carry out the welfare of Tatmadaw service personnel and to implement other necessary matters for the Tatmadaw.

The "vision" of the MEC, operating under the management of the Office of the Quartermaster General, is "to support the economic development of the Nation, to promote the living standard of the people and to eradicate poverty".[9] The government authorized the MEC to undertake a wide range of economic activities. It had initial investment capital of 10 billion kyat, since significantly increased, as its business activities have expanded in recent years. Most of the MEC's business activities are in the manufacturing sector and in heavy industry. It now operates steel plants, cement factories, marble slab factories, and sugar factories, along with other businesses. While mostly kept secret until quite recently, the MEC's activities are now openly advertised. In 2017, twenty years after its establishment, publicly available information indicated that it ran forty-three businesses, as shown in Table 4.9.

While the MEC established many new businesses in the most recent decade, it also closed a number of firms. The Maw Taung Coal Production plant, which exported coal to Thailand, was closed down, as the operation was no longer economical. Likewise, Innwa Trading, which used to export beans and pulses, was also closed. The Myanmar International Insurance Service Corporation, a subsidiary of the MEC, was transferred to the Ministry of Finance and Revenue in the early 2000s. In its stead, the MEC now operates Aung Myint Mo Min Insurance Co. Ltd.

Among the MEC's business activities, banking, telecommunications, insurance, and beer production are well known. As mentioned earlier, its Dagon Brewery has a sizable market share. The MEC's steel plants produce steel frames for bridge construction. While its declared business activities are in the areas of heavy industry and capital intensive undertakings, the MEC also engages in the production of consumer goods, such as instant coffee, soft drinks, tea bags, condensed milk, and so on. It even moved into the entertainment sector by opening an indoor skydiving facility in Yangon in October 2017. And it recently opened the DENTOMEC Toothbrush and Toothpaste Factory and the Royal Sportainment Complex for ice skating, both in Yangon—on 3 January and 1 May 2019, respectively.

TABLE 4.9
Businesses under the Myanmar Economic Corporation, 2017

Factory/Plant/Firm	Location	Products/Remarks
No. 1 Steel Plant	Kyauk Swe Kyo	iron nails/wire coils
No. 2 Steel Plant	Myaung Dagar	bridge frames
No. 3 Steel Plant	Insein (Ywama)	iron nails, square-matches, bulb wire
Ship Scrapping Plant	Thilawa	raw iron for No. 1 Steel Plant
No. 1 Cement Plant	Myaing Gale	cement (900 ton capacity)
No. 2 Cement Plant	Kyaukse	cement (4000 ton capacity)
Roofing Sheet Factory	Than Hlyin	corrugated zinc/galvanized iron sheet
SIGMA Wire Factory	Hlaing Tharyar	wire cable
Gawdan Mine (1)	Thibaw	gypsum
Gawdan Mine (2)	Hlain Bwe	gypsum
Marble Slab Factory	Mandalay	marble slabs
Granite Slab Factory	Loikaw	granite slabs
Oxygen Factory	Yangon-Mindama	oxygen gas
Refractory Plant	Aung Lan	fire bricks
Disposable Syringe Factory	Hmawbi	syringes
Gas Plant (1)	Yangon	gas for hospital and industrial use
Gas Plant (2)	Mandalay	oxygen and acetylene
Tri Star Tyre Factory	Ywama	car tyres (rubber plantation)
No. 1 Sugar Mill	Kant Balu	sugar
No. 2 Sugar Mill	Kan Hla	sugar
No. 3 Sugar Mill	Dayin Gabo	sugar
Ethanol Plant	Taung Zin Aye	ethanol
Glass Factory	Than Hlyin	
Dagon Brewery	Shwe Pyithar	beer, soda, and soft drinks

TABLE 4.9 (*continued*)

Factory/Plant/Firm	Location	Products/Remarks
Innwa Bank	Yangon	banking services
Aung Myint Mo Min Insurance	Yangon	insurance services
MECTel	Yangon	telecommunication services
Myanmar Mobile Money Service	Yangon	financial services
No.1 International Port Terminal	Yangon-Ahlone	port services
Freight Handing Service	Yangon-Ywama	container service
Okkalar Golf Resort	Yangon	golf course and resort
Tyre Retreading Plant	Yangon-Ywama	recycled tyres
Rice Mill and Rice Storage	Yangon-Htee Dan Port	rice
Dagon/Army Rum Factory	Yangon-Shwe Pyi Thar	rum
Drinking Water Plant	Naypyitaw	bottled drinking water
Tea Powder and Tea Mix Factory	Pyinmapin	Swen Phi Oo Tea-Mix (tea plantation)
Dagon Dairy Plant	Pyinmapin	condensed milk and milk powder
Nan Myaing Coffee	Pyin Oo Lwin	coffee beans and powder (coffee plantation)
MyTel	Yangon	joint venture with Viettel (Vietnam)
Star High Company Ltd.	Yangon	financer of MyTel
Vertical Wind Tunnel	Yangon	sports and entertainment
Kantharyar Hospital	Yangon	medical and health care services
Cotton Ginning Plant	Myitthar	cotton wool

Source: Author's compilation.

Telecommunications and healthcare services are the latest major lines of business for the MEC. On 12 January 2017, the Myanmar government awarded a telecoms licence to Myanmar National Tele & Communications Co. Ltd., now renamed Telecom International Myanmar Co. Ltd. or MyTel. The firm is a joint venture of Vietnam's military-run Viettel Global, the MEC's subsidiary Star High Public Company, and Myanmar National Telecom Holding Public Co. Ltd (MNTH)—a consortium of eleven local companies. MyTel thus became the fourth telecoms operator in Myanmar. Viettel has a 49 per cent stake in this US$1.5 billion investment, while MNTH and Star High were to have stakes of 23 and 28 per cent, respectively (*Straits Times* 2017). Star High Public Company reportedly offers access to 1,000 existing towers and more than 13,000 kilometres of fibre optic cables (Hammond and Trautwein 2016). Along with MECTel, MyTel, chaired by U Khin Maung Soe, is the MEC's second telecoms service provider.[10]

When the USDP government introduced economic reforms, the Tatmadaw complied with these measures. During his meetings in early 2015 with Emeritus Senior Minister Goh Chok Tong of Singapore, Senior General Min Aung Hlaing told his guest that "military businesses, which are being operated for the welfare of personnel, retirees and their families and for the economic development of the country, will be transformed into public companies at an opportune time" (*Global New Light of Myanmar* 2015a). The senior general also explained to Mr Wang Yingfan, a special envoy from the Chinese Ministry of Foreign Affairs, that "military-related businesses are conducted in line with the law" (*Global New Light of Myanmar* 2015b).

Accordingly, the Tatmadaw decided to transform UMEHL from a special company into a publicly listed company. It was announced on 11 February 2019 that the UMEHL had been renamed the Myanma Economic Holdings Public Company Limited. It started to pay taxes to the government. In the past, UMEHL enjoyed many monopolies, especially in import and export, thanks to the control of Trade Council, effectively chaired by Vice Senior General Maung Aye. Its most well-known imports were edible oils, fuel, and automobiles; exports included cigarettes, beans and pulses, gems, and marine products. The near monopoly of the import and local distribution of edible palm oil, imported from Malaysia, was a major business with a large patronage network for UMEHL. Likewise, before the liberalization of car imports in 2012, UMEHL was one of the very few enterprises that imported cars from overseas, generating a huge income. However, since 2011, UMEHL has lost its monopolies in these sectors. The import and distribution of edible oils, fuel and automobiles are, for example, no longer major businesses lines for UMEHL. In 2013, it started paying commercial tax and income tax on its business activities. It declared that it was among the business entities in Myanmar paying the highest taxes. And, in fact, Myawaddy Trading and Myawaddy Bank were top commercial tax and income tax payers in the 2013–14 and 2014–15 fiscal years.

The Tatmadaw has business undertakings besides UMEHL and the MEC. The collapse of the centrally-planned state-owned socialist economic system in 1988 essentially drove Myanmar toward a state-managed, market-based, capitalist economy. The combination of the legacy of patronage under the socialist political and socio-economic system and the economic sanctions imposed by the West during the SLORC/SPDC era give birth to a new class of cronies and to crony capitalism, firmly grounded in rent-seeking in association with military leaders. Many of these cronies were allowed to engage in extractive businesses, such as timber production or mineral exploration. In exchange for favours in such business deals, the military could ask these cronies to provide financial support for its off-budget spending.

In recent years, some cronies have been involved in land development in connection with the Tatmadaw. One prominent case was the Dagon City 1 development project, with its price tag of US$300 million. It is one of five projects planned on 71 acres of land owned the Tatmadaw near the renowned Shwe Dagon Pagoda. Because of protests on the part of civil society groups and monks, the project was finally cancelled (Ko Ko Aung 2015). Likewise, a US$200 million project on a six acres of land near the famous Inya Lake on Yangon's Pyay Road, the former site of the Sinphyushin quarters for officers, has been jointly developed by Korea's POSCO, Daewoo, Lotte Hotels and Resorts and by Myanmar's IGE Group of Companies, another crony business firm, as service apartments and an office tower (*Frontier Myanmar* 2017b; *Kyemon* 2013b, p. 9). Yet another project is the "redevelopment of the Defence Services Museum site in Yangon". When the museum was moved to Naypyitaw, the Tatmadaw decided to develop a commercial centre on this 16,000-square-metre site. This US$320 million project will be carried out jointly by several Japanese companies working with the Ayeyar Hinthar Group, a known crony firm reportedly close to the Tatmadaw (Japan Overseas Infrastructure Investment Corporation for Transport and Urban Development 2017).[11]

A further issue closely related to the Tatmadaw's business activities is land grabbing by military units for business purposes or to support troops' welfare. The local self-sufficiency policy practised until 2010 tasked each military unit with generating income for monthly financial support for troops and with the free distribution of rice for their family members. During the SLORC/SPDC period, and mainly because of the considerable expansion of military units, the Tatmadaw claimed millions of acres of land for military use. In addition, many local units grabbed lands for the purpose of providing for regimental welfare. According to information from the Ministry of Defence, 461,323.75 acres of land were grabbed by local military units beyond their parameters. In other words, the units used this land not for military purposes but rather for other activities, such as income generation.

The practice of local fund-raising and income-generation created opportunities for corruption, the abuse of power, and so on. Some officers used these opportunities to enrich themselves. The most notorious cases were the business activities conducted by officers in the military intelligence service prior to their dismissal in 2004. But local income generation also led to renting out regimental electricity facilities or storage places or even military trucks for commercial purposes; running small-scale factories to produce goods such as candles, cheroots, ice, bricks, or charcoal; and providing road transportation and producing vegetables and raising cows, pigs, and chickens. In some cases, local military units confiscated farm land for inclusion in their cantonments, so that they could rent that land—whether back to the original owners or to new tenants—for income. These confiscations added to the many cases of land disputes across Myanmar.

In his explanation at the Union Parliament on 16 July 2013, Defence Minister Lt. Gen. Wai Lwin explained that there had been 488 cases of complaints against the Tatmadaw for land grabbing, and that in a first round of investigations 382 cases had already been looked into. After investigation, 7,664.49 acres were to be returned. In addition, another 10,700 acres, which were not involved in the 382 cases investigated, were also to be returned. The minister added that the ministry had recently received an additional 167 complaints, taking the total number of complaints to 655 (*Myanma Alin* 2013).

On 13 September 2013, the Hluttaw Land Commission submitted 745 cases to the government for investigation, so that the land could be returned to its original owners if it had been inappropriately or unnecessarily confiscated. In the process, it was found that 46 of these cases overlapped; the total number of cases for actual investigation was 699, covering 473,979.739 acres. After investigation was completed, the government decided to return a total of 72,686.201 acres in 171 cases.

TABLE 4.10
Findings of the Report on Land Confiscation in Myanmar, 2014

	Category	Number of Cases	Number of Acres
1	Land retained, as it is necessary	386	351,733.738
2	Land returned, as reclaim were excessive.	62	43,717.740
3	Land returned, as it was not used,	109	28,968.461
4	Private and civil code settlement.	142	4,924.720
	TOTAL	699	473,979.739

Source: Kyemon (2014a).

Out of 699 cases, 565 cases, involving a total area of 321,435.280 acres, were related to the Tatmadaw (*Kyemon* 2014a, p. 1; 2014b). They accounted for 80.83 per cent of the cases and 67.82 per cent of the land area.

When the Tatmadaw returned land to its original owners after the first round of investigations in November 2013, out of the total of 54,255 acres, only 24,855 acres were related to the cases under investigation; the remaining 29,400 acres were voluntarily returned. The second round of returns was in February 2014, and the total area of land returned was 154,892 acres (*Kyemon* 2014a, p .4). By

15 December 2017, the Tatmadaw announced that it had returned a total of 258,013.559 acres to its owners (*Myanma Alin* 2017). Many more complaints were subsequently filed, and the investigation is an ongoing process. The Tatmadaw will still need to return more land to its previous owners or to the state.

While most of the land confiscated for new military units was virgin or state-owned land, it also included a significant amount of farm land. Further, not all land confiscations were undertaken for the benefit of the Tatmadaw. Many cases involved land for government projects and regional development. Since they occurred under a military regime, and since regional commanders were the chairmen of regional SLORC/SPDC bodies, the common view was that confiscations were undertaken by the Tatmadaw. Of course, there were abuses of power by local authorities at all levels, most likely military officers, involving grants of land to colleagues and cronies. In an interview conducted on 30 May 2015 by a scholar working on land issues in Myanmar, one interviewee complained,

> land is hard to access because everywhere you go, someone owns the land, like a general or general's son or daughter. It is all under individual names and they all take it. ... In the Ministry of Agriculture, there was map of land holdings along Yangon-Mandalay expressway, according to seniority, the highest general up to 500 acres, colonel 100 acres, and lower is 20 acres. It is getting worse now, their greed level is worse than before. (Mark 2017, p, 147)[12]

The parliamentary question and answer session at the twelfth regular session of the first Pyidaungsu Hluttaw or Union Parliament on 12 June 2015 illustrated the extent of the problem of land grabbing on the part of Tatmadaw units. According to questions from four members of the parliament, in 2009 the newly established No. 24 Defence Industry seized about 4,000 acres, including 3,400 acres of farm land, in Pauk Township. No. 438 Light Infantry Battalion seized 617 acres, including 37 acres of farm land, in 1996. No. 503 Light Infantry Battalion seized 963 acres, including 40 acres of farm land, in 1995. Finally, No. 51 Infantry Battalion took about 20 acres of farm land, to be rented out to eight farmers, and 130 palm trees on the land, in Myan Aung in 1992. The deputy minister of defence came to answer the questions of members of parliament concerning the return of land, and, with the exception of the Tatmadaw's agreeing to return about 15 acres with 89 palm trees in Myan Aung, his replies were negative. The ministry would neither offer additional compensation nor return the land.

From the details that emerged in this session of parliament, one can generally conclude that a military unit of battalion size could use some 800 acres of land for facilities and other purposes.[13] Factories belonging to defence industries, military hospitals, artillery battalions, air defence battalions, air bases and regional naval commands need larger plots of land. For instance, six new air bases have been established since the 1990s, making a total of ten across Myanmar. Likewise, the Myanmar Navy created two new regional commands and four fleets.

In other words, land grabbing, which is closely related to income generation by local military units, is widespread. These activities tarnish the image of the Tatmadaw. Therefore, the Tatmadaw leadership started to restrict them in 2005. After the purge of intelligence establishment in that year, the Tatmadaw leadership introduced measures to curtail the business activities of local units. All income generated from these was to go directly to the Office of the Quartermaster General, rather than remaining in regimental funds for expenditure at that level. By 2010, before the general elections and political transition, all business activities on the part of local military units were banned, and income from cantonment development offices was to be transferred directly to the same office.

About the same time, and in order to ease the financial burden on local military units, they were encouraged to buy shares in UMEHL. According to some observers, each military battalion was asked to buy up to 50 million kyat in shares from the Regimental Fund. In some cases, regional command headquarters needed to help to fulfill this quota. The annual payouts on these shares became income for each battalion, to be used for welfare purposes and other subsidies for troops. The 30 per cent dividend rate meant that each battalion would receive some 15 million kyat a year to use for the welfare of troops and their families.

Conclusion

Cutting official defence spending would at present not be easy, since the Tatmadaw leadership is firmly committed to making Myanmar's military a "Standard Army"—even though the term is never clearly defined. At present, the share of defence expenditure in the Union Government Expenditure is around 14 per cent, and it appears that the amount spent has not changed significantly since 2011. Nevertheless, critics point out that the percentage of defence spending in Union Government Expenditure is slightly larger than the combined spending on health and education. The percentage is likely to decline if and when the government expands revenue collection because the Tatmadaw does not in fact insist on receiving a fixed percentage of government spending.

It is not currently feasible to put the Tatmadaw solely and fully on the government budget. At the same time, the revival of the Tatmadaw's commercial interests is closely related to its unstated policy of self-sufficiency in almost all aspects. In the area of human resources, it has for instance established medical and engineering academies. Similarly, in the area of financial resources, the Tatmadaw seeks to maintain and retain self-sufficiency. While the income of UMEHL is mostly for the welfare of the troops, military units, and veterans, little is known about the use to which the revenues of the MEC are put.

There is a debate about the forceful termination of the Tatmadaw's commercial activities. The termination of such military businesses could trigger illegal activities on the part of service personnel. Myanmar's internal security situation and the weak rule of law in the country mean that many soldiers could end up involved in criminal activities because of the need to cope with rising living costs.

The Tatmadaw's commercial enterprises and interests obviously require good public relations if they want to be meaningful and socially acceptable. It is particularly true in the case of UMEHL, which has been a target of criticism. It needs a face-lift and a major reorganization so that it can claim that, in the absence of a "General Providence Fund", it is a pension fund for the benefit and welfare of soldiers and their families while ensuring that proceeds from its activities are not used as off-budget support for the military. There is as of now no information on whether the Tatmadaw uses money generated by UMEHL and the MEC for off-budget military spending. Both public relations and managerial efficiency argue for the transformation of both UMEHL and the MEC into portfolio investors in certain profitable sectors. Today, not all the commercial enterprises under these entities in fact make profits. Yet they provide employment opportunities, and could serve as vehicles for the demobilization of soldiers.

In his keynote speech delivered to the Union of Myanmar Federation of Chambers of Commerce and Industry on 9 December 2017, the renowned economist U Myint highlighted the important role of the Tatmadaw in Myanmar's economic development strategy, "Myanmar Eco Vision" or MEV. The critical role of the Tatmadaw in the achievement of peace and stability was a national imperative, and he considered the Tatmadaw a key stakeholder. "To ensure a successful outcome for MEV", U Myint stated, the "Tatmadaw has a critical role to play. Its cooperation and support are essential to achieve goals set in MEV. It is further envisaged in the Vision that the Tatmadaw will be transformed into professional, well equipped and modern armed forces."[14] Yet U Myint did not explicitly mention whether the Tatmadaw should play a role beyond the maintenance of peace and stability. His recommendation to "transform" the Tatmadaw into a "professional" military could mean, in the Western sense of professionalism, that the Tatmadaw should not be a business entity.

Meanwhile, for as long as the national government has limited resources to finance a modern armed force and the military's entrenched business interests are deep and wide, whether for troops' welfare or for off-budget spending, it is difficult to foresee that the Tatmadaw would go out of business and subsist on the budget alone.

NOTES

1. In 1948, the Tatmadaw had 15 infantry battalions. During the civil war that followed, three Karen battalions were abolished. Therefore, from about 12 battalions in 1949, the Tatmadaw grew into a total of 57 battalions by 1958. In the 1950s, the Tatmadaw waged not only counter-insurgency warfare against various rebels but also combat against external aggression on the part of Kuomintang troops.
2. In some cases, particularly in the early 1980s, reported absolute expenditure on defence also varies between the Union Government Expenditure and the State Administrative Organizations Expenditure, with the former slightly larger than the latter. This suggests that some defence spending was undertaken by the state, not by the Ministry of Defence. However, this difference disappeared in later years.
3. The figures shown in the deputy minister's PowerPoint presentation were slightly lower than the latest revised budget. For instance, the defence budget for 2015–16 was reported as 3040.08 billion and that for 2016–17 as

2990.57 billion. However, the revised version released in early 2018 showed that those budgets were 3141.15 billion and 3000.66 billion, respectively.
4. Six of these planes were commissioned in December 2017.
5. As of the end of 2017, none of these aircraft had been commissioned.
6. For instance, the DSI established the Burma Five Star Line Co. Ltd. on 5 February 1959 with paid-up capital of 1.2 million kyat. Along with the Five Star Line, on 26 November 1959, the DSI formed both the Rangoon Agency Ltd. as a shipping agency, and the Burma Trading House.
7. At present, UMEHL is under the Office of the Adjutant General. In the early days of its existence, it was chaired by generals from various offices. However, the managing director was and still is the director of procurement. The first chairman was Lieutenant General Myo Nyunt, commander of the Yangon Command, and the first managing director was Brigadier General David Abel. They were succeeded by Major General Than Oo, the judge advocate general, and Brigadier General Win Hlaing, the director of procurement, in 1996. Major General Than Oo was succeeded by Lieutenant General Win Myint, of the Office of the Adjutant General, in 1998; Lieutenant General Tin Aye, chief of the Office of Defence Industries, in 2002; Lieutenant General Khin Zaw Oo, of the Office of the Adjutant General, in 2011; and Lieutenant General San Oo of that same office in 2014. Successive directors of procurement held the post of managing director.
8. For example, UMEHL took over the state-owned Myanma Five Star Line from the Ministry of Transport in 2010, just before the political transition, and transformed it into a limited company. Along with the shipping line, UMEHL operates a container yard and a jetty. Some of the ships owned by Myanma Five Star Line are very old and have been suspended from operation. In recent years, at least two ships, the *ThanLwin* and the *ChinDwin* were transferred to Myanmar Navy to be refurbished and commissioned as coastal hospital ships.
9. Author's confidential sources.
10. When Senior General Min Aung Hlaing visited Vietnam in March 2017, he took with him on the trip the chairman of Myanmar National Tele & Communications Co. Ltd. The men visited Viettel Group's research and development department (*Myawaddy* 2017a). When General Secretary of the Central Committee of the Communist Party of Viet Nam Mr Nguyễn Phú Trọng visited Myanmar, together with Vice President U Myint Swe he opened the MyTel Head Office in Yangon on 26 August 2017 (*Kyemon* 2017b). Senior General Min Aung Hlaing visited the office soon thereafter (*Myawaddy* 2017b). U Khin Maung Soe was reported to be the chairman of the MNTC during the Senior General's visit to Vietnam and to be the chairman of MyTel when the Vietnamese General Secretary opened the head office in Yangon.

11. See also Yee Ywal Myint (2017).
12. Following Karl Marx's theory of history centred on the ownership of means of production—the primitive age, the age of slave ownership, the feudal age, the capitalist age and the socialist age—some people even privately joke that Myanmar has entered into the sixth historical age: the age of military officers' land-ownership (*sit-thu-gyi-mye-paing-shin-khit*).
13. For detail, please see Pyithu Hluttaw (n.d.).
14. Statement in author's possession.

REFERENCES

Burma Socialist Programme Party (BSPP). 1971. *Tatmadaw atwinshi pati aphwe-asi-myar-ei phwae-si-pon hnit loke-ngan tarwunmyar* [The structure and tasks of party organizations within the Tatmadaw]. Yangon: Burma Socialist Programme Party.

Democratic Voice of Burma. 2015. "Request to Support Those Who Lost Land in the Kyesindaung Project", 18 November 2015.

Ei Ei Toe Lwin. 2013. "Letpadaung Community Bands Together". *Myanmar Times*, 27 May 2013. https://www.mmtimes.com/national-news/6868-letpadaung-mine-communities-form-compensation-body.html (accessed 30 January 2018).

Flight Global. 2015. "Grob Aircraft Begins G120TP Deliveries to Myanmar", 14 July 2015. https://www.flightglobal.com/news/articles/grob-aircraft-begins-g120tp-deliveries-to-myanmar-414605/ (accessed 11 June 2019).

Frontier Myanmar. 2017a. "Myanma lay-tat atwek wal-yuhtar thi JF-17 taike-lay-yin ko san-that pyan-than nay" [Test flight of JF-17 for Myanmar Air Force], 15 June 2017a. https://frontiermyanmar.net/mm/news/5064 (accessed 11 June 2019).

———. 2017b. "Lotte Yangon Hotel Opens at Site Overlooking Inya Lake", 1 September 2017b. https://frontiermyanmar.net/en/lotte-yangon-hotel-opens-at-site-overlooking-inya-lake (accessed 28 January 2018).

———. 2018. "Myanmar to Buy Russian Fighter Jets in Deal Worth More Than $200m", 23 January 2018. https://frontiermyanmar.net/en/myanmar-to-buy-russian-fighter-jets-in-deal-worth-more-than-200m (accessed 11 June 2019).

Fuller, S.L. 2017. "Russian Helicopters Repairs First Batch of Mi-24Ps for Myanmar". *Rotor and Wing International*, 13 October 2017. http://www.rotorandwing.com/2017/10/13/russian-helicopters-repairs-first-batch-mi-24ps-myanmar/#.WmgCXKiWa70 (accessed 11 June 2019).

Global New Light of Myanmar. 2015a. "Senior General Min Aung Hlaing Receives Emeritus Senior Minister of Singapore", 4 February 2015a. http://globalnewlightofmyanmar.com/senior-general-min-aung-hlaing-receives-emeritus-senior-minister-of-singapore/ (accessed 11 June 2019).

———. 2015b. "Senior General Stresses Reciprocal Relationship Between Politics and Economy", 5 February 2015b. http://globalnewlightofmyanmar.com/senior-general-stresses-reciprocal-relationship-between-politics-and-economy/ (accessed 11 January 2019).

Grevatt, Jon. 2017. "Russia Expands Myanmar Mi-24P Repair Programme". *Jane's Defence Weekly*, 17 October 2017. http://www.janes.com/article/74947/russia-expands-myanmar-mi-24p-repair-programme (accessed 30 January 2018).

Hammond, Clare, and Catherine Trautwein. 2016. "Viettel Picked for Fourth Telecoms Tie-up with Military Partner". *The Myanmar Times*, 25 March 2016. https://www.mmtimes.com/business/technology/19662-viettel-nears-contract-for-fourth-telecoms-operator.html (accessed 30 January 2018).

Han Zar Myay Mon. 2016. "Request to Support Those Who Lost Land in the Kyesindaung Project". *Mizzima*, 6 October 2016. http://www.mizzimaburmese.com/article/18813 (accessed 30 January 2018).

The Irrawaddy. 2010. "Burma Buys 50 Fighter Jets From China", 15 June 2010. http://www2.irrawaddy.com/article.php?art_id=18726 (accessed 11 June 2019).

Japan Overseas Infrastructure Investment Corporation for Transport and Urban Development. 2017. Statement issued 28 July 2017. http://www.join-future.co.jp/english/news/pdf/ 20170728_01_01.pdf (accessed 30 January 2018).

Ko Ko Aung. 2015. "Government Scuttles $300m Dagon City Project". *Frontier Myanmar*, 23 July 2015. https://frontiermyanmar.net/en/government-scuttles-300m-dagon-city-project (accessed 11 June 2019).

Kyemon. 2013a. "Letpadaungtaung kyaeni simankein hnit pat-thet thi sone-sansitsae yay asiyinkhansar apawakaungahtaephaw saung-ywet myi kawmati nhyinai asiaway kyinpa" [Coordinating meeting for implementation of investigation report on Letpadaung copper mine project held], 14 September 2013a.

———. 2013b. "Karkweyay wungyi-htarna hnit sipwa-yay konepanimyar B.O.T sanit phyint myay-yar sarchoke letmetyayhtoe pwe kyinpa" [Signing ceremony for land rent agreement based on B.O.T system between Ministry of Defence and business companies held], 14 September 2013b.

———. 2014a. "Tatmadaw ka thein-yu-htar-thaw myay-yar ar dutiya akyein sesit-sun-hlut-pay hlet-shi" [Tatmadaw returns confiscated land for second time], 6 February 2014a.

———. 2014b. "Thihnan hnit thit-taw yaw-hnaw sikekhinmyar toechae sik pyochin phyit dae-thakhanmyar win-ngway toe lar myi" [Local people will generate more income by extending mixed planting of crops and forests], 3 July 2014b.

———. 2017a. "Dutiya akyein pyidaungsu hluttaw sa-toke-hta ponhman-asi-away dutiya nae set-let kyinpa" [Second day of the fourth regular session of the second Union Parliament held], 1 February 2017a.

———. 2017b. "Naing-ngan atwin myan-hnone-myint telephone set-thweyay sanit saung-ywet-myi MyTel konpani yone-choke yangon myoe hnike phwintlit" [Headquarters of MyTel Company that will carry out high-speed telephone communication system within the country opens in Yangon], 27 August 2017b.

———. 2018. "2018 khu-hnit pyidaungsu ei-ban-dar-ngway aya-thone saing-yar upadaygyan par yathone-ngway-myar hnit sat-hlyin-ywe hluttaw tho shinlin tinpya" [Income and expenditure in the 2018 Union budget bill explained], 17 January 2018.

Mark, SiuSue. 2017. "Land Tenure Reform in Myanmar's Regime Transition: Political Legitimacy verses Capital Accumulation". Doctoral dissertation, Erasmus University Rotterdam.

Maung Aung Myoe. 2009. *Building the Tatmadaw: Myanmar Armed Forces Since 1948*. Singapore: Institute of Southeast Asian Studies.

Min Min. 2017. "Lower Defence Budget Estimated in Coming Fiscal Year". *Mizzima*, 1 February 2017. http://www.mizzima.com/news-domestic/lower-defence-budget-estimated-coming-fiscal-year (accessed 11 June 2019).

Mizzima. 2017. "Myanmar Air Force to Induct JF-17 Fighters by End-2017", 31 October 2017. http://www.mizzima.com/news-domestic/myanmar-air-force-induct-jf-17-fighters-end-2017 (accessed 11 June 2019).

Myanma Alin. 1999. "Nga-saet-lay hnit-myauk tatmadaw nae (taw-hlan-yay nae) sityaypya akhananar hnike tatmadaw karkweyay oo-si-choke bogyoke-hmu-gyi Than Shwe myot-kyar thi meinkhun" [Address of the Commander-in-Chief of Defence Services Senior General Than Shwe on 54th Anniversary of Armed Forces Day (Resistance Day)], 28 March 1999.

———. 2013. "Myay-thein saung-ywet yartwin loke-htone-loke-nimyar hnit anyi sanit-takya sisit saung-ywet khe" [Land confiscation was systematically carried out in accordance with rules and regulations], 17 July 2013.

———. 2017. "Karkweyay wungyi-htarna hma pyan-lae-sunt-hlut myay-myar naing-ngan daw-tho at-hnan pyi-si-hmu thadin-htokepyan-chat" [Press release on the return of land to the state by the Ministry of Defence], 17 December 2017.

Myawaddy. 2017a. "Tatmadaw karkweyay oo-si-choke bogyoke-hmu-gyi Min Aung Hlaing Viettel Group ei loke-ngan saung-ywet-hmu-myar ar thwar-yauk lae-lar" [Commander-in-Chief of Defence Services Senior General Min Aung Hlaing studies activities of Viettel Group], 8 March 2017a.

———. 2017b. "Tatmadaw karkweyay oo-si-choke bogyoke-hmu-gyi Min Aung Hlaing Telecom International Myanmar Co. Ltd. (MyTel) yone-choke tho thwar-yauk lae-lar" [Commander-in-Chief of Defence Services Senior General Min Aung Hlaing visits headquarters of Telecom International Myanmar Co. Ltd. (MyTel)], 12 October 2017b.

Nyein Nyein. 2017. "Parliament Approves Reduced Budget for 2017-2018". *The Irrawaddy Online*, 17 March 2017. https://www.irrawaddy.com/news/burma/parliament-approves-reduced-budget-for-2017-2018.html (accessed 11 June 2019).

Paddock, Richard C. 2018. "An Army in Myanmar at War with Its People". *International New York Times*, 23 January 2018.

Pyithu Hluttaw. N.d. Website of the Myanmar Parliament. https://www.pyithuhluttaw.gov.mm (accessed 11 June 2019).

Russian Aviation. 2016. "Irkut Reportedly Received an Order from Myanmar for Yak-130 Combat Trainer Aircraft", 18 January 2016. https://www.ruaviation.com/news/2016/1/18/4672/ (accessed 11 June 2019).

———. 2017a. "The First Pictures of Two Myanmar Air Force Yak-130 Trainer Jets", 17 November 2017a. https://www.ruaviation.com/news/2017/11/17/10185/ (accessed 11 June 2019).

———. 2017b. "Myanmar Army Commissions 10 New Military Planes into Service Including Six Russian Yak-130 Fighter", 18 December 2017b. https://www.ruaviation.com/news/2017/12/18/10404/ (accessed 11 June 2019).

San Nyein and Mya Han. 1993. *Myanma naingnganyay sanit pyaung karla (1962-1974)* [Myanmar's politics in the period of systemic change]. Volume Two. Yangon: Universities' Historical Research Center.

Stockholm International Peace Research Institute (SIPRI). Various years. *SIPRI Yearbook: Armaments, Disarmament and International Security*. Stockholm: SIPRI.

Straits Times. 2017. "Myanmar Awards Fourth Telecoms Licence as Mobile Market Heats Up", 13 January 2017. http://www.straitstimes.com/asia/se-asia/myanmar-awards-fourth-telecoms-licence-as-mobile-market-heats-up (accessed 30 January 2018).

Union of Myanmar Economic Holdings Ltd. (UMEHL). Various years. *Ayetyet saing yar hnit pat lae asiyinkhansar* [General Annual Report]. Yangon: UMEHL.

WeapoNews. 2017. "Myanmar Navy Received Two Israeli Gunboat", 5 May 2017. http://weaponews.com/news/6635-myanmar-navy-received-two-israeli-gunboat.html (accessed 11 June 2019).

Yee Ywal Myint. 2017. "Legislator Questions Hotel Project at Defence Museum". *Myanmar Times*, 4 October 2017. https://www.mmtimes.com/news/legislator-questions-hotel-project-defence-museum.html (accessed 11 June 2019).

5

THE ECONOMIC ROLE OF THE THAI MILITARY: A COMMERCIAL LOGIC TO COUPS?

Kanda Naknoi

Since the replacement of Thailand's absolute monarchy with a constitutional regime in 1932, the country's armed forces have attempted *coups d'état* at the rate of one every four years. Two thirds of these attempts have been successful. The resultant military juntas have typically promulgated new regulations, laws and constitutions before holding elections or themselves falling victim to coups. These new rules and the changes that they have introduced suggest the role of the Thai military as a significant economic-policy maker. At the same time, the military is also a consumer and a producer of goods and services. In fact, the Thai military produces both services related to security and services with no relation to security.

The goal of this chapter is to document the role of the Thai military as producer of the latter, services with no relation to security. The chapter draws on publicly available information from the Bank of Thailand, the Department of Business Development of the Ministry of

Commerce, the Royal Gazette (*Ratchakitchanubeksa*), the Stock Exchange of Thailand, and the country's Securities and Exchange Commission (*Khanakammakan kamkap laksap lae talat laksap*).

The chapter makes three arguments. First, the Thai military has produced a wide range of services unrelated to security for six decades. It directly provides services through, or holds shares in, companies in banking and asset management, facilities for banquets and recreation, real estate and hotels, and radio and television broadcasting. Second, banking, radio broadcasting and television broadcasting have been regulated by laws enacted during military regimes to maintain strict barriers to entry. The roles of the Thai military as both producer of services and policymaker are in this sense complementary. Finally, besides the military budget, the factors of production crucial to the military's involvement in services unrelated to security include bank deposits; capital raised on the Stock Exchange of Thailand, including that from foreign sources; substantial land holdings; and conscripts. The military has thus benefitted not only from financial globalization but also from access to effectively subsidized low-wage labour.

The chapter sheds light both on the production activities of the Thai military in service sectors unrelated to security and on its success in shaping regulations to favour its own businesses. The role of the Thai military as producer has received little scholarly attention, unlike its role as consumer and policymaker.[1] But these production activities may well suggest economic motives for Thailand's frequent military coups, and for the armed forces' engagement in the political and policy spheres more generally.

Thai Military Involvement in the Provision of Services Unrelated to Security

The Thai military entered the commercial banking and television broadcasting sectors in 1957. Although it had also established radio stations a decade earlier, its radio broadcasting was initially for national security, especially as part of anti-communist campaigns. The commercialization of military radio broadcasting took place after 1957, as was the case with services of the Thai military unrelated to security more broadly. For this reason, the story of such services really begins with the military's involvement in banking and asset management.

Banking and Asset Management

The military established its own commercial bank just months after Field Marshal Sarit Thanarat's successful coup of September 1957. The bank was explicitly named the *Thanakhan thahan thai* or Thai Military Bank; it had registered capital of 10 million baht. Its major shareholders were military institutions, whose holdings accounted for 57.68 per cent of shares. Of this total, 53.68 per cent of the new bank's shares belonged to the Army Welfare Department, 2.0 per cent to the Air Force Welfare Department, and 2.0 per cent to the War Veterans Organization of the Ministry of Defense. The remaining shares were held by individual shareholders—officers in all three branches of the military, including the Navy; civilian employees of the Ministry of Defense; and retired military officers. It is noteworthy that the junta leader Sarit himself was the largest non-institutional shareholder in the bank, with a holding of 10 per cent of shares. The total number of shareholders, including institutional shareholders, in the year of the bank's founding was 6,559 (Department of Business Development n.d. a).

The inaugural board of directors of the Thai Military Bank comprised fourteen high-level officers from all three branches of the military, and included Sarit as its first chairman (Department of Business Development n.d. a). However, the bank's first "manager" (*phuchatkan*)—effectively, its managing director—was a civilian, Jote Gunakasem. In 1958, Jote would leave the bank to become the governor of the Bank of Thailand, the country's central bank, and he would briefly hold both that post and that of the military regime's finance minister (Noranit n.d.).

In the following four decades, the bank increased its capital many times, but the military remained the top shareholder. Over time, a select few civilians joined the Thai Military Bank's board of directors. From 1982 to 1994, two or three out of its fifteen directors were civilians at any given time (Department of Business Development n.d. a). Having been listed on the Stock Exchange of Thailand since 1983 (Stock Exchange of Thailand n.d.), the bank became a public limited company (*borisat mahachon chamkat*) eleven years later (Department of Business Development n.d. c). Increases in capital and the surge in foreign capital inflows into the Thai economy via the Bangkok International Banking Facility fuelled the expansion of the Thai Military Bank in this period. Prior to the Asian Financial Crisis of the late 1990s, the bank had become the sixth largest in Thailand by deposits. However, rapid growth combined with poor oversight eventually led to a serious non-performing loan problem.

Following the financial crisis, the Thai government bailed the Thai Military Bank out, and the Ministry of Finance replaced the military as its top shareholder. In 2004, DBS Bank of Singapore became a major shareholder in the bank as a result of a recapitalization (Thai Military Bank 2004). The next year, it was renamed TMB Bank as part of a re-branding strategy in anticipation of further recapitalization (TMB Bank 2005). That recapitalization saw the Netherlands' ING Bank N.V. became another major shareholder in 2007 (TMB Bank 2007). The direct consequence of these recapitalizations was a decline in the Thai military's stake in the bank.

As of 2018, the top two shareholders in TMB Bank were the Ministry of Finance with a 25.92 per cent holding, and ING Bank with a 25.02 per cent direct holding (TMB Bank 2018).[2] The military is the sixth-largest shareholder with a mere 1.25 per cent share in the bank. However, as Thailand was under military rule from 2014, and as the military thus controlled the Ministry of Finance, it was effectively the top shareholder by voting shares.

The composition of the bank's board of directors has reflected changes in its ownership structure. Under terms set in 2007, ING Bank has the right to nominate at least one board member, and so does the Ministry of Finance (TMB Bank 2007). As the military's shareholding in the bank declined, the number of military officers on its board also declined. In mid-2019, the deputy commander-in-chief of the Royal Thai Army was the only military officer on its board of directors (TMB Bank n.d. c).

In its early years of operation, the Thai Military Bank limited its commercial banking services to the military and its personnel, including former officers. The bank began to open branches to provide commercial banking services to the general public from 1973 (TMB Bank n.d. a). Today, TMB Bank has more than 400 branches throughout Thailand and foreign branches in the Cayman Islands and Laos. It holds as much as 4.62 per cent of total deposits in the Thai commercial banking system.[3]

The bank aspires to become a universal bank providing a full range of financial services. In pursuit of that end, it has taken substantial ownership stakes in three additional companies in the financial services sector. First, until Designee for ETA Contract Company was wound up in June 2018, TMB Bank owned 99.5 per cent of the shares in this business support company, established in 1989 (TMB Bank n.d. b; Department of Business Development Data Warehouse n.d.).[4] Second, it owns 87.5 per cent of the mutual fund company TMB Asset Management, established in 1996 (Department of Business Development n.d. g). Finally, it owns 100 per cent of the shares in Phayathai Asset Management, established in 2000 (Department of Business Development n.d. h). Overall, the TMB Bank is ranked the seventh-largest Thai commercial bank by assets.[5]

However, such rankings are not necessarily useful indicators of the bank's competitive position. The reason is that new entries into commercial banking in Thailand were strongly discouraged under the Commercial Banking Act of 1962, enacted by Field Marshal Sarit's military regime a mere five years after the establishment of the Thai Military Bank. The act has been amended a number of times, but the strict barriers to entry into the sector remain. The Commercial Banking Act allowed the finance minister to authorize, or not, new banking licences (Royal Gazette 1962). The number of Thai commercial banks has never exceeded twenty. The financial liberalization undertaken in 1993, which established the Bangkok International Banking Facility, permitted foreign banks only to enter the interbank market.

Foreign banks were later permitted to enter the retail banking sector, as an inevitable part of the process of restructuring and recapitalizing troubled banks after the Asian Financial Crisis. Very soon after the military regime that seized power in the coup of September 2006 gave way to an elected government, February 2008 saw enactment of the Financial Institutions Business Act (Royal Gazette 2008)—doubtless months or years in preparation. This act replaced the 1962 Commercial Banking Act as the legal framework for regulating banking, including investment banking. Up to that time the Act on the Undertaking of Finance, Securities, and Credit Foncier Business, enacted in 1979 and amended a number of times, had regulated the latter sector (Royal Gazette 1979).

In practice, the new Financial Institutions Business Act unified the legal framework for bank regulation and strengthened the role of the Bank of Thailand in supervision and enforcement. It gave the central bank the power to relax the limits on foreign ownership applicable to local banks, from 25 per cent to 49 per cent, on a case-by-case basis. Furthermore, the 2008 act also allowed the finance minister to authorize foreign ownership of more than 49 per cent, if recommended by the central bank. The TMB Bank subsequently received permission for foreign ownership exceeding 25 per cent. Currently, the foreign ownership share in the bank is 33.81 per cent (Stock Exchange of Thailand 2019).

Radio Broadcasting

Before the establishment of the National Broadcasting and Telecommunications Commission (*Khanakammakan kitchankan krachai siang kitchakan thorathat lae kitchakan thorakhamanakhom haeng chat*, NBTC) in 2010, the National Committee on Radio and Television Activities (*Khanakammakan kitchakan withhayu krachai siang lae witthayu thorathat haeng chat*), a division within the government's powerful and influential Public Relations Department (*Krom prachasamphan*), regulated broadcasting in Thailand.[6] Nevertheless, the Thai military—primarily the Army, but also the Air Force and Navy—has long owned a much larger number of radio frequencies than any other government agency, including the Public Relations Department (National Broadcasting and Telecommunications Commission n.d.; National Committee on Radio and Television Activities n.d., p. 142; Kunlawadi 2002, p. 3). Until the end of the Cold War, military radio channels were primarily used for purposes relating to national security. More recently, however, some of them have been used for commercial purposes, through concessions to the private sector and especially to firms that use these channels to operate stations that play music. As the process of allocating concessions and setting their terms is not public information, the financial dimensions of military radio broadcasting remain unclear, though doubtless significant.

Television Broadcasting

The Royal Thai Army Television Station (*Sathani witthayu thorathat kongthap bok*, RTATS) was established in 1957, the same year in which the Thai Military Bank was founded. The Army has owned the station ever since, without the involvement of the Air Force or the Navy. In other words, the station was set up as a unit within the Army, and it began its free television broadcasting via one channel. In 1967, RTATS gave a long-term concession for a new channel to Bangkok Broadcasting and Television Company (*Borisat krungthep thorathat lae witthayu*), in which the wife of then Army commander-in-chief Field Marshal Praphat Charusathian and members of her family had a substantial stake (Department of Business Development n.d. b; Dueanphen 1996).

RTATS originally broadcast as Channel 7, but it became Channel 5 in 1974. Since then, Channel 7 has been solely operated by Bangkok Broadcasting and Television Company, while the Army continued to let the two stations broadcast a wide range of programmes: news, dramas, concerts, talk shows and more.

Subsequent decades saw these two Army television channels face competition from two additional channels: one owned by the Public Relations Department and another by a state enterprise, the Mass Communications Organization of Thailand (*Ongkan sue muanchon haeng prathet thai*). Nevertheless, the small total number of channels meant that, as in the commercial banking sector, competition in the television sector was limited.

In 1997, the Army created a holding company called Tho Tho Bo 5 (Department of Business Development n.d. d). The new firm's registered capital was 10 million baht, with a 40 per cent share owned by the Army and the remaining 60 per cent share by six generals. Its board of directors consisted of four generals and three civilians, of whom one was also a member of the board of the Thai Military Bank. Its memorandum of association (*nangsue borikhonsonthi*) listed satellite-related businesses including sales, purchases and leasing; broadcasting; publishing; and mass media among its business purposes. The memorandum thus implied that the company could receive a concession from the Royal Thai Army Television Station. The Tho Tho Bo 5 holding company held shares in at least two other companies, which it absorbed in 2003: RTATS Channel 5 Publishing Company and RTATS Channel 5 Publication Company. These companies were established in 1997 and 1999, respectively (Department of Business Development n.d. e and n.d. f). The chapter returns to them below.

Over time, RTATS Channel 5 continued to upgrade its equipment in order to expand its broadcasting network. A major turning point came in 1998, when the channel began broadcasting digital television via a satellite network called Thai TV Global Network or TGN. Today, TGN broadcasts its programmes to more than 170 countries around the world.

The expansion of broadcasting led the Tho Tho Bo 5 holding company to embark on an ambitious path. In 2003, it became a public company called RTA Entertainment. The directors of this new company included ten generals, one colonel and four civilians (Department of Business Development n.d. i). Shortly before the conversion of the extant holding company to RTA Entertainment, the managing director of the company gave a rare interview touching on its operations and finances. He indicated that the company had received a concession for satellite television from RTATS Channel 5. Expected revenues and profits for 2003 alone were 570 million baht and 120 million baht, respectively. Furthermore, the company was in the process of a capital increase, from 250 million to 440 million baht, and it was anticipated that its future listing on the Stock Exchange of Thailand would raise its capital to 1.1 billion baht (*Phuchatkan raiwan* 2003).

In the event, the planned listing did not occur. According to a statement from Thailand's Securities and Exchange Commission, the company withdrew its application (Securities and Exchange Commission 2004). The statement also emphasized that the commission took into account two aspects of any application for listing. First, when no regulatory body oversaw some of the operations of an applicant, there was substantial risk that the establishment in the future of such a body would have important implications for the applicant's operations. Second, when a concession was extended by a government agency, the commission requested that the applicant disclose details of the process through which it obtained the concession, to enable prospective shareholders to evaluate the level of risk associated with the concession (Securities and Exchange Commission 2004). RTA Entertainment does not appear to have released financial information to the public from 2003 to 2012. The company recorded profits from 2013 onward, but their scale has generally been less than the 10 per cent rate projected in 2003 (Department of Business Development n.d. i).

The establishment in 2010 of the National Broadcasting and Telecommunications Commission as the new regulatory body responsible for the broadcasting industry gave it authority extending to both television and radio broadcasting. Its establishment also led to the creation of the NBTC Research and Development Fund (*Kongthunwichai lae phatthana kitchakan krachai siang kitchakan thorathat lae kitchakan thorakhommanakhom phuea prayot satharana*). The source of money in the NBTC Research and Development Fund is the licensing fees paid by radio and television broadcasters.

Within two months of its 2014 coup, the National Council for Peace and Order junta changed the governance structure of the NBTC and expanded its authority (Royal Gazette 2014). It authorized the NBTC's chairman, the secretary general of the cabinet office, the secretary general of the Ministry of Defense and two "experts" to serve as the managers of the research and development fund. The original NBTC Act of 2010 had only authorized the two secretaries general to serve on the committee responsible for selecting NBTC commissioners, and in no other capacity. The junta also stipulated that fees collected by the research and development fund before this new order took effect be turned over to the Ministry of Finance as fiscal revenue. Further, the fund would now be permitted to extend loans to that ministry. The NBTC now had eleven commissioners, of whom six came from the military. The chairman of the commission held the rank of air chief marshal; the other five military commissioners were Army officers (National Broadcasting and Telecommunications Commission 2014).

In 2017, the junta's appointed legislature, or National Assembly (*Sapha nittibanyat haeng chat*), enacted a new NBTC Act. It reduced the number of commissioners to seven and raised their minimum age from 35 to 40 years (Royal Gazette 2010 and 2017). Military officers continued to dominate the commission; its chairman remained an Air Force officer of the highest rank. And that same year saw the NBTC approve a budget covering the cost of rental of the satellite used to transmit RTATS's TGN for the 2017–20 period (National Broadcasting and Telecommunications Commission 2017). Other Thai radio and television operators would thus effectively subsidize RTATS, with funds falling outside the military's share of the country's annual budget.

Construction, Distribution, Manufacturing, Mining, Publishing, Hospitals and More

As is common in Thailand, the memoranda of association for RTATS Channel 5 Publishing and RTATS Channel 5 Publication listed an extremely wide range of businesses in which they might operate (Department of Business Development n.d. e and n.d. f). Examples of these businesses were construction subcontracting; producing goods such as rice, fruit and herbs; mining; publishing books and magazines; distributing a variety of products, including alcoholic beverages and jewelry, through retail and wholesale trade; and operating private hospitals, medical schools, restaurants and bars.

Nevertheless, these firms' initial registered capital was low. That of RTATS Channel 5 Publishing was 10 million baht, and that of RTATS Channel 5 Publication only half that amount (Department of Business Development n.d. e and n.d. f). It is difficult to assess the real business purposes of these firms. One hypothesis is that each was established with a plan to increase capital and become a conglomerate in the future.

The largest shareholder in these two firms was the Tho Tho Bo 5 holding company, whose attempt to list on the Stock Exchange of Thailand failed. The stakes held by that company in RTATS Channel 5 Publishing and RTATS Channel 5 Publication were 75 per cent and 99.99 per cent, respectively (Department of Business Development n.d. e and n.d. f). It is thus not surprising that the two companies had some of the same senior Army officers on their boards of directors, or that one these generals was also on the board of Tho Tho Bo 5. Had the attempted listing of the company on the stock exchange proved successful, the company would perhaps have used these subsidiaries to engage in a wider range of business activities.

Real Estate and Hotels

At least since 1966, the Royal Thai Army has had rules governing the leasing of its land and properties to the private sector for commercial purposes. The rules promulgated in that year prohibited subletting to third parties (Royal Thai Army 1966). However, revised rules introduced in compliance with a 1975 royal decree on government properties permitted such subletting; the decree granted discretion in this area to the Ministry of Finance (Royal Gazette 1975). Examples of military properties available for rent are hotels and vacation homes. There are at least nine such properties on Navy and Army bases in Chonburi, Phetchabun, Prachuapkhirikhan, Rayong and Samutprakan provinces (*Painaidii* 2018).

Another aspect of the military's use of land under its ownership is housing development under the programme called "Homes for the Welfare of Government Officers and Regular Employees of the Army".[7] These residential properties are available for long-term lease or sale, with subsidized mortgages, to military officers and other Army employees (Real Estate Division, Royal Thai Army 2005). In the case of properties for lease, after five years the original tenant may sublet her or his home to a third party, whether or not the latter is an Army officer or employee (Baania n.d. b). In the case of properties for sale, buyers purchase the dwellings, but the Army retains ownership of the land (Narong n.d). Heirs with no connection to the military may inherit these homes. Among the provinces in which such residential properties have been constructed are Bangkok, Chiangmai, Chiangrai, Lopburi, Nakhon Sawan, Nakhon Nayok, Nakhon Ratchasima and Phuket.

Banquet and Recreation Facilities

All three branches of the Thai military operate recreation facilities. The Army operates the Royal Thai Army Club and the Royal Thai Army Sports Center, the Air Force the Royal Thai Air Force Club and the Royal Thai Air Force Golf Course, and the Navy the Royal Thai Navy Club and the Royal Thai Navy Golf Course.

These clubs are located on bases in Bangkok and outside the capital. While entry onto the bases requires a military identification card, the clubs' facilities are at the same time available to the public for private events, such as wedding receptions. The golf courses are open to the public, including foreigners and foreign tourists. Offering these services to outsiders appears to be of only secondary economic importance—really just a means of revenue management. However, it does raise the question of whether the facilities are critical to the primary function of the military.

Factors of Production in Thai Military Services Unrelated to Security

This section briefly describes three factors of production that the Thai military uses in the delivery of services unrelated to security: capital, labour and land.

The chapter has noted four sources of capital that have funded the business activities of the Thai military. First, its budget has financed equity in various concerns held by military institutions and the operating costs of military radio stations and of RTATS Channel 5. Second, the Thai Military Bank managed to increase its capital by listing on the Stock Exchange of Thailand. Third, deposits in the Thai Military Bank have allowed the bank to extend loans to companies owned by the military, such as RTA Entertainment (Thai Military Bank 2003). Finally, foreign capital was necessary to the restructuring of the Thai Military Bank after the 1997 financial crisis. Limitations in available data, above all concerning the costs of operating military radio stations and Channel 5, mean that comparison of the relative contributions of capital from the four sources is not possible.

Thailand maintains a regime of conscription, which assures its military a ready supply of labour to support undertakings unrelated to security. While high-ranking officers, especially generals, become members of the boards of companies owned by the military, conscripts often find themselves deployed as service workers at recreation facilities, including hotels and golf courses.

The Royal Thai Army owns more land than—following estimates in Porphant (2008)—even the Crown Property Bureau itself. While the value of its land may be lower, the Army's landholdings are 110 times greater in area than those of the bureau (Royal Thai Army War College 2013). Among government agencies, Army landholdings are second only to those of the Department of Forestry. And this is to consider only the Army; research on the land owned, occupied and controlled by the Air Force and the Navy remains necessary.

Conclusion

This chapter draws on publicly available information to document some of the economic activities of the Thai military outside the area of security. For six decades, the Thai military has provided services in banking, asset management, radio broadcasting, television broadcasting, real estate and hotels, banquet services and recreation. These services are provided by companies owned and controlled by the military or by units within the military. Among the three branches of the Thai military, the Army has been a much more active economic actor than the Air Force or the Navy.

The involvement of the Royal Thai Army in the provision of services unrelated to security provides a possible incentive for it to seize political power as a means of gaining direct influence over economic policy and enacting or amending laws relating to its own lines of business and to the sectors in which it is commercially active. New rules, written under post-coup military regimes, have immensely benefitted military firms in banking and broadcasting. These rules have been designed purposely to restrict entry into those sectors and hence to limit competition. These developments suggest the possibility of a commercial logic to coups in Thailand, and a complementarity between the military's roles as provider of services and as political actor and policymaker.

ACKNOWLEDGEMENTS

The author is indebted to Thongchai Winichakul and Yupana Wiwattanakantang for valuable discussions of the business activities of the Thai military. She also thanks Ravin Thomya for her research assistance. An earlier version of this chapter appeared in Thai, in Kanda (2012a and 2012b).

NOTES

1. See Chambers and Napisa (2017) for the most recent major work devoted to study and analysis of military roles in and influence on the economies of Southeast Asia.
2. The shareholding information is as of 24 April 2018 (TMB 2018).
3. The deposit share is calculated using the deposit balance in TMB Bank's financial statements, as submitted to the Stock Exchange of Thailand, and the total deposit balance of Thailand's commercial banking system according to data from the Bank of Thailand.
4. This company was established through a syndicated loan contract with the Bangkok Tollway Company, to facilitate the transfer of concessionary construction rights to the Special Highway Authority of Thailand. As the security agent, the Thai Military Bank became the major shareholder in the company (Thai Military Bank 2002).
5. The top six commercial banks in Thailand, by assets, are the Bangkok Bank, the Siam Commercial Bank, Kasikorn Bank (formerly the Thai Farmers Bank), Krungthai Bank, the Bank of Ayudhya and Thanachart Bank.

6. See Royal Gazette (2000), esp. p. 31.
7. That is *Ban sawatdikan phuea kharatchakan lae lukchang pracham kongthap bok*; see Baania (n.d. a).

REFERENCES

Baania. N.d. a. *Ban sawatdikan phuea kharatchakan lae lukchang pracham kongthap bok* [Homes for the welfare of government officers and regular employees of the Army]. https://baania.com/th/project/บ้านสวัสดิการเพื่อข้าราชการและลูกจ้างประจำกองทัพบก (accessed 21 June 2019).

———. N.d. b. *Ban sawatdikan phuea kharatchakan lae lukchang pracham kongthap bok khrongkan ban thanarak* [Homes for the welfare of government officers and regular employees of the Army, Ban Thanarak project]. https://baania.com/th/project/%E0%B8%9A%E0%B9%89%E0%B8%B2%E0%B8%99%20E0%B8%AA%E0%B8%A7%E0%B8%B1%E0%B8%AA%E0%E2%80%A6 (accessed 3 February 2018).

Chambers, Paul, and Napisa Waitoolkiat, eds. 2017. *Khaki Capital: The Political Economy of the Military in Southeast Asia*. Copenhagen: NIAS Press.

Department of Business Development, Ministry of Commerce, Thailand. N.d. a. Registration file on Thanakhan thahan thai chamkat [Thai Military Bank], registered 5 November 1957; file number 202/2500.

———. N.d. b. Registration file on Borisat krungthep thorathat lae witthayu chamkat [Bangkok Broadcasting and Television Company], registered 25 October 1967; file number 575/2510.

———. N.d. c. Registration file on Thanakhan thahan thai borisat mahachon chamkat [Thai Military Bank Public Company], registered 3 January 1994; file number Bo Mo Cho 248.

———. N.d. d. Registration file on Borisat tho tho bo 5 chamkat [Tho Tho Bo 5 Company], registered 14 June 1997; file number (1)273/2540.

———. N.d. e. Registration file on Borisat tho tho bo 5 phaplitching chamkat [RTAS Channel 5 Publishing Company], registered 24 December 1997; file number (5)1757/2540.

———. N.d. f. Registration file on Borisat tho tho bo 5 phapblikhechan chamkat [RTAS Channel 5 Publication Company], registered 24 December 1997; file number (1)139/2542.

———. N.d. g. Registration file on Borisat laksap borihan kongthunruam thahan thai chamkat [TMB Asset Management Company], registered 16 October 1996; file number 2165/2539.

———. N.d. h. Registration file on Borisat borihan sinsap phayathai chamkat [Phayathai Asset Management Company], registered 9 August 2000; file number (1)28/2543.

———. N.d. i. Registration file on Borisat a thi e entoethenmen mahachon chamkat [RTA Entertainment Public Company], registered 19 August 2003; registration number 40854600024.

Department of Business Development Data Warehouse. N.d. Data on Borist desikni fo i thi e khonthraek chamkat [Designee for ETA Contract Company], registered 21 March 1989; registration number 0105532025842. http://datawarehouse.dbd.go.th/bdw/company/profile/ (accessed 16 July 2019).

Dueanphen Limsitrakun. 1996. "Chong 7 si thi wi phuea khrai?" [Channel 7 for whom?]. *Phuchatkan raiduean*, July 1996.

Kanda Naknoi. 2012a. "Setthasat samansamnuek 55 pi thun kongthap thai (ton thi 1)" [Common-sense economics: 55 years of Thai military capital (part 1)]. *Prachatai*, 23 March 2012a. https://prachatai.com/journal/2012/03/39802 (accessed 25 June 2012).

———. 2012b. "Setthasat samansamnuek 55 pi thun kongthap thai (ton thi 2)" [Common-sense economics: 55 years of Thai military capital (part 2)]. *Prachatai*, 25 April 2012b. https://prachatai.com/journal/2012/04/40226 (accessed 25 June 2019).

Kunlawadi Wangdisirikun. 2002. "Setthasat kanmueang waduai kanchatsan sapphayakon khluenkhwamthi nai prathet thai" [The political economy of radio frequency allocation in Thailand]. Master's thesis, Department of Economics, Chulalongkorn University.

Narong Dunlayaphaptham, Colonel. N.d. "Khrongkan sawatdikan banphak tho pho 2 phuenthi cho wo no mo 'nakhon ratchasima moden'" [Welfare housing project, Second Army Region, Nakhon Ratchasima Province zone: "Nakhon Ratchasima model"]. Nakhon Ratchasima: *Samnakngan khrongkan sawatdikan banphak kharatchakan tho pho* 2.

National Broadcasting and Telecommunications Commission, Thailand. 2014. Annual Report, 2014. http://www.nbtc.go.th/getattachment/Information/AnnualReport/รายงานผลการปฏิบัติงานประจำปี-2557/NBTC-Annual-Report-2014.pdf.aspx (accessed 4 October 2019).

———. 2017. Annual Report, 2017. http://www.nbtc.go.th/getattachment/Information/AnnualReport/36067/เอกสารแนบ.pdf.aspx (accessed 4 October 2019).

———. N.d. "Raichue sathani witthayu krachai siang thua prathet" [List of radio stations across the country]. *Khanakammakan kitchakan krachai siang kitchakan thorathat lae kitchakan thorakhommanakhom haeng chat*.

National Committee on Radio and Television Activities, Public Relations Department, Thailand. N.d. "Raichue sathani witthayu krachai siang nai khet krungthepmahanakhon (chamnaek tam nuai-ngan ton sangkat)" [List of radio stations in Bangkok (by agency)].

Noranit Setthabut. N.d. "Chot Khunnakasem khunkhlang khong chomphon Sarit" [Jote Gunakasem, Field Marshal Sarit's treasury lord]. King Prajadhipok's

Institute Data Bank. http://wiki.kpi.ac.th/index.php?title=โชติ_คุณะเกษม (accessed 25 June 2019).

Painaidii, 2018. "Thiphak khong nuai-ngan ratchakan" [Government agency housing], 17 October 2010. http://www.painaidii.com/wheretogo/wheretogo-detail/000173/lang/th/?block=1 (accessed 30 September 2019).

Phuchatkan raiwan. 2003. "Tho tho bo 5 rap sampathan thi chi en leng khao talat traimat sam" [Tho Tho Bo 5 with TGN concession, aims to list in third quarter], 2 July 2003. http://info.gotomanager.com/news/details.aspx?id=7090 (accessed 25 June 2019).

Porphant Ouyyanont. 2008. "The Crown Property Bureau in Thailand and the Crisis of 1997". *Journal of Contemporary Asia* 38, no. 1: 166–89.

Real Estate Division, Royal Thai Army. 2005. "Krom thanarak kho khuen thi ratphatsadu phuea chattham khrongkan ban thanarak" [Treasury Department requests return of land for Ban Thanarak project]. *Kong asangharimmasap kongthap bok*, Memorandum 0404/11033, 8 October 2005.

Royal Gazette, Thailand. 1962. "Phraratchabanyat kanthanakhan phanit pho so 2505" [Commercial banking act of 1962]. *Ratchakitchanubeksa*, Volume 79, Special Section 19, pages 1–23, 30 April 1962. http://www.ratchakitcha.soc.go.th/DATA/PDF/2505/A/039/1.PDF (accessed 1 October 2019).

———. 1975. "Phraratchabanyat thi ratphatsadu pho so 2518" [Royal decree on government properties, 1975]. *Ratchakitchanubeksa*, Volume 92, Special Section 54, pages 1–6, 5 March 1975. http://www.ratchakitcha.soc.go.th/DATA/PDF/2518/A/054/1.PDF (accessed 30 September 2019).

———. 1979. "Phratchabanyat kanprakop thurakit ngoenthun thurakit laksap lae thurakit khredit fongsie pho so 2522" [Royal decree on the undertaking of finance, securities and credit foncier business, 1979]. *Ratchakitchanubeksa*, Volume 96, Special Section 74, pages 39–90, 9 May 1979. http://www.ratchakitcha.soc.go.th/DATA/PDF/2522/A/074/39.PDF (accessed 1 October 2019).

———. 2000. "Phratchabanyat ongkon chatsan khluenkhwamthi lae kamkap witthayu krachai siang witthayu thorathat lae kitchakan thorakhammanakhom" [Royal decree on allocation of radio frequencies and regulation of radio, television and telecommunications]. *Ratchakitchanubeksa*, Volume 117, Special Section 16(a), pages 1–33, 7 March 2000. http://www.ratchakitcha.soc.go.th/DATA/PDF/00018720.PDF (accessed 7 October 2019).

———. 2008. "Phraratchabanyat thurakit sathaban kanngoen pho so 2551" [Royal decree on the business of financial institutions, 2008]. *Ratchakitchanubeksa*, Volume 125, Section 27(1), pages 1–58, 5 February 2008. http://www.ratchakitcha.soc.go.th/DATA/PDF/2551/A/027/1.PDF (accessed 1 October 2019).

———. 2010. "Phraratchabanyat ongkon chatsan khluenkhwamthi lae kamkap kanprakop kitchakan witthayu krachai siang thorathat lae kitchakan thorakhamanakhom pho so 2553" [Royal decree on the organization for allocating frequencies and regulating radio and television activities and telecommunications activities, 2010]. *Ratchakitchanubeksa*, Volume 127, Special Section 78(1), pages 1–46, 19 December 2010. http://www.ratchakitcha.soc.go.th/DATA/PDF/2553/A/078/1.PDF (accessed 4 October 2019).

———. 2014. "Prakat khana raksa khwamsangop haeng chat chabap thi 80/2559 rueang kankaekhai phoemtoem kotmai waduai ongkon chatsan khluenkhwamthi lae kamkap kanprakop kitchakan witthayu krachai siang thorathat lae kitchakan thorakhamanakhom" [Announcement of the National Council for Peace and Order on amending the law on the organization for allocation of frequencies and regulation of radio, television and telecommunications activities]. *Ratchakitchanubeksa*, Volume 131, Special Section 134(d), pages 3–4, 21 July 2014. http://www.ratchakitcha.soc.go.th/DATA/PDF/2557/E/134/3.PDF (accessed 4 October 2019).

———. 2017. "Phraratchabanyat ongkon chatsan khluenkhwamthi lae kamkap kanprakop kitchakan witthayu krachai siang thorathat lae kitchakan thorakhamanakhom (chabap thi 2) pho so 2560" [Royal decree on the organization for allocation of frequencies and regulation of radio, television activities and telecommunications activities (second version), 2017]. *Ratchakitchanubeksa*, Volume 134, Special Section 65(1), pages 59–75, 22 June 2017. https://ictlawcenter.etda.or.th/files/law/file/98/5295f29e6521c69fbc4806200e64ce1b.pdf (accessed 4 October 2019).

Royal Thai Army. 1966. "Rabiap kongthap bok waduai kanpokhrong lae withikan chatkan thi din pho so 2509" [Army rules for the oversight and management of land, 1966]. *Kongthap bok*.

Royal Thai Army War College, Thailand. 2013. "Khrongkan namrong kankaekhai panha kanbukruk thidin nai khwamkhropkhrong khong kongthap bok duai rabop phumisonthet koranisueksa nai phuenthi changwat thahan bok kanchanaburi" [Pilot project on using geo-information systems to solve the problem of encroachment on Army lands: case study of Kanchanaburi Military District]. *Witthayalai kanthap bok*.

Securities and Exchange Commission, Thailand. 2004. "Ko lo to chichaeng khothetching korani kankrachai hun khong tho tho bo 5" [SEC explains facts on the distribution of shares in Tho Tho Bo 5]. Memorandum 45/2547. *Khanakammakan kamkap laksap lae talat laksap*, 25 June 2004.

Stock Exchange of Thailand. 2019. Company Factsheet: TMB Bank. *Talat laksap haeng prathet thai*, 16 September 2019. https://www.set.or.th/set/factsheet.do?symbol=tmb (accessed 27 September 2019).

———. N.d. "Khomun raiborisat/laksap TMB" [Data by company/security: TMB]. *Talat laksap haeng prathet thai*. https://www.set.or.th/set/companyprofile.do?symbol=tmb (accessed 25 June 2019).

Thai Military Bank. 2002. Annual Report 2002.

———. 2003. Annual Report 2003.
———. 2004. Annual Report 2004.
TMB Bank. 2005. Annual Report 2005.
———. 2007. Annual Report 2007.
———. 2018. Annual Report 2018.
———. N.d. a. "About TMB". https://www.tmbbank.com/en/about (accessed 30 September 2019).
———. N.d. b. "About TMB: Corporate Group Structure". https://www.tmbbank.com/en/about/corporate_group_structure (accessed 3 June 2019).
———. N.d. c. "Board of Directors". https://www.tmbbank.com/en/about/bod (accessed 25 June 2019).

6

EPILOGUE: CONTROLLING OR PLAYING POLITICS?

Robert H. Taylor

> ... when [the army] was mistaken enough to come down into the arena and to play politics instead of controlling them, it began a descent which ended in its abject defeat – militarily, politically, spiritually. (Wheeler-Bennett 2005 [1953], p. xxxii)

To whom or what does an army—as the primary force of the sole legitimate yielder of violence on behalf of a community with its own internationally recognized territory, the state—owe its loyalty? To representations of the state—the constitution, the head of state, the nation, a noble ideal, its own professional *éclat*? Or to the government—the president or prime minister, the legislature, the ruling party of the day? This dilemma is at the heart of all discussions of civil-military relations. Those who believe that armies are not faced with this dilemma live in fantasyland. The army, as a central pillar of the modern state, is inevitably a political institution, and the answer to the opening question above is quintessentially a political one. The answers given to this question at various times have determined the role of the armies of Thailand and

Myanmar, and of most of the other countries in Southeast Asia if not the world, since the formation of the modern, professional militaries of independent states. Both of those armies, since 1911 in the case of Thailand[1] and since 1948 in the case of Myanmar,[2] have been deeply involved in politics, but to different degrees at different times. The devil, as always, is in the detail, as the contributions to this volume make amply clear.

The extensive theoretical literature on the political role of the military has provided a variety of taxonomies for the degree of military involvement in politics during the course of the past century and more. For example, Samuel Finer, in his classic *The Man on Horseback*, set out six levels of involvement—from normal constitutional mechanisms through to intimidation and threats, and to failure to protect or outright violence against civilian authorities (Finer 2005, p. 140). Like Finer, other analysts lay out various continua of degrees to which the military directly involves itself in politics, up to and including direct military rule such as that in Myanmar between 1988 and 2011 and in Thailand between—most recently—2015 and 2019.[3]

If we think of an army as essentially an institution by means of which a state makes war upon or defends itself against another state or other states, then we must confront Clausewitz's view that to address the issue of civil-military relations with reference to the locus of loyalty is to create a preposterous proposition. However, Clausewitz was writing before the maturation of those twins of the modern state, a professional army and popular government. He wrote in his classic *On War*,

> The subordination of the political point of view to the military would be contrary to common sense, for policy has declared the War; it is the intelligent factor. War is only the instrument, and not the reverse. The subordination of the military point of view to the political is, therefore, the only thing which is possible. (Rapoport 1968, p. 405)

Clausewitz's view is no longer tenable. The armies of Thailand and Myanmar have never been used to fight a significant war with any of either country's neighbours, but they have been involved in a myriad of other activities—from the yielding of violence against domestic insurgents and dissidents, to so-called nation-building tasks and economic and infrastructural development and generating resources for themselves or their leaders. They may justify their claim on a significant proportion of government budgets by asserting a need to defend the nation, but that purpose has never required more than a fraction of this largess. Rather, involvement in domestic affairs has preoccupied these armies.

The domestic orientation of Southeast Asian armies raises a different question from that posed by Clausewitz, particularly in the post-Cold War era. Not only has democratization become an academic industry, but it is also held up as an ideal to which all states must aspire. This ideal is usually achieved where, amongst other things, the military is clearly subordinate to a popularly chosen civilian government. The army therefore ceases to appear to be a political actor and ideally becomes a tool of the civilian government of the day, near to—if not actually achieving—the ideal of a professional army under the control of civilian politicians.[4] However, constitutional government and civilian control of the military are two different, if related, things. In fact, it is probably easier for dictatorships than for popularly chosen governments to control armies. The conundrum of civilian control of the military as framed by Michael Howard is an analytically

> double problem ... [involving] the subordination of military force to the political government, and control of the government in possession of such force by legal restraint and the popular will. (Howard 1957, p. 214)

What matters, then, is not only that a government is popularly elected but also that it is constrained in its activities, including the use of its military, by the force of law. That is, the civilian authorities respect, as does the army, the constitution and its subordinate laws, rather than morphing into a dictatorship or autocracy. The literature on the role of the military in politics rather assumes that this is the case. It therefore concentrates on the first of Howard's problems: "the subordination of the military force to the political government". To avoid the second problem is, however, to duck many awkward issues.

Armies are sometimes described as being composed of armed bureaucrats.[5] Such a description is misleading. Their uniforms, training and day-to-day living arrangements, along with their organizational ethos, set armies apart from civilian society. Through a process of socialization, soldiers are bound together as a caste apart; hence the distinctive uniforms and hierarchical organizational structures (Janowitz 1960).[6] For the officer corps, in particular, trained from early age

> in the drill of military discipline, the psychological effect of an order from a superior officer is compelling and cannot be ignored. Every military command has a power over him that is logically inexplicable, but cancels out his own will. (Zweig 2013, p. 432)

This discipline, in addition to an army's weapons, makes it effective as a political agent. If that socialization is undermined, both an army and the society from which it is formed fall prey to division and manipulation. The Philippine case, in which factionalism subverted the military's political independence, illustrates such an outcome (McCoy 1999, especially pp. 4–42).

The effort to conceptualize the relationship between civilian control of the military and the military's intrusion into what is generally conceived of as the civilian sphere of government highlights that "civilian control is not a fact but a process" (Kohn 1997, p. 143). There is a spectrum of relationships, and at some point on that spectrum the balance of power between the civilian arms of government and the military tips in favour of one or the other. Those arms require effective countervailing power to control the military, or the military will become the dominant, if not dictatorial, power. That is to say, if on the civilian side of the equation the institutions of rule—such as political parties, civilian traditions and public opinion in opposition to military rule—are deeply embedded and so recognized by the military, the probability of the balance swinging in the direction of the military is weak. While the military maintains influence, that influence is limited to its defined defence functions, however elastic.

On the other hand, if the civilian power morphs into an autocracy or dictatorship, then the army is in danger of losing its constitutional position and obligations. Analytically, this insight is not easy to operationalize. One has to look at the facts on the ground. Again, the devil is in the detail.

John Wheeler-Bennett sought to understand the role of the military in politics in *The Nemesis of Power* (Wheeler-Bennett 2005 [1953]), from which the quotation at the beginning of this epilogue was taken. He drew a distinction—to which I return below—between an army which controls politics and an army which plays politics. Such a distinction assumes that the army is necessarily a powerful political actor, thanks to its essential position as a central prop of the state. However, when an army involves itself in civilian politics unwisely, it begins to play politics, and in the German case that Wheeler-Bennet examined, the army lost control over its own sphere of action—with disastrous consequences for itself and the state that it had been formed to defend. That result, under the Nazi regime, was both the army's and the state's undoing. Wheeler-Bennett takes for granted the truism that a government which is not supported by its army is a government which is in imminent threat of being ousted by a coup, unless countervailing powers have effectively neutered that army. In order for both the army and the government to avoid these respective fates, governments and armies must deal carefully with each other's interests. Adherence to implicit, as well as written, constitutional norms is essential on both sides.

Thus armies need to respect the preserves of civilian governments as long as offering this respect does not threaten the peace and security of the country. If that threat presents itself, should the army be in a position to re-establish the state on an equanimous basis even if this means that it takes power temporarily in its own name? When the German army attempted to ask that question after the rise of Adolf Hitler, it had already lost control of its fate to a megalomaniac who was the architect of the destruction not only of the German army but also of the German state. Hitler undermined the military's ability to take power from him. The consequence was abject defeat because the army's leadership made the mistake, as Wheeler-Bennett wrote, of playing politics rather than controlling them.

Germany's army was formed in 1871 as a result of the unification of the country under the auspices of Prussia.[7] For nearly fifty years, the traditions of the aristocratic Prussian officer corps, including above all its loyalty to the King of Prussia *cum* Kaiser of Germany, remained intact despite the development of representative institutions under the country's constitution. Like the officer corps, the chancellor, as head of government, was appointed by and responsible solely to the Kaiser. This situation remained the case until two days before the official end of the First World War. At that time, the German military had suffered defeat at the hands of foreign foes, but it remained a force within Germany. However, rebellion was growing in the ranks.[8] Sailors based at Kiel mutinied, and desertions and the formation of communes with links to Communists, Spartacists and other left wing political forces were becoming common. Civil war was in the air. The government in Berlin, led by Prince Max of Baden, agreed with Social Democratic

Party (SDP) leader Friedrich Ebert that the only way to avoid that war was the abdication of the Kaiser and the formation of an SDP government. As Ebert said, "A revolutionary gesture is necessary to forestall the revolution." The Kaiser, then at the army's headquarters at Spa, Belgium, agreed to abdicate and go into exile in Holland, but only after the recently appointed quartermaster general, General Karl Groener, told him in the presence of the commander in chief, Field Marshal Paul von Hindenburg, "The army will re-enter Germany as an organised force under the orders of its Generals, but not under those of Your Majesty. The army is no longer with Your Majesty."[10] The date was 9 November 1918.

On the same day, in Berlin, where the spectre of revolution was in the streets below his windows, Ebert—to whom Prince Max had handed power and who therefore now occupied the chancellor's office—sought "a means to buttress his flimsy authority". On his desk was a secret telephone linked directly to Spa. The phone rang, Ebert picked it up, and a voice said, "Groener speaking." He asked whether the government was "willing to protect Germany from anarchy and to restore order". Ebert said that it was, to which Groener replied, "The High Command will maintain discipline in the Army and bring it peacefully home." He laid down conditions, however, including the suppression of Bolshevism, the provisioning of the army and the security of transport communications (Wheeler-Bennett 2005 [1953], pp. 20–21).

On 11 December, a month after the armistice, the army marched into Berlin. Less than two weeks later, at the request of Ebert, loyal troops were called to suppress the mutinous People's Marine Division, which was besieging his office. Ebert ignored subsequent efforts on the part of a newly formed, radical national assembly to bring the army under civilian control and to disband the military high command. The week of 10–17 January 1919 was particularly bloody, with the Spartacists crushed by the Frei Corps—a paramilitary force loyal to the army. And when the national assembly met at Weimar after elections that had been held the previous month, "it did so under military protection" (Wheeler-Bennett 2005 [1953], pp. 28–37). In mid-1920, Groener resigned as chief of the German general staff and entered Ebert's cabinet. Having left the cabinet in 1923, he was called back to serve as defence minister, and frequently as acting chancellor, from 1928 to 1932 (Wheeler-Bennett 1956, pp. 538–41).

From an initial attitude of "sullen unreliability", under its new commander, Groener's successor General Hans von Seeckt, the army leadership came to understand that, to achieve its ambition to re-establish Germany as a strong military power despite the strict limitations imposed by the Treaty of Versailles,[11] it would have to work through and not against the government of the Weimar Republic (Wheeler-Bennett 2005 [1953], p. 82). Von Seeckt shared with Groener the view that, as Groener said, the German army existed "To serve the State – far from all party politics, to save and maintain it against the terrible pressure from without and the insane strife at home – this is our only goal" (Wheeler-Bennet 2005 [1953], pp. 108–9). Throughout the 1920s, "despite various crises, rumours, coups, and royalist and attempted rightist Nazi infiltration of the army, the army and the government maintained their cooperative but distant relationship" (Wheeler-Bennet 2005 [1953], p. 82). This posture did not, however, stop the army from developing its own economic enterprises or working alone and with others—including the hated Bolsheviks in the Soviet Union—to rebuild Germany's military by secretly circumventing and subverting the restrictions placed on the rearmament of Germany by the Treaty of Versailles.

In 1926 von Seeckt resigned and was succeeded by General Kurt von Schleicher, a man who took a different view of the role of the military in politics. Following the death of Ebert, who had been elected president of the Weimar Republic, Field Marshal von Hindenburg, then seventy-eight years old and a "wooden titan" in Wheeler-Bennett's analysis (Wheeler-Bennett 1936), became head of state. Via his connection to von Hindenburg's son and assistant Oskar, a junior officer in von Schleicher's earlier command, von Schleicher "saw his chance to meddle in politics" (Wheeler-Bennett 2005 [1953], p. 152). With the support of von Hindenburg, he had become by the end of 1932 chancellor, minister of defence and Reich commissioner of Prussia—effectively but briefly in control of the key levers of power in the German Republic. However, he would overreach, and Hitler and the Nazis engineered his murder as soon as the end of June 1933. By that time the army as a guarantor of its own interests and the security of Germany was becoming in political terms effectively neutered, surrounded as it was by forces both armed and unarmed that were loyal to Adolf Hitler and the Nazi Party.

At this point in his narrative, Wheeler-Bennett comes as close as he ever does to defining what he meant by playing politics as opposed to controlling politics.

> The Reich Government which took office on December 2, 1932, marked the apogee of power of the Army – and Kurt von Schleicher – in German politics. In influence the Army had undoubtedly been stronger under von Seeckt, who had established and maintained it as a detached and final arbiter of fate within the Reich. This influence, however, had been only oblique and indirect – and for that reason it had been all the stronger – but in December 1932 the Army and the military caste had the highest offices of the State concentrated in their hands. (Wheeler-Bennett 2005 [1953], p. 266).

The political power that the German army had attained by 1932 was in part the consequence of the recall to the cabinet of General Groener as minister of defence four years earlier. Groener insisted on the army remaining out of politics, but that insistence did not stop von Schleicher from his political scheming. Following Defence Minister Groener's suppression of the storm troopers of the Nazi Party's *Sturmabteilung*, Hitler's paramilitary brown-shirts, Commander in Chief von Schleicher organized a right-wing attack on Groener in the legislature, and then informed him, in the presence of another officer, that he no longer had the support of the army (Wheeler-Bennett 1956, pp. 538–42). Groener was forced from office. Von Schleicher continued to scheme with Oskar von Hindenburg, manipulating the increasingly feeble President Paul von Hindenburg in a failed attempt to split the Nazi Party and to bring its allegedly tamer wing into government in league with the army. Hitler had a similar idea, and he proved a more effective political manipulator, grasping not only the chancellorship but also—following von Hindenburg's death the following year—the presidency.

Von Schleicher, with whom Wheeler-Bennett rode horses in Berlin's Tiergarten, possessed "no vestige or loyalty or innate decency. ... He operated in the dusk behind the throne, spying on all and sundry, tapping their telephones, bugging their offices. He betrayed patron after patron. ..." (Wheeler-Bennett 1974, p. 36).[12] Having helped engineer the removal of the SDP Chancellor Hermann Müller in 1930, he engineered the selection of his replacement under President von Hindenburg. That man was Heinrich Bruning, the leader of the Catholic Centre

Party. Bruning remained in office for two years and saw through the eventual re-election of von Hindenburg primarily because of support from a left, including the SPD, determined to defeat Hitler, his primary opponent. Bruning, however, was soon ousted from power, when the army withdrew its support for him, and his replacement, again chosen by von Schleicher, was the witty but inept Franz von Papen. Von Schleicher had met secretly with Hitler in order to bring down Bruning. Von Papen soon proved his ineptitude and was replaced by von Schleicher himself. He remained in office for thirty-three days before, in January 1933, his erstwhile ally von Papen and others convinced von Hindenburg that Hitler should take the chancellorship.

Initially, Hitler seemed to please both the generals and the many lower-ranking officers already in sympathy with his party, thanks to his pledge to undertake a massive rearmament programme in a government composed of two props—the Nazi Party and the army. As Robert O'Neill sets out in *The German Army and the Nazi Party, 1933-1939*, the party exploited Hitler's initially "favourable impression on the army" to make it obedient to him—including incorporating Nazi insignia into the army's own uniforms, using the army to train Hitler's Waffen-SS—the armed wing of the party, which grew from three regiments to thirty-eight divisions—and altering the army's pledge of loyalty from one to the constitution to one to the person of Hitler as the Führer (O'Neill 1966, p. 54).[13] Having overcome the resistance of the army high command to a war that it felt that it could not win, Hitler launched Germany and its army on an aggressive war which led to their utter annihilation. The German army was now indeed the servant of the civilian government, despite the best intentions of its leaders.[14] By the same methods described by political analysts as the means by which armies involve themselves in politics, including blackmail and intimidation, Germany's once proud officer corps became the servant of the man that its members once called Corporal Schicklgruber, using the original surname of his father.

In fifteen years, the German army had gone from being the central pillar and prop of the constitutional order of Weimar Germany to merely one of a number of yielders of violence in Nazi Germany, in the end no longer able to be the master of its own fate and therefore of the fate of the German state. What does this lesson have to say about the political role of armies in Southeast Asia? It would seem to apply to at least four of the ten armies of the region. The armies of Malaysia, Singapore, Brunei, Cambodia, Laos and Vietnam have—for various reasons having to do with a combination of factors including historical legacy, ethnicity, autocracy, and integration into a ruling party and civilian bureaucracy—by and large appeared unlikely either to control or to play a dominant role in politics of their own volition. Nevertheless, they are not without significant political, and economic, influence.[15] It is obvious, however, from the studies included in this volume that the armies of Myanmar and Thailand have at one time or another both played politics and controlled politics.

It would appear, on balance, that the army of Thailand has been more willing to play politics and less able to control the outcome of politics than the army of Myanmar. For example, the army of Thailand has governed in its own right—without the assistance of civilian allies such as the monarchy, the civil service, foreign supporters or civilian political parties—for a mere six or seven years since its first successful entry into politics at the time of the end of absolute monarchy in 1932. On the other hand, the Myanmar army has controlled the state directly during twenty-six years and indirectly during fifteen years of the country's first seventy years of independence. In other years, it can be said that the army has had a veto power over all civilian governments. Since the end of the Second World War, Thailand has experienced repeated *coups d'état* and the introduction, by most counts, of twenty different, if similar, constitutions—approximately one every four years. During that same period of time, Myanmar has experienced one coup and two half-coups and three new constitutions. The most recent Myanmar constitution, written by the army, guarantees that there will be no more coups, for it gives the army the power effectively to abolish the elected government and rule until new elections take place and a new government is formed under the same constitution.

Each country's army, or at least factions of the officer corps of each country's army, has both played and controlled politics at one time or another. Military allies of Stable Anti-Fascist People's Freedom Party leaders Kyaw Nyein and Ba Swe sought unsuccessfully to sway the 1960 elections in Myanmar. The so-called Thai Young Turks attempted a coup on April Fool's Day 1981, without royal backing. The attempt failed three days later, but not without exposing the undemocratic nature of the authoritarian government of Prime Minister General Prem

Tinsulanonda. Both armies have attempted in other ways to influence politics by attempting to change how people think and behave politically. In the late 1950s, the Myanmar army established the National Solidarity Association to inculcate anti-communist ideology into the population as well as to check the behaviour of elected politicians. In recent years the army of Thailand has used "Information Operations" to inform, shape, and "correct" public opinion (Puangthong 2017). Armies, unlike civilian politicians, have extensive psychological-warfare capabilities, available both for confusing enemies and for cultivating support for themselves and their purposes.

The problems that armies face when they do chose to intervene in politics is partially a function not merely of the armies themselves, but of the societies in which they are rooted. Myanmar, in comparison with Thailand, has experienced relatively little social or economic change until very recently. Between 1962 and 1988, General Ne Win's Burmese Road to Socialism terminated Myanmar's brief and partial post-independence opening to foreign capital and ideas. The succeeding quarter-century, during which broad Western economic sanctions constrained Myanmar, ended any prospect of rapid change. Even after the partial lifting of sanctions, change has been slow, and Myanmar remains an overwhelmingly peasant society riven by seemingly interminable ethnic conflicts. Thailand, in contrast, has been transformed from a peasant society into an urbanized export-oriented manufacturing and services economy, with less than ten per cent of its gross domestic product dependent on agriculture.

Unlike the era in which both armies first ventured into politics, politics in Thailand is no longer in the hands of a tiny elite. The clashes in recent years between Red Shirts and Yellow Shirts, and the divisions between those who voted for Thaksin Shinawatra and his successors on the one hand and the Bangkok and Southern voters who opposed Thaksinite forces on the other, bore witness to a society in which politics is highly factionalized but vibrant. Myanmar, on the other hand, and as demonstrated by its first elections in decades in 2010 and 2015, remains very much a mass society in which public opinion is swayed not by economic and social issues but by the appeal of one person, Daw Aung San Suu Kyi.

For the time being at least, the army in Myanmar is unlikely to intervene in politics directly, unless political or constitutional stability is threatened or the army's financial interests and budgetary appropriations are at risk. The same would be the case in Thailand had the army not felt threatened by the deep divisions in Thai politics and by challenges to the role of the monarchy. The army took a direct hand forging that role from the late 1950s onwards; it is now tightly bound to and almost dependent on the palace. Use of the hyper-royalism that Thongchai Winichakul described before the death of King Bhumibol in 2016 persists under his successor King Vajiralongkorn (Thongchai 2016). As—along with the judiciary and civil service—the Thai officer corps sees itself as the servant of the king who appoints its members, the army will remain tied to the preferences of the royal family, at least until a profound crisis occurs. An officer in the army of Myanmar once told me that, while he hated the British for colonizing his country, he had to thank them for abolishing the Burmese monarchy. The defeat of the German state at the end of the First World War and the prospect of revolution at home forced the German army to abandon the Kaiser. The army of Thailand has yet to face the question of whether the continuation of the monarchy is worth the political price.

While the political role of the armies of the Philippines and Indonesia are beyond the scope of this volume, both provide comparative lessons. Whereas the Philippine army once appeared to come very near to behaving as the ideal servant of elected governments, during the 1965–86 rule of President Ferdinand Marcos, his dictatorship suborned the military to such a degree that it was unable to conduct a coup without the assistance of anti-Marcos civilian crowds backed by the United States in the so-called EDSA Revolution of 1986. From then forward, the officer corps became highly factionalized, as the army's chain of command had been broken and patron-client ties generated opportunities for officers to manipulate politics and to gain office for themselves, and more generally encouraged mutinies and disorder. In many ways, army politics reflects the nature of Philippine civilian elite politics.[16] Because of the post-Marcos factionalism of the Armed Forces of the Philippines, the army as an institution has been unable to take power in its own name despite at least thirteen attempts to do so since 1986.

The Indonesian case, on the other hand, has its parallels with the role of the army in Myanmar. It has conducted only one coup, with the ouster of President Sukarno in 1965. Under the successor regime led by General Soeharto, initially the army was the main prop of the government. Over time, however, Soeharto became more reliant on support from business, family and party affiliates so that a form of sultanism[17] emerged. When eventually faced with the decision of whether to support Soeharto in the face of widespread demonstrations against his autocratic management, the army withdrew its support, and he was forced to resign. Having realized that direct army rule would be as unpopular as the former dictatorship, the Indonesian officer corps also set out to constrain its place in politics.

At that time, the officer corps sought to withdraw from the front lines of politics while reorienting its political role from "occupying" to "influencing" the political sphere and using indirect methods to do so. It became willing "to engage in political role-sharing (joint decision making in case of important national and government issues) with other components of the nation" (Crouch 1999, pp. 138–39; Honna 2003, p. 166). In Wheeler-Bennett's terms, the army of Indonesia stopped playing politics but sought indirectly to control politics in order to protect the core interests of the army and the state as it saw them. That army remains a powerful political force today, and the period since its withdrawal from front-line politics has not yet tested its willingness to obey a civilian government in a crisis that threatens either its corporate autonomy or the stability of the state.

It is one of the ironies of history that probably the most vibrant times in Myanmar's history, as measured by the practice of what is known as democratic politics, occurred in the 1920s and 1930s—under British colonial rule. Elections with free and open campaigning were regularly held until 1939. Political parties were organized, and party leaders formed their own "private armies" without hindrance from the colonial authorities. There was a free press, and student and worker politics was turbulent but largely tolerated. How did this come about? The shorthand explanation was that not only in Myanmar but also in India, of which British Burma was an integral part until 1937, the British had created a political order in which the colonial authorities—including the civil service, police and the British Indian Army—"held the ring" for domestic politics to thrive openly. While the Second World War destroyed that system in Myanmar, it continued in India. As a result, India is heralded as the world's largest multi-party democracy and one which has found a means to largely regulate its army's involvement in politics (Wilkinson 2015).

After independence, however, when a former colony's civil service and army are no longer under the control of an alien power, it is tempting for the holder of the ring, particularly the army, to step into the ring. Finding a relatively impartial referee for the political contest is a highly difficult task, for interests and egos are involved. Armies, like kings, might take heed from the words of Lord Castlereagh, written a month before the Battle of Waterloo and the defeat of Napoleon, himself the father of the modern mass national army.

> Tyrants may poison and murder an obnoxious character, but the surest and only means a *constitutional* sovereign has to restrain such a character is to *employ him* ... the essence of a free state is to manage the party warfare, as to reconcile it with the safety of the sovereign ... to do this, the King [or army] must give contending parties facilities against each other, and not embark too deeply in any way.[18]

NOTES

1. See, *inter alia*, Batson (1984), Chai-anan and Morell (1981), Chai-anan (1982), Murashima et al. (1986), Suchit (1987), Chai-anan and Suchit (1985), Sukhumbhand (1987), Yos (1989), Chambers (2013), and Pavin (2014).
2. See Silverstein (1972), Taylor (1985, 1987, 1989), Callahan (2003), Maung Aung Myoe (2009), Selth (2002), and Nakanishi (2013).
3. Claude E. Welch laid out a more elaborate version of the same; see Welch (1976). Also see Feaver (1999) and Luckman (1971).
4. By a different line of reasoning, Samuel P. Huntington posed the idea that, as armies become increasing professional, they will become less willing to intervene in civilian politics (Huntington 1957). Finer (2005, pp. 24–25) effectively refuted this argument. The American scholar of military-civil relations Zoltan Barany has, nevertheless, recently restated that classic Huntingtonian formulation (Barany 2018).
5. See, for example, Feit (1973).
6. See also Freeman (1948).
7. The classic study is Craig (1955).
8. Famously depicted in novel form in Erich Remarque's novel *All Quiet on the Western Front* (Remarque 1929).
9. Quoted in Baumont (1931, p. 50).
10. Quoted in Baumont (1931, p. 98). Groener was a Württemberg sergeant's son and therefore not a Prussian. His commander, Marshal Paul von Hindenburg, a Prussian, could not bring himself to speak disloyally to his

Kaiser. Similarly, General Wiranto told President Soeharto on 20 May 1998 that the Indonesian army could not maintain the stability of the country, with the implication that the latter would have to resign. He did so on the following day (Honna 2003, p. 161).
11. The treaty limited the German army to 100,000 men, including officers; prohibited forces other than cavalry and infantry; limited the navy to six ships; banned the import or export of arms; and, among other things, placed arms manufacture under British, French and American control.
12. It was said that von Schleicher should have been an admiral, as "his military genius lies in shooting under the water at his political friends" (Wheeler-Bennett 1974, p. 66). He and his wife were murdered in their home by the members of the Nazi regime's Gestapo on what became known as the Night of the Long Knives, 30 June 1934.
13. See also Cooper (1978).
14. See the introduction to O'Neill (1966) and also Müller (1987).
15. See for example the essays in Ahmad and Crouch (2001), in Mietzner (2011), and in Chambers and Napisa (2017).
16. See Chambers (2014) and Arugay (2011).
17. See Chehabi and Jinz (1999).
18. Bew (2011, p. 397), quoting Castlereagh to Sir Charles [Castlereagh], 8 May 1815; see Webster (1931).

REFERENCES

Alaggapa, Muthiah, ed. 2001. *The Declining Role of the Military in Southeast Asia*. Stanford: Stanford University Press.

Arugay, Aries A. 2011. "The Military in Philippine Politics: Still Politicised and Increasingly Autonomous". In *The Political Resurgence of the Military in Southeast Asia*, edited by Marcus Mietzner, pp. 85–105. Abingdon: Routledge.

Barany, Zoltan. 2018. "Burma: Suu Kyi's Missteps". *Journal of Democracy* 29, no. 1 (January): 5–19.

Batson, Benjamin A. 1984. *The End of the Absolute Monarchy in Siam*. Singapore: Oxford University Press.

Baumont, Maurice. 1931. *The Fall of the Kaiser*, translated by E. Ibbetson James. London: George Allen and Unwin.

Bew, John Bew. 2011. *Castlereagh: Enlightenment, War and Tyranny*. London: Quercus.

Callahan, Mary P. 2003. *Making Enemies: War and State Building in Burma*. Ithaca: Cornell University Press.

Chai-anan Samudavanija. 1982. *The Thai Young Turks*. Singapore: Institute of Southeast Asian Studies.

Chai-anan Samudavanija and David Morell. 1981. *Political Conflict in Thailand: Reform, Reaction, Revolution*. Cambridge, Massachusetts: Oelgeschlager, Gunn & Hain.

Chai-anan Samudavanija and Suchit Bunbongkarn. 1985. "Thailand". In *Military-Civilian Relations in South-East Asia*, edited by Zakaria Ahmad and Harold Crouch, pp. 78–117. Singapore: Oxford University Press.

Chambers, Paul, ed. 2013. *Knights of the Realm: Thailand's Military and Police, Then and Now*. Bangkok: White Lotus.

———. 2014. "Superficial Consolidation: Security Sector Governance and the Executive Branch in the Philippines Today". In *Security Sector Reform in Southeast Asia: From Policy to Practice*, edited by Felix Heiduk, pp. 102–30. London: Palgrave Macmillan.

Chambers, Paul, and Napisa Waitoolkiat, eds. 2017. *Khaki Capital: The Political Economy of the Military in Southeast Asia*. Copenhagen: NIAS.

Chehabi, Houchang E., and Juan J. Linz, eds. 1999. *Sultanistic Regimes*. Baltimore: Johns Hopkins University Press.

Cooper, Matthew. 1978. *The German Army 1933-1945: Its Political and Military Failure*. London: Macdonald and Jane's.

Craig, Gordon A. 1955. *The Politics of the Prussian Army, 1640-1945*. Oxford: Oxford University Press.

Crouch, Harold. 1999. "Wiranto and Habibie: Military-Civilian Relations since May 1998". In *Reformasi: Crisis and Change in Indonesia*, edited by Arief Budiman, Barbara Hatley, and Damien Kingsbury, pp. 127–48. Clayton, Victoria: Monash Asia Institute.

Feaver, Peter D. 1999. "Civil-Military Relations". *Annual Review of Political Science* 2: 211–41.

Feit, Edward. 1973. *Armed Bureaucrats: Military Administrative Regimes and Political Development*. New York: Houghton Mifflin.

Finer, Samuel E. 2005. *The Man on Horseback: The Role of the Military in Politics*. 2nd ed. London: Pall Mall Press.

Freeman, Felton D. 1948. "The Army as a Social Structure". *Social Forces* 27, no. 1 (October 1948–May 1949): 78–83.

Honna Jun. 2003. *Military Politics and Democratization in Indonesia*. London: RoutledgeCurzon.

Howard, Michael. 1957. "Introduction: The Armed Forces as a Political Problem". In *Soldiers and Governments: Nine Studies in Civil-Military Relations*, edited by Michael Howard, pp. 9–24. Westport, Connecticut: Greenwood Press.

Huntington, Samuel P. 1957. *The Soldier and The State: The Theory and Politics of Civil-Military Relations*. New York: Vintage Books.

Janowitz, Morris. 1960. *The Professional Soldier: A Social and Political Portrait*. Glencoe, Illinois: The Free Press.

Kohn, Richard H. 1997. "How Democracies Control the Military". *Journal of Democracy* 8, no. 4 (October): 140–53.

Luckman, A.R. 1971. "A Comparative Typology of Civil-Military Relations". *Government and Opposition* 6, no. 1 (Winter): 5–35.

Maung Aung Myoe. 2009. *Building the Tatmadaw: Myanmar Armed Forces since 1948*. Singapore: Institute of Southeast Asian Studies.

McCoy, Alfred W. 1999. *Closer than Brothers: Manhood at the Philippine Military Academy*. New Haven: Yale University Press.

Mietzner, Marcus, ed. 2011. *The Political Resurgence of the Military in Southeast Asia*. Abingdon: Routledge.

Müller, Klaus-Jürgen. 1987. *The Army, Politics and Society in Germany, 1933-1945: Studies in the Army's Relation to Nazism*. Manchester: Manchester University Press.

Murashima Eiji, Nakharin Mektrairat, and Chalermkiet Phiu-nual. 1986. *Political Thoughts of the Thai Military in Historical Perspective*. JRP Series 55. Tokyo: Institute of Developing Economies.

Nakanishi Yoshihiro. 2013. *Strong Soldiers, Failed Revolution, the State and the Military in Burma, 1962-1988*. Singapore and Kyoto: NUS Press and Kyoto University Press.

O'Neill, Robert. 1966. *The German Army and the Nazi Party, 1933-1939*. London: Cassell.

Pavin Chachavalpongpun. 2014. *"Good Coup" Gone Bad: Thailand's Political Development since Thaksin's Downfall*. Singapore: Institute of Southeast Asian Studies.

Puangthong R. Pawakapan. 2017. *The Central Role of Thailand's Internal Security Operations Command in the Post-Counter-Insurgency Period*. Trends in Southeast Asia, no. 17/2017. Singapore: ISEAS – Yusof Ishak Institute.

Rapoport, Anatol, ed. 1968. *Clausewitz on War*. Harmondsworth: Penguin.

Remarque, Erich. 1929. *All Quiet on the Western Front*. New York: Little Brown.

Selth, Andrew. 2002. *Burma's Armed Forces: Power without Glory*. Norwalk, Connecticut: EastBridge.

Silverstein, Josef. 1972. *Burma: Military Rule and the Politics of Stagnation*. Ithaca: Cornell University Press.

Suchit Bunbongkarn. 1987. *The Military in Thai Politics, 1981-1986*. Singapore: Institute of Southeast Asian Studies.

Sukhumbhand Paribatra. 1987. "Thailand: Defence Spending and Threat Perception". In *Defence Spending in Southeast Asia*, edited by Chin Kin Wah, pp. 75–198. Singapore: Institute of Southeast Asian Studies.

Taylor, Robert H. 1985. "Burma". In *Military-Civilian Relations in South-East Asia*, edited by Zakaria Ahmad and Harold Crouch, pp. 13–49. Singapore: Oxford University Press.

———. 1987. "Burma: Defence Expenditure and Threat Perceptions". In *Defence Spending in Southeast Asia*, edited by Chin Kin Wah, pp. 252–80. Singapore: Institute of Southeast Asian Studies.

———. 1989. "Burma: Political Leadership, Security Perceptions and Policies". In *Leadership Perceptions and National Security: The Southeast Asian Experience*, edited by Mohammed Ayoob and Chai-anan Samudavanija, pp. 205–23. Singapore: Institute of Southeast Asian Studies.

Thongchai Winichakul. 2016. *Thailand's Hyper-royalism: Its Past Success and Present Predicament*. Trends in Southeast Asia, no. 16/2016. Singapore: ISEAS – Yusof Ishak Institute.

Webster, Charles K. 1931. *The Foreign Policy of Castlereagh, Vol. 1, 1812-1815: Britain and the Reconstruction of Europe*. London: G. Bell and Sons.

Welch, Claude E. 1976. "Civilian Control of the Military: Myth and Reality". In *Civilian Control of the Military: Theory and Cases from Developing Countries*, edited by Claude E. Welch, pp. 1–42. Albany: State University of New York Press.

Wheeler-Bennett, John. 1936. *Wooden Titan: Hindenburg in Twenty Years of German History, 1914-1934*. New York: William Morrow.

———. 1956. "Men of Tragic Destiny: Ludendorff and Groener". In *Essays Presented to Sir Lewis Namier*, edited by Richard Pares and A.J.P. Taylor, pp. 506–42. London: Macmillan.

———. 1974. *Knaves, Fools and Heroes in Europe between the Wars*. London: Macmillan.

———. 2005 [1953]. *The Nemesis of Power: The German Army in Politics 1918-1945*. London: Palgrave Macmillan.

Wilkinson, Steven I. 2015. *Army and Nation: The Military and Indian Democracy since Independence*. Cambridge, Massachusetts: Harvard University Press.

Yos Santasombat. 1989. "Leadership and Security in Modern Thai Politics". In *Leadership Perceptions and National Security: The Southeast Asian Experience*, edited by Mohammed Ayoob and Chai-anan Samudavanija, pp. 83–109. Singapore: Institute of Southeast Asian Studies.

Zweig, Stefan. 2013. *Beware of Pity*, translated by Anthea Bell. London: Pushkin Press.

INDEX

A
Abel, David, 127n7
Abhisit Vejjajiva, 4
Admiral Panteleyev, 63
Agbayani, Aguedo F., 1–2, 11, 16
Air Force Welfare Department, Thailand, 134
Al-Qaeda, 42
ambivalent state, 2, 3, 11, 12, 20, 22, 23
anti-communism, 76, 77
Apirat Kongsompong, 91
Arakan Army, 40
Arakan Rohingya Salvation Army (ARSA), 41–42, 46, 61
armed forces, modernizing, Myanmar, 47–58
Armed Forces Day Parade, 98
Armed Forces of the Philippines, 2, 21
arms imports of Myanmar, 49
Army Welfare Department, Thailand, 134
Asian Financial Crisis, 134–36
Association of Southeast Asian Nations (ASEAN) Defense Ministers' Meeting, 64
Ata Ullah, 41
Aung Myint Mo Min Insurance Co. Ltd., 113, 116, 118
Aung San Suu Kyi, 4, 61, 160
 leadership, 4
Aung Thit Sar Oo Insurance, 113
Ava Bank, 110
Ayeyar Hinthar Group, 121

B
Bangkok Broadcasting and Television Company, 138
Bangkok International Banking Facility, 136
Bank of Thailand, 132, 134, 136, 144n3
Ba Swe, 159
Beatrice Food (Burma) Limited, 110
Berlin, Donald, 2, 16
"Bike for Dad", 81
"Bike for Mom", 81
"Black May" incident of 1992, 3, 13, 89
Blaufarb, Douglas, 18
Border Guard Forces, Myanmar, 36, 40, 66n4
Boris Butoma, 63

Index

British Burma, 162
Bruning, Heinrich, 157
Buddhist monks, 72
Burma
 defence budget, 8
 H.R.5819 bill, United States, 61
 long-term military control of, 2
 Burma Economic Development
  Corporation (BEDC), 109–10
 Burma Five Star Line Co. Ltd.,
  127n6
 Burma Human Rights and Freedom
  Act of 2018, S.2060, United
  States, 61
 Burma Independence Army, 32
 Burma International Inspection
  Company Limited, 110
 Burma Orchids Limited, 110
 Burma Socialist Programme Party
  (BSPP), 5, 97, 111, 112
  BSPP Tatmadaw Organizing
   Committee,
 "Burmese Way to Socialism", 30

C
Callahan, Mary, 19
Catholic Centre Party, Germany,
 157–58
ceasefire agreements, Myanmar, 40
"ceasefire capitalism", Myanmar, 39
Central Intelligence Agency, United
 States, 38
Central Statistical Organization
 (CSO), Myanmar, 99
Chaisit Shinawatra, 78
Chalard Hiransiri, 76
Chamlong Srimuang, 87
Chaohu (Hull 890), 62
"chaos" of democracy, 82
Chavalit Yongchaiyudh, 77, 87
ChinDwin, 127n8

Chinese Kokang ethnic armed group,
 62
Chulachomklao Royal Military
 Academy, Thailand, 13
Class 7, 8?
civilian government's authority, 36
Civil Services Personnel Law of 2013,
 Myanmar, 34
Clausewitz, Carl von, 151–52
Cobra Gold exercises, 59
Cold War, 89, 137, 152
Commanding Officer Conference,
 Myanmar, 111
Commercial Banking Act of 1962,
 Thailand, 136
communism, 76
Communist Party of Burma (CPB),
 37, 43
Communist Party of Thailand (CPT),
 19–20, 76, 77
Connors, Michael, 2, 3, 20
constitutionalism, 20
crony capitalism, 30
Cyclone Nargis, 108

D
Daewoo, 120
Dagon Brewery, 113, 116, 117
Dagon City 1 project, 120
DBS Bank, Singapore, 135
Defence Expenditure, Myanmar,
 101–3
Defence Services Academy, Myanmar,
 34
Defence Services Act of 1959,
 Myanmar, 34
Defence Services Council, Myanmar,
 34–35
 Defence Services Council Order
  1/2016 (DSCO 1/2016), 35
 Defence Services Council Order
  4/2014 (DSCO 4/2014), 35

Defence Services Council Order 6/1990 (DSCO 6/1990), 35
Defence Services Council Order 18/1973 (DSCO 18/1973), 35
Defence Services Institute (DSI), Myanmar, 109
Head Office, 110
defence strategy, Myanmar
external threats, 43–46
internal threats, 39–43
Defense POW/MIA Accounting Agency, United States, 60
"Democratic Soldiers", Thailand, 77, 87
DENTOMEC Toothbrush and Toothpaste Factory, 116
Designee for ETA Contract Company, 136
developmentalist nationalism, 84
developmental militarism, 14, 73, 75, 77, 79, 81
Directorate of Defence Services Intelligence, Myanmar, 33
"discipline-flourishing democracy", Myanmar, 7, 36
DSI No. 1 and General Provision Store and Canteen, 110
dwifungsi, 73

E
Ebert, Friedrich, 155
EDSA Revolution of 1986, 161
8888 Uprising, 32
ethnic armed groups, Myanmar, 18, 39–40, 45
ethnic armed organizations. *See* ethnic armed groups
ethnic chauvinism, 21

F
Faith Movement. *See* Harakah al-Yaqin

federalism, 39, 40
F-7 fighter jet, 50
Financial Institutions Business Act, Thailand, 136
financial liberalization, 136
Finer, Samuel, 151
First Army Region, Thailand, 88
1st Infantry Battalion, Thailand, 88
First World War, 21
Five Provinces Bordering Forest Preservation Foundation, Thailand, 84
5-series patrol boats, 57
"Four Cuts" strategy, Myanmar, 42
Frei Corps, 155
Future Forward Party, 23

G
General Administration Department, Myanmar, 10
General Providence Fund, Myanmar, 125
The German Army and the Nazi Party (O'Neill), 158
Global Magnitsky Human Rights Accountability Act, United States, 61
Goh Chok Tong, 119
GROB Aircraft, 107
Groener, Karl, 155–57, 163n10
Guardian Magazine, 109, 111
Guardian Newspaper, 109, 111
guerrilla warfare, 44

H
Harakah al-Yaqin (Faith Movement), 41
Harn Leelanon, 87
Hitler, Adolf, 154, 156, 158
Hla Htay Win, 34
Hluttaw Land Commission, Myanmar, 122

"Homes for the Welfare of Government Officers and Regular Employees of the Army" programme, Thailand, 142
human rights organizations, 42

I
IGE Group, 120
"Immediate Guideline 3.8", Thailand, 82
India-Myanmar Bilateral Military Exercise 2017 (IMBAX-2017), 63
India-Myanmar Coordinated Patrol (IMCOR), 62
India-Myanmar Naval Exercise 2018 (IMNEX-18), 63
"Information Operations", Thailand, 160
ING Bank, 135
Inn Din massacre, 65
Innwa Trading, 116
Internal Security Operations Command (ISOC), Thailand, 87
International Force for East Timor (INTERFET), 78
International New York Times, 113
Islamic terrorism, 42
Islamophobia, 6

J
Jingzhou (Hull 532), 62
Jote Gunakasem, 134
Justice for Victims of Corrupt Foreign Officials Act, Canada, 61

K
Kachin Independence Organization, 39
Karen National Union, 37, 39
Khana ratsadon, 73
Khattiya Sawasdipol, "Seh Daeng", 88

Khin Aung Myint, 63
Khin Maung Soe, 127n10
Khin Nyunt, 33
Khin Zaw Oo, 127n7
"Khon Kaen Model", 92
King Bhumibol, 80, 84, 91, 161
King Chulalongkorn, 12, 72
King Mongkut, 72
King Naresuan the Great, 81
King's Guard (*kong thahan mahatlek raksa phra-ong*), Thailand, 72, 88, 91
King Vajiralongkorn, 91, 161
King Vajiravudh, 12, 72
KIRIN Beer, 113
Kokang. *See* Chinese Kokang ethnic armed group
Ko Ko, 34
Krit Sivara, 76, 77, 86, 87
Kukiat Srinaka, 91
Kuomintang (KMT), 38
Kyaw Nyein, 159
Kyaw Soe, 111
Kyaw Soe Oo, 65

L
land confiscation, 122–23
Lashkar-e-Taiba, 41
lèse majesté, 80, 90, 93n7
Lotte Hotels, 120

M
Mandalay Brewery, 110, 112
The Man on Horseback (Finer), 151
Manoon Rupkachorn, 87
Manopakorn Nititada, Phraya, 85
Marcos, Ferdinand E., 2, 161
Mass Communications Organization of Thailand, 138
Maung Aye, 33, 119
Maung Maung Soe, 61

Maw Taung Coal Production plant, 116
MECTel, 118, 119
"Men in Black", 88
military authoritarianism, 6
Min Aung Hlaing, 60
  arms imports, 48
  to China, 61
  generation leadership of the Tatmadaw, 7
  in India, 62
  and Ko Ko, 34
  leadership of the Tatmadaw, 64
  military businesses, 119
  in Moscow, 63
  and new Tatmadaw leadership, 35
  and post-SPDC era, 57
  in Thailand, 66
  in Vietnam, 127n10
  vision of a Standard Army, 19, 46, 98
  and welfare programme for military families, 58
  and "world-class Tatmadaw", 47
Ministry of Defense Act of 2008, Thailand, 82
Ministry of Finance, Thailand, 135, 140, 141
Ministry of Finance and Revenue, Myanmar, 116
"monarchised military", 71, 84, 90
monarchization, 21, 77, 79, 81
monarchy-centric national security, 90
Moscow Conference on International Security 2018, 63
Mujahideen separatist movements, 41
Müller, Hermann, 157
Myan Aung, 123, 124
Myanma Economic Holdings Public Company Limited, 119
Myanma Five Star Line, 127n8
Myanmar, 4, 6, 151

armed forces, 4–7
arms imports of, 49
defence budget, 47–48
democratic reforms, 8
military, 9
military, defence strategy of, 46
paramount government agency, 10
rural society in, 10
Tatmadaw's role in, 7
Thailand and, 3–4
weapons to, 51–56
Myanmar Air Force (MAF), 58, 107
Myanmar Armed Forces, 61
Myanmar Brewery, 112
Myanmar Defence Expenditure, 100
Myanmar Economic Corporation (MEC)
  businesses, 2017, 117–18
  Ministry of Defence and, 115
  revenues of, 125
  telecommunications and healthcare services, 119
  UMEHL and, 9–10, 17, 112, 113, 120
  "vision" of, 116
"Myanmar Eco Vision" (MEV), 126
Myanmar International Insurance Service Corporation, 116
Myanmar National Democratic Alliance Army, 40, 62
Myanmar National Telecom Holding Public Co. Ltd (MNTH), 119
Myanmar National Tele & Communications Co. Ltd. *See* MyTel
Myanmar Navy, 57
Myanmar Police Force, 36
Myanmar-U.S. Human Rights Dialogue, 59
Mya Sein Yaung operations, 112
Mya Tun Oo, 60
Myawaddy Bank, 114, 120
Myawaddy magazine, 109

Myawaddy Trading, 114, 120
Myint Nwe, 104–6
Myo Nyunt, 127n7
MyTel, 118, 119, 127n10

N
Nakanishi Yoshihiro, 5, 18
National Assembly, Thailand, 140
National Broadcasting and
  Telecommunications Commission
  (NBTC), Thailand, 137, 139, 140
National Committee on Radio and
  Television Activities, Thailand,
  137
National Council for Peace and Order
  (NCPO) junta, Thailand, 3, 80–82,
  90, 140
National Defense Academy, Japan,
  59
National Defense Authorization Act,
  Myanmar, 60, 61
"nationalistic militarism", 12, 72
National League for Democracy
  (NLD), 4, 40
National Solidarity Association,
  Myanmar, 160
Nationwide Ceasefire Agreement,
  Myanmar, 40, 42
Nazi Party, 158
Nazi regime, 154
NBTC Act of 2010, Thailand, 140
NBTC Research and Development
  Fund, Thailand, 140
The Nemesis of Power (Wheeler-
  Bennett), 153
"neocolonialism", 44
Ne Win, 33
  between 1962 and 1988, 160
  in Burma Army, 32
  "caretaker government", 1
  civilian government in Rangoon, 2
  March 1962 coup, 5
  Revolutionary Council rule, 111
  and Than Shwe, 35
Ngwetaryi magazine, 109
1950 Special Company Act, Myanmar,
  113, 115
1960 Defense Act, Thailand, 76
No. 24 Defence Industry, Myanmar,
  123
No. 438 Light Infantry Battalion,
  Myanmar, 123
No. 51 Infantry Battalion, Myanmar,
  123
No. 503 Light Infantry Battalion,
  Myanmar, 123
non-Bamar ethnic groups, 7
NORINCO, 114, 115

O
Office of the Adjutant General,
  Myanmar, 114, 127n7
Office of the Quartermaster General,
  Myanmar, 116
Official Secrets Act, Myanmar, 65
O'Neill, Robert, 158
On War (Clausewitz), 151

P
Pallop Pinmanee, 87
parliamentary democracy, 30
partial regime, 3, 5, 6, 11–16, 18, 20,
  21, 23
People's Liberation Army (PLA), 61
People's Militia Forces, Myanmar, 36
People's Party, Thailand. *See Khana
  ratsadon*
People's Volunteer Organization,
  Myanmar, 37
People's War, 44
Phahonphonphayuhasena, Phraya, 85
Phibun. *See* Plaek Phibunsongkhram
Phin Choonhavan, 74
Phuea Thai Party, 86

Plaek Phibunsongkhram, 14, 17, 73–74
Plan 09/10 of 1967, Thailand, 76
Plan 110/2012 of 1969, Thailand, 76
POSCO, 120
Pracharat, 82
Prajak Sawangjit, 87
Praphat Charusathian, 138
Prawit Wongsuwan, 79, 82
Prayut Chanocha, 4, 23, 64, 80, 86, 91, 159–60
Premium Gold cigarettes, 114
Prem Tinsulanonda
   civil-military relations, views on, 93n6
   1980 ascension to power of, 89
   1980–88 premiership, 13, 77
   premiership of Thaksin Shinawatra, 88
   Sonthi's leadership, 79
Pridi Banomyong, 74, 86
Pridi Ramasoot, 87
Prince Boworadet, 85
pro-democracy movement, 32
"professional military", 47, 126
Public Relations Department, Thailand, 137, 138
Pyidaungsu Hluttaw, Myanmar, 123
"Pyithu Tatmadaw", 111

Q

"Queen's Tiger Guard" faction, Thailand, 88, 91

R

"Radio Coup" of 1951, Thailand, 75
Rakhine State, 8
Ratchaphak Park, 81
Ravi Wanpen, 87
recreation clubs, belonging to Thai military, 142
"Red Shirts", 88

Regimental Funds, Myanmar, 112, 124
"Returning Happiness to the People", television programme, 81
Revolutionary Council, Myanmar, 109–11
Rohingya crisis, 59
Rohingya issue, 41, 43, 63
Rohingya militant groups, 41–43, 45
Rohingya Patriotic Front, 41
Rohingya people, 4
Rohingya rights, 42
Rohingya Solidarity Organization, 41
"royal-centric military ideology", 72
Royal Guard, Thailand, 904, 88–89
Royal Guard Command, Thailand, 91
Royal Guards Security Command, Thailand, 88
Royally Initiated Projects, Thailand, 83, 84
Royal Siamese Armed Forces, 72
Royal Sportainment Complex, 116
Royal Thai Armed Forces, 83
Royal Thai Army, 15, 16, 64, 83, 135, 141, 143, 144
   ideological orientation, 13
   political ideology and economic interests, 11–16
   Tatmadaw and, 17
Royal Thai Army Television Station (RTAS), 137–38
RTA Entertainment, 139, 143
RTATS Channel 5 Publication, 140–41
RTATS Channel 5 Publishing, 138, 140–41

S

Sangad Chaloryu, 86
San Yu, 111
Sarit Thanarat, 2, 13, 17, 75, 86, 134, 136
Second World War, 159, 162

Securities and Exchange Commission, Thailand, 133, 139
Shwe War Myay operation, 112
SLORC Law No. 4/97, Myanmar, 115
SLORC Law No. 6/97, Myanmar, 115
SLORC Law No. 9/89, 115
SLORC/SPDC bodies, Myanmar, 123
SLORC/SPDC era, Myanmar, 10, 17, 99, 120–21
SLORC/SPDC period, Myanmar. *See* SLORC/SPDC era
Social Democratic Party (SDP), Germany, 154–55, 157
Soeharto, 162, 164n10
Somdhat Attanand, 78
Sonthi Boonyaratglin, 79, 86
SPDC-era defence policy, Myanmar, 40
Special Company Act of 1950, Myanmar, 109
Special Economic Zone, disputed between Myanmar and Bangladesh, 108
Stable Anti-Fascist People's Freedom Party, 159
"Standard Army" concept, Myanmar, 7–10, 32, 46–65, 98, 124
Star High Public Company, 118, 119
State Administrative Organizations Expenditure (SAOE), Myanmar, 99, 101–3, 126n2
State Law and Order Restoration Council (SLORC) junta, Myanmar, 5, 32, 66n1, 97
State-Owned Economic Enterprise Law, Myanmar, 115
State Peace and Development Council (SPDC) junta, Myanmar, 5, 32, 47, 66n4, 97
Stock Exchange of Thailand, 133, 134, 139, 141, 143, 144n3
Stockholm International Peace Research Institute (SIPRI), 99
sufficiency economy concept, 82
Surachart Bamrungsuk, 11
Surayud Chulanont, 78

T
Ta'ang National Liberation Army, 40
Tatmadaw
    defence expenditures and commercial interests of, 97–98
    commercial activities of, 108–24
    defence budget, 99–108
    with old characteristics, 30–32
    defence strategy, 39–46
    emerging new leadership, 32–35
    Standard Army, 46–65
    and Thai Army, 17
    third constitutional, 38
    third-generation leadership, 7
    transformation and economic interests, 5–11
    Western criticism of, 7
Tatmadaw Party Committee, 111
Telecom International Myanmar Co. Ltd. (MyTel). *See* MyTel
Thai armed forces, 13, 70, 88
Thai Army. *See* Royal Thai Army
Thai democracy, 77
Thai identity, 76
Thailand, 151
    "Black May", 3
    and Myanmar, 3–4
Thai Military Bank, 134–37, 143, 144n3
Thai Military Day, 81
Thai military ideology, 70–71
    in post-2014 Thailand, 80–84
    officers, 84–89
    since 1852, 71–80
Thai monarchy, 12, 76, 84
"Thai-ness", 73, 89, 90

Thai peasantry, 87
Thai race, 73
Thai Rak Thai Party, 79
Thai TV Global Network, 139
Thai Young Turks, 77, 86, 87, 92, 159
"Thaksinomics", 88
Thaksin Shinawatra, 14, 78, 79, 86, 88, 90, 160
Thanakhan thahan thai. See Thai Military Bank
Thanin Kraivichien, 77
ThanLwin, 127n8
Thanom Kittikhachon, 17
Than Oo, 127n7
Than Shwe, 33–35, 98
Thant Myint-U, 19
Thaung Kyi, 111
Thawan Thamrongnawasawat, 85
Thein Sein, 4, 33
Third Anglo-Burmese War, 21
Thirty Comrades, 32
Thongchai Winichakul, 161
Tho Tho Bo 5, 138, 139, 141
"Three Main National Causes", Myanmar, 37, 38
Thura Kyaw Htin, 111
Thura Myint Aung, 34
Thura Shwe Mann, 33
Thura Thet Swe, 34
Thura Tin Oo, 111
Tin Aung Myint Oo, 33
Tin Aye, 127n7
TMB Bank. *See* Thai Military Bank
total-war approach, Myanmar, 44
transitional democracy, 6
Treaty of Versailles, 156
21st Infantry Regiment in the 2nd Division of the First Army Region, Thailand, 88
2015 Defence White Paper, Myanmar, 37, 38, 40, 44, 45

U
Ukrist Pathmanand, 2, 3, 20
UMS *Anawrahta*, 62
UMS *Aung Zeya* (F-11), 57, 62
UMS *Inlay*, 63
UMS *King Sin Phyu Shin*, 63
UMS *Kyan Sittha* (F-11), 57
UMS *Mahar Bandoola* (F-21), 57
UMS *Mahar Thiha Thura* (F-23), 57
UMS *Sinbyushin* (F-14), 57
UMS *Tabinshwehti* (773), 57
U Myint, 126
Union Government Expenditure (UGE), Myanmar,
    defence expenditure in, 99, 101–4, 125
    State Administrative Organizations Expenditure, 126n2
    2017–18 defence budget, 8
Union of Myanmar Economic Holdings Ltd. (UMEHL)
    business activities, 114
    businesses lines, 120
    firms, 114
    income of, 125
    and MEC, 9–10, 17, 112
    shares, 113, 124
    state-owned Myanma Five Star Line, 127n8
    tax exemption, 115
    transformation, 119
Union of Myanmar Federation of Chambers of Commerce and Industry, 126
Union of Myanmar Ship (UMS), 57
Union Parliament, Myanmar, 47
Union Peace Conference, Myanmar, 40, 42
Union Solidarity and Development Party (USDP), 31, 33, 104
United Nations peace-keeping missions, 90

United Nations Security Council, 45
United States Military Academy (West Point), 75
University Training Corps, Myanmar, 58
U.S. Department of Defense, 60

V
Viettel, 118, 119, 127n10
von Hindenburg, Oskar, 156, 157
von Hindenburg, Paul, 155–58, 163n10
von Papen, Franz, 158
von Schleicher, Kurt, 156–58, 164n12
von Seeckt, Hans, 156

W
Wai Lwin, 34, 121
Wa Lone, 65
War Department (*krom kalahom*), Thailand, 72

War Office Council, Myanmar. *See* Defence Services Council
War Veterans Organization, Thailand, 17
"Watermelon" soldiers, 88, 92
Weimar Republic, 21–22
Western liberal democracies, 10
"West Point" model, 75
Wheeler-Bennett, John, 22, 153–54, 156, 157, 162
"white flag" communists, 37
Wild Tigers (*suea pa*), 72, 85
Win Hlaing, 127n7
Win Myint, 127n7
Wongthewan ("Divine Progeny") faction, 88, 91

Y
Young Military Officers Group (*Khana thahan num*). *See* Thai Young Turks

www.ingramcontent.com/pod-product-compliance
Lightning Source LLC
Chambersburg PA
CBHW070944230426
43666CB00011B/2552